To Stake a Claim

To Stake a Claim

Mission and the Western Crisis of Knowledge

Edited by

J. Andrew Kirk

and

Kevin J. Vanhoozer

ORBIS BOOKS

Maryknoll, New York 10545

The Catholic Foreign Mission Society of America (Maryknoll) recruits and trains people for overseas missionary service. Through Orbis Books, Maryknoll aims to foster the international dialogue that is essential to mission. The books published, however, reflect the opinions of their authors and are not meant to represent the official position of the society. To obtain more information about Maryknoll and Orbis Books, please visit our website at www.maryknoll.org.

Manufactured in the United States of America

Library of Congress Cataloging-in-Publication Data

To stake a claim : mission and the Western crisis of knowledge / J. Andrew
    Kirk, Kevin J. Vanhoozer, editors.
      p.   cm.
    Includes bibliographical references and index.
    ISBN 1-57075-274-5 (pbk)
      1. Missions—Theory. 2. Knowledge, THeory of (Religion) I. Kirk, J.
    Andrew. II. Vanhoozer, Kevin J.

BV2063, T6 1999
266'.001—dc

99-052363

Contents

Preface

J. ANDREW KIRK

This book began its life as a part of an international, multiyear study project that convened for the first time in Paris in January 1992. It was called "Toward a Missiology of Western Culture," and was directed overall by Wilbert R. Shenk. In Paris one of the seven working groups for the project was identified to do research on the relationship between what counted for "knowledge" in the West, how it had changed over the years, and how those changes related to the evangelistic mission of the church within Western culture. The issue we were addressing, in effect, was the "epistemological predicament" of Christianity in "postmodern" Western culture. With an eighteen-month hiatus because of a lapse in funding, the group met a number of times before finishing the final conference of the larger project in September of 1997 at the Bon Secours Spiritual Center near Baltimore, Maryland.

Adding members in three stages as we entered more deeply into the subject matter, we became known as the "epistemology and mission" group. In the first stage, Bert Hoedemaker of the University of Groningen, Holland, Lars Johansson of the Örebro Seminary in Sweden, and myself, of the School of Mission at the Selly Oak Colleges in Birmingham, England, met twice, each of us writing a preliminary paper setting out our respective ideas and approaches.

The second stage saw the addition of two people expert in the interaction between theology and philosophy—Andy Sanders of Groningen University in Holland and Kevin Vanhoozer of the University of Edinburgh. This now expanded group of five had a memorable and productive meeting in Birmingham, producing the detailed outline of a process that had the potential to fulfil the group's aims and aspirations.

We identified four key areas for study. The first was to "analyze and evaluate the dominant positions in contemporary philosophy in the areas of truth, rationality and pluralism, indicating what kind of predicaments and consequences for humanity they imply." This is essentially covered in the first three chapters of the book. The second was envisaged as the attempt to "analyze and evaluate the predicament of faith, religion and revelation in the light of the dominant positions in contemporary philosophy." The third was designed to "analyze and evaluate the dominant positions of contemporary theology in their attempts to deal with this predicament." The final phase aimed to tackle the ambitious task of "summarizing the epistemological problems involved in the process of communicating the Gospel within Western culture, and attempting a theological/missiological evaluation of those processes."

In a third stage, Nancey Murphy of Fuller Theological Seminary and Philip Clayton of Sonoma State University, both located in California, joined the group. These two helped to balance the preponderance of European membership in the group and, more importantly, brought the knowledge and training of professional philosophers to our efforts.

Asked to prepare a short statement to spell out what the group attempted to achieve in relationship to Christian mission in the West, the following paragraph was drafted:

> One of the most characteristic features of modern culture is epistemological uncertainty: i.e. there is a decreasing confidence about an adequate basis for knowing. The crisis is often explained in terms of a shift between what is commonly called modernity and postmodernity. The aim of this subgroup is to analyze and evaluate both the opportunities and difficulties for mission of this particular aspect of Western culture. To achieve this end we intend to focus on questions in contemporary epistemological discussion relating to truth, rationality, and pluralism.

Murphy, Clayton, and Vanhoozer undertook to produce the mapping exercise envisaged in phase one, with two significant sections to be written by Sanders. The text is the result of a process in which the whole group has been involved. It has been through a number of revisions. No one person would have written it quite as it stands. All can find parts that they would wish to rephrase, reorder, or reconfigure. Therefore, it does not represent the full position of any individual member of the group. Nevertheless, the group stands behind it as a serviceable guide for those who are unfamiliar with the state of the debate regarding epistemology in the Western world. Those already well versed in the discussions may wish to skip this first part and move on to those parts where the interdisciplinary debate between philosophy, theology, and missiology is taken up.

Concurrently with the mapping exercise, a number of colaborators were invited, along with some members of the group, to write what we called "analytical essays" on the responses of leading theologians to the epistemological crisis—Colin Gunton, John Hick, George Lindbeck, Wolfhart Pannenberg, Arthur Peacocke, D. Z. Phillips, Alvin Plantinga, Rosemary Radford Ruether, Juan Luis Segundo, and Mark C. Taylor. No doubt another group would have come up with a different list. The rich fare we enjoyed in discussing these representative theologians provided us with concrete points and a common experience utilized in phase three of our project—writing "constructive papers" in which each member of the group would explore "from their own perspective, the nature of the challenge of the epistemological predicament to the nature and work of mission and missiology, and to suggest ways in which the Christian message can make its own contribution to the present epistemological predicament." These essays form Part Two of this volume.

At about this time, the group began to consider how to put together a summary message for the concluding symposium of the project as a whole at Bon Secours. It was agreed that this final document would "indicate the difficulties and opportunities for mission of the epistemological questions, some attempts to address these and an agenda for further research in the area of a missiological evaluation of the process of communicating the Gospel in the light of the epistemological questions."

The group met for a final time in Groningen in the Netherlands in August 1997, shortly before the plenary symposium of the entire Missiology of Western Culture Project. By this time a notable rapport had been established in the group, indicating the real value of research and reflection within the discipline of intense peer interaction. This rapport did not hide the substantial differences we discovered, but it did enable a fruitful and creative debate around complex, emotive, and important basic themes. In the final part of this meeting, the group discussed in detail each of the constructive essays and once again made suggestions for changes and additions. We also spent time discussing the major Christian articles of faith in relation to the epistemological challenges. This proved to be a highly fertile exercise, although not recorded for posterity because of its provisional nature. Both the content of the programmatic statement, suggestions for future work (which appear as part of the Epilogue), and the contents of the book you now hold were discussed at that meeting.

This description of the process gives a brief idea both of how the group worked and how the book came to be written. Essays identified by an author's name are the work of that individual, but all these chapters have benefited from the criticisms and suggestions of the rest of the group. Essays not identified by an author's name are products of the group as a whole. Not every member agrees with everything that is said in these sections, but they are all arrived at through a long process of conversation and sharing. Each member of the group has been glad for the opportunity to be involved in an exciting project doing pioneer work. We are conscious that we have fallen short of our aspirations, that our findings are tentative, and that much remains to be done. We believe that we have shown at least that the area of epistemology is not marginal to mission reflection and action, but raises acute, central concerns that missiology cannot afford to ignore if it wishes to engage realistically and self-consciously with the relevance of Christian faith in societies shaped by the history, culture, and ideals of the West. We will be exceedingly pleased if we stimulate others to further significant study in this area.

Introduction:
Epistemology and Mission

Across the disciplines something has changed in how the Academy views its own quest for knowledge: physicists read Thomas Kuhn and wonder what their "paradigms" might be; social scientists reflect on how to do research after the "demise of objectivity"; students of literature struggle with questions of the canon; and artists are faced with the "construction of art by the reader or viewer." The change everyone seems to be discussing bears many names: "postmodernism," "poststructuralism," and "deconstruction," among others. Yet little doubt remains that the traditional self-understanding of a whole string of disciplines, from physics to theology, is under attack.

A number of the issues being discussed fall within a field not in itself so new: epistemology, or the theory of knowledge. The claim being made (and widely debated) is that there is something mistaken about traditional epistemology which has concentrated on such questions as the status of knowledge claims and how one makes them, their objectivity, how one goes about justifying them, and how they function, both in the Academy and in human society more generally.

This debate is of crucial importance to the discipline of missiology. The new criticisms and concerns being debated throughout the Western intellectual world (and beyond) express an intellectual crisis that touches on the work of the missiologist in two ways: first, they preoccupy many of those who are in conversation with the Christian faith; and secondly, they raise severe questions about the study of mission itself.

The general survey that occupies the first three chapters does not attempt to reduce this widespread cultural phenomenon that many are calling postmodernity to a simple formula, nor to dictate how missiology ought to be carried out in light of it. Instead, it attempts to give an account of the questions being raised and the answers being given, making a case for the vital importance of these questions. In our view, it is essential that missiologists understand exactly what is being said about "the crisis of knowledge" today and why so many people think these questions are crucial. The book's goal, then, is to provide the resources for all interested readers to enter into, and to understand, this debate.

MODERNITY AND POSTMODERNITY

One of the features characteristic of modern Western culture is epistemological uncertainty, seen in the generally decreasing confidence that any adequate basis for knowing can be found. The crisis is often explained in terms of a distinctive shift of mood between what is called modernity and postmodernity.

Modernity is the name given to the most influential way of understanding the vast changes that have happened to Western culture during the past two centuries or more. It speaks of a cultural condition that has permeated every aspect of human life, denoting a serious rupture with the culture that preceded it. Modernity is characterised by the rise of capitalism, defined as "a competitive market system in which goods and labour power are commodities,"[1] by confidence in the power of reason, as exemplified in the scientific method and its achievements, by the triumph of liberal democracy over other political systems, by a decline in the public importance of religion, and by belief in progress.

This modern self-understanding emerged with the modernization process alongside the increasing technological innovations initiated in the industrial revolution and the changes to political and social life that were made necessary by economic growth, urbanization, universal suffrage, the rise of the welfare state, colonial expansion, international trade, and war on a hitherto unimagined scale. These changes have given rise to modernism, an ideological defense of modern culture as the best of all possible worlds. The modern world, according to its own self-understanding, is free from the old magical worldview, from political absolutism, from arbitrary moral norms and cultural conventions. Modernism highlights the power of cultural debate to bring enlightened, rational solutions to all human problems.

Postmodernity, on the other hand, breathes a very different atmosphere. Its essence, at least for thinkers such as Jean-François Lyotard, Jacques Derrida, and Richard Rorty, is a carefree scepticism about every possible attempt to make sense of history. It anarchically rejects "all the metanarratives of progress—whether Marxist or liberal."[2] Those who embrace this understanding of postmodernity deliberately reject all possibility of arriving at a defining, universally valid explanation of the phenomena of the world, whether that explanation is understood as already given or still anticipated.

The reasons for this unprecedented shift in perception are many. For the postmodernists just mentioned, they include at least the following beliefs:

---

1. Anthony Giddens, *Beyond Left and Right: The Future of Radical Politics* (Cambridge: Polity Press, 1994), 11.

2. J.O. Urmson and J. Ree (eds.), *The Concise Encyclopedia of Western Philosophy and Philosophers* (London: Routledge, 1989), 256.

1. the increasing dominance of technological reason has led to a loss of human values;
2. different rational systems for interpreting the world are seen as self-referring, and there is no superior vantage point from which their adequacy may be judged;
3. if truth claims are, by their very nature, ideological manoeuvres to achieve dominance, as French and German postmodernists assert, they will tend to squeeze out difference and ignore the inviolability of the other;
4. there is no given, stable, inner self that affords an absolute reference point for knowing;
5. an uncomplicated, univocal correspondence between an external reality and any human interpretation of it is not possible;
6. all knowledge is socially and culturally conditioned, which means that it simply expresses a point of view (never *the* point of view);
7. all human understanding is bound by conventional explanation and the language in which it is expressed.

Once the cultural shift, inherent in the transition from modernity to post-modernity, is acknowledged, various responses are possible. Some see it not as a problem but as heralding a glorious liberation from the imposition of a putative uniform rationality that is actually based on a narrow cultural consensus. From now on, culture can legitimise an endless plurality in which the value of all opinions may be acknowledged. Human discourse can be comprehensively democratised. Each person and social group can construct reality for themselves. Others wish to declare the epistemological quest—the quest for well-justified or objective knowledge claims—dead and buried. Human beings, the refrain goes, should be free from theoretical concerns to concentrate on significant practical issues such as global economic justice, the end of discrimination, the survival of the planet, the diminution of individual and corporate violence.

Others are less optimistic about the consequences of the postmodern shift. For example, they believe that a kind of criterionless plurality poses a fundamental ethical dilemma with very practical consequences: not only does it make such notions as human rights exceedingly problematic,[3] it also questions any possibility of speaking about falsehood and evil. As a result, some[4] explore the possibility of uncovering serviceable criteria for distinguishing between adequate and inadequate systems of belief and morals.[5]

---

3. Cf. R. Bellamy (ed.), *Theories and Concepts in Politics: An Introduction* (Manchester: Manchester University Press, 1993).

4. Most especially, A. MacIntyre, *Whose Justice? Which Rationality?* (London: Duckworth, 1988).

5. Technically known as a move from "foundationalism" to "holism."

IMPLICATIONS FOR MISSIOLOGY

Whatever conclusions one draws from the debate about the predominant mood of late twentieth-century Western culture as a whole (and there are vigorous disagreements), missiology (as systematic, critical reflection on the nature and practice of Christian mission) has to be concerned with the issues raised by contemporary epistemological discussion. There are three major strands to this concern:

1. *The Challenge to Christian Believing.* Under the conditions of modernity, particular truth claims are challenged against the norm of scientific rationality. By contrast, in the postmodern perspective, described above, the very possibility of objective truth claims is questioned. The notion that a given body of beliefs is true to "the way the universe is" is not considered so much false as inconceivable. If there is no agreed epistemological basis for judging the adequacy of particular beliefs and values, it would seem to follow that the claims that Christians make for the gospel are no more valid than any other religious or secular claims.

2. *The Challenge to Christian Mission.* If the postmodern perspective is right in its radical pluralism, then it is no longer possible either to speak of one universal human context (the unity of the human race is dissolved as a utopian dream), or to assert that the Christian message is universally applicable (i.e., true for every generation in every context), or to hold that it ought to be proclaimed to every human being under heaven. If the universality of the gospel vanishes in the face of epistemological relativism, would not the mandate to make it known universally have to be rejected as epistemological imperialism?

3. *The Opportunities for Missiology.* In spite of the sobering impact of both modernity and postmodernity on Christian self-understanding, the new situation affords new possibilities both for missiological reflection and for missionary communication. In the first case, a changed intellectual climate may help to bring to light neglected elements in the Christian tradition. Whether fortuitously or by design, serious discussion of pneumatology (the work of God's Spirit) and eschatology (the consummation of God's kingdom) has come to the fore in the last quarter of the twentieth century. In the second case, reaction against an excessive emphasis on the controlling nature of "instrumental reason" has led to the recognition of wider dimensions to knowledge—in particular the place of community, tradition, and action in the process of knowing ourselves and the world in which we live. This new focus on the interaction between conceptual knowing and knowing through action is an area where missiology has both much to learn and much to offer.

The epistemological crisis in the Western world is important for missiology because it undergirds this culture's awareness of its vulnerability and alienation from the certainties of the past. An understanding of the transformations taking place in human modes of thinking—in consciousness, in attitudes to ethical discourse, in the perception of culture itself—is a prerequisite for understanding changing social and political processes and the current defense of the hegemony of the world economic order. It also helps to explain the current crisis of the Western church, manifested, among other areas, in the transition from territorial and/or cultural predominance to minority status, in the church's ambivalent attitudes toward ethical dilemmas like divorce, abortion, and homosexuality, and in wrestling with cultural trends that impinge on styles of worship, leadership, use of language, and methods of evangelism.

Whether one understands missiology as a reflection on Christian mission *ad intra* (the questions of authentic renewal) or *ad extra* (how does one communicate the Christian message to non-Christians or seek to be an effective agent for the right kind of social change?), epistemology as reflected in the cultural rupture between modernity and postmodernity is a necessary (if not always prior) ingredient of serious and engaged thinking in this field today.

PART ONE

Understanding the
Epistemological Predicament
of the Contemporary West

CHAPTER ONE

Epistemological Trends in the West

The epistemological predicament that today confronts the Academy (and, many would say, Western society at large) challenges at least three traditional claims in the area of philosophy: to objective rationality, to truth, and to a "realist" interpretation of our language as corresponding with "the way things really are." In order to grasp the nature of the contemporary predicament, we begin with a brief survey of distinctive features of the theories of knowledge in three of the major Western traditions—the Anglo-American, French, and German—before moving on to a summary of their seven most important common features. In the next chapter we will move on to a systematic reconstruction of the predicament as laid out by recent work in the theory of knowledge.

Quick generalizations are often made about "the epistemological situation" in the West without considering the significantly different forms that the critique of knowledge has taken in different Western traditions. In order to avoid superficial generalizations, we have undertaken separate surveys of the English, French, and German linguistic communities, which are summarized here. These make clear that the problems being raised are not identical: when one crosses the English Channel, what is meant by "the postmodern predicament" may be as different as what is meant by "drive on the 'right' side of the road"! The reader will find these differences also reflected in the systematic treatment further below, for example in the contrasts highlighted between the mostly Anglo-American "logocentrics" and the mostly French "logoexcentrics."

THE PREDICAMENT IN ANGLO-AMERICAN EPISTEMOLOGY

At least four major components of the recent history of Anglo-American philosophy should be listed: the linguistic turn, the rise and fall of positivism, the attack on foundationalist epistemologies, and the continuation of pragmatism.

THE LINGUISTIC TURN

Modern philosophy is sometimes distinguished from medieval by its turn to epistemology as a first philosophy: that is, the assumption that traditional philosophical problems could only be approached after or by means of answers to the question, How can we know? The linguistic turn represents a second shift of equal importance. The philosophy of language becomes a first philosophy, and all other philosophical questions, including epistemological questions, must be addressed through the study of the language in which those questions are framed.[1]

Anglo-American philosophy has been closely associated with analytic philosophy throughout the twentieth century. Analytic philosophy began at Cambridge a century ago, with the reactions of G. E. Moore and Bertrand Russell against British Idealism. Early linguistic analysis was largely inspired by careful work in the foundations of logic (by Gottlob Frege, by Russell and A.N. Whitehead in their *Principia Mathematica*, and by Ludwig Wittgenstein in the *Tractatus*). Its assumption was that the formal structure of an ideal language would also show the metaphysical structure of reality. This early approach to linguistic analysis had an important influence on the logical positivists.

Between the two world wars this formal approach to language and reality was rejected, more or less independently, by Wittgenstein at Cambridge and Gilbert Ryle and J.L. Austin at Oxford. A second form of linguistic analysis was developed, the goal of which was largely to dissolve philosophical problems by showing that they arise from misconstruals or the improper use of language. While "ordinary language philosophy," as was practiced by pupils of Wittgenstein and Austin, has fallen into disrepute, a lingering legacy remains in the recognition of language as the key to philosophy and in the caution about the dangers of language "going on holiday."[2]

One motive that stimulated analytic philosophy was the quest for certitude. Just as Kant had hoped to stake philosophy's certitude on the unvarying categories of the mind, so analytic philosophers hoped to find a sphere of certain knowledge in the analysis of (unchanging, universal) concepts. W.V.O. Quine's attack on the analytic-synthetic distinction and his resulting elaboration of a "truth-meaning holism" has shown the futility of this quest.[3] Conceptual analysis has fallen prey, along with all other branches of knowledge, to historicism.

Not all philosophers of language have been affected, however, by the move from formalism to ordinary language and thence to historicism. The

---

1. Cf. Richard Rorty (ed.), *The Linguistic Turn: Recent Essays in Philosophical Method* (Chicago and London: University of Chicago Press, 1967).

2. For an excellent account of the development of analytical philosophy, see P.M.S. Hacker, *Wittgenstein's Place in Twentieth-Century Analytical Philosophy* (Oxford: Blackwell, 1996).

3. W.V.O. Quine, "Two Dogmas of Empiricism," in *From a Logical Point of View* (Cambridge, MA: Harvard University Press, 1953), first published in 1951.

attempt to develop formal semantic theories is an important emphasis in contemporary Anglo-American philosophy, along with increasingly technical work in formal logic.[4]

THE RISE AND FALL OF POSITIVISM

Logical positivism, originating in the Vienna Circle in the 1920s (of which Moritz Schlick was the most influential founding member), has had an influence on Anglo-American philosophy equal to that of linguistic analysis, and was itself strongly influenced by both the "physicalism" of Ernst Mach and the logical atomism of Russell and Wittgenstein. A.J. Ayer was responsible for conveying its influence to Britain and Rudolf Carnap its most influential exponent in the U.S.

Logical positivism attacked metaphysical reflection and attempted to develop a scientific empiricism in its place, modeled on logic and scientific standards of knowledge. Its influence on Anglo-American philosophy departments, especially in the 1940s and 1950s, was enormous, even though the logical positivist positions were very quickly replaced by the more moderate positions of the neopositivists (e.g., Karl Popper and Carl Hempel).

The critique of positivism as an epistemology and philosophy of science (especially by Stephen Toulmin, N.R. Hanson, and Thomas Kuhn) and of its sharp distinction between theory and observation (by Hilary Putnam) has been as thorough and effective as any refutation in the history of philosophy. As a result, few philosophers today officially espouse a positivist epistemology. Still, the interest in scientific knowledge and a quasi-positivist suspicion of religion and traditional metaphysics remain strong in analytic philosophy departments.

THE ATTACK ON FOUNDATIONALIST EPISTEMOLOGIES

Foundationalism is a theory of knowledge inspired by Descartes' image of a belief system as a building. Philosophy's job has been construed as the examination or reconstruction of the foundations of knowledge. In twentieth-century Anglo-American philosophy, however, this account of knowledge and philosophy has been called into question. Two kinds of problems have come to be seen by many as insuperable. First, there is the problem of finding suitable foundational beliefs. The two options have seemed to be either a Cartesian-style intuition or sense experience. Cartesian intuitions are now seen to be dependent upon language (conceptual systems) and therefore questionable.

The second problem for the foundationalist is that of construction: how to reason from the foundation to the rest of knowledge. Theories of empir-

---

4. See, e.g., Michael Dummett, *Truth and Other Enigmas* (Cambridge, MA: Harvard University Press, 1978).

ical knowledge suffer from the dilemma that, although sense data (reports of immediate sensory experience) in the logical positivists' scheme have the requisite foundational indubitability, the problem of construction (i.e., how to use them to justify any interesting knowledge claim) was soon recognized as insuperable. The later (neopositivist) move to found empirical knowledge on ordinary observations of medium-sized objects or scientific data represents a severe weakening of the classical foundationalist theory.

It would be mistaken to claim that foundationalism no longer has advocates among analytical philosophers. The movements, however, that have attracted the main philosophical attention over the last forty or so years have, almost without exception, proposed alternatives to the foundationalist approach to knowledge. Quine's "holism," based on the web metaphor discussed below, has had an influence on the major figures of the last twenty years (e.g., Donald Davidson, Hilary Putnam, and their followers) that is difficult to overestimate. The philosophy of science since 1960 has been increasingly preoccupied with nonfoundational theories of scientific knowledge (e.g., Toulmin, Kuhn, Lakatos, Feyerabend, Bas van Fraassen, Wesley Salmon, and Philip Kitcher).

In addition, there have been numerous attacks on the entire paradigm of knowledge as justified true belief. Richard Rorty and other neopragmatists and "post-philosophers," for example, have challenged altogether the need for justification. In the U.S. in particular, feminist critiques of traditional "male" epistemology and feminist reconstructions of the concept of knowledge are having a large impact. This movement includes the work of feminist philosophers of science such as Sandra Hardy, feminist epistemologists such as Rosie Tong, and, most recently, feminist theoreticians of critical thinking such as Dianne Romain.[5]

THE RISE OF PRAGMATISM

Classical American pragmatism (as exemplified in the work of C.S. Peirce, William James, and John Dewey) took some account of pragmatic usefulness as the chief criterion for, and even as the definition of, knowledge. Questions of what we know should be answered in terms of what is useful to the knower (James explained this in terms of the "cash value" of truth). In recent years neopragmatism, which attempts to overcome the unsolved difficulties raised by traditional pragmatic theories of science and by notions such as Peirce's idea of a "final convergence of expert opinion," has begun to remove science from its former dominant position in pragmatic theory (although there are some signs that, reading between the lines, science remains as foundational as ever). According to the neopragmatists, such as Rorty, epistemology as a serious (or at least soluble) set of questions must

---

5. Dianne Romain, *Thinking Things Through: Critical Thinking for Decisions You Can Live With* (Mountain View, CA: Mayfield Publishing Co., 1997).

be abandoned; henceforth, all philosophy becomes "conversation." A more moderate pragmatic element, a legacy from Carnap and C.I. Lewis, has been incorporated into Quine's holist epistemology.

CONTINENTAL INFLUENCES

Finally, and not unrelated to the last heading, German and (even more) French epistemology continues to gain followers in the analytical world. Numerous formerly staunch analytical epistemologists have attempted either to integrate analytical with Continental thought (e.g., Hubert Dreyfus and Richard Bernstein) or have rejected the former in favor of the latter.

MAJOR RESPONSES

There have been three main responses to these difficulties in analytical philosophy. For one group of philosophers, epistemology in something like the traditional sense of the term is still a live option. And here there are a variety of strategies: *(a)* There are those who try to counter Humean (and other) skeptical arguments with more sophisticated accounts of the foundations of knowledge. *(b)* There are others who attempt to develop a "weak foundationalism," structurally similar to classical foundationalism, yet without the latter's shortcomings (e.g., William Alston and Keith Lehrer). *(c)* Coherence-based epistemologists proceed in classical analytical terms and with the rigor typical of this style of philosophy, yet they offer a theory of justification based not on foundations but on the coherence between sets of statements (e.g., Nicholas Rescher, Ernst Sosa, and Lawrence Bonjour). *(d)* A variety of developments have occurred among epistemologists (now the majority) who reject the foundationalist model entirely. These include Quine and other 'holist' epistemologists, 'holist' philosophers of science such as Thomas Kuhn, and what we might call "traditionalists," whose account of justification is linked to particular intellectual traditions, while still allowing for comparative assessments of adequacy (e.g., Imre Lakatos, Alasdair MacIntyre, and, several decades ago, Michael Polanyi).

For another group of Anglo-American philosophers, the job traditionally assigned to epistemology has been taken over by linguistic analysis, in particular by the analysis of concepts of truth. Truth, some of these thinkers argue (e.g., Albert Taski), may be analyzed as a relation between two sets of statements: an "object language" and a "metalanguage." For such views, reference is a semantic, that is, a language-internal question (e.g., Peter Strawson). All truth claims involve the interpretation of a linguistic situation and, therefore, require careful semantic analysis, using either pragmatic or formal semantic techniques (e.g., John Searle and Bas van Fraassen). In some cases the semantic approach is expanded into a "deflationary theory of truth," according to which the predicate "is true" adds nothing to the mere assertion of the statement in the first place; it can (in most cases) simply be omitted.

Finally, a variety of philosophers dispute that epistemology as an organized area of study is even a live option any longer. It should be replaced, they maintain, by a variety of successor disciplines such as neopragmatism (Rorty), by a Wittgensteinian language-game analysis (Peter Winch and D. Z. Phillips), by hermeneutics (Richard Bernstein and Mary Hesse, who draw on Continental thinkers such as Paul Ricoeur, H.-G. Gadamer, and Jürgen Habermas), by an analysis of power dynamics in society (the Anglo-American followers of Michel Foucault), or by the study of knowledge as a social phenomenon, as in the so-called strong program in the sociology of knowledge (Barry Barnes and David Bloor).

TRUTH, RATIONALITY, AND PLURALISM:
SOME SUMMARY POINTS

Clearly, there is no consensus within Anglo-American philosophy. One encounters instead a great variety of positions. Still, several general trends can be identified. First, French thinkers have exercised a growing influence on Anglo-American philosophy; the French influence is much more strongly felt in the U.S. today than it was fifteen years ago. The frequent discussion of what "postmodernism" means (and whether it has arrived) hints at this trend. Similarly, German critiques of traditional theories of knowledge have played an important role in Anglo-American philosophy, running from a renewed interest in hermeneutics to the increasing attention paid to Habermas and neo-Marxism (e.g., Richard Bernstein and Mary Hesse).

Second, books with titles such as *Beyond Analytical Philosophy* and *After Philosophy* express some people's sense that the analytical tradition as a whole must be left behind. Some "postepistemologists" are motivated by factors internal to analytical philosophy itself, others by the sense that an alternative approach to philosophy will yield a more accurate account of the question of knowledge.

Third, others, attempting to avoid the morass of relativism, have turned back to the history of philosophy and classic philosophical texts in an effort to find more satisfactory solutions to the problems of knowledge. Extensive recent work has been carried out in ancient, Hellenistic, medieval, and early modern philosophy. Arguably, scientific realism is an analogous attempt, within the philosophy of science, to reclaim the empiricist past.

Fourth, increasingly the distinction between philosophy and other disciplines has been blurred in the study of knowledge. Cognitive science, neurophysiology, psychology, artificial intelligence, and various subfields within linguistics are now viewed as indispensable for answering traditional philosophical questions about knowledge.

Finally, it would be fair to say that the field of epistemology itself has lost some of its former hegemony in analytical philosophy. Like Quentin Skinner's *Return of Grand Theory* in the social sciences, one increasingly finds a return to the "big questions" raised within philosophical disciplines such as metaphysics, ethics, and philosophical theology.

Perhaps the most significant shift in all of this is the recognition that philosophy, too, has a history. That is, philosophers have long been willing to grant the historicity of other knowledge claims: first, in the "soft" sciences, and then, in the 1960s, in the "hard sciences." However, the goal of analytic philosophy was to isolate a sphere of knowledge that was not subject to the same vicissitudes as empirical knowledge—i.e., the realm of the conceptual. Quine's undoing of the analytic-synthetic distinction has blurred the lines between the conceptual and the empirical, and, in so doing, has ended analytical philosophy's hope of finding a sphere of universal, certain knowledge. The successor to analytical philosophy is, in the words of Jeffrey Stout, "conceptual archaeology."[6]

THE PREDICAMENT IN FRENCH PHILOSOPHY

What is the shape and significance of French philosophy? Perhaps one theme on which all contemporary French philosophers could agree is that the subject of philosophy (in both senses—the subject matter and the one who philosophizes) is in crisis. Descartes had tried to found knowledge (and philosophy) in the subject. French thinkers after 1945 had turned to the three H's (Hegel, Husserl, and Heidegger) in order to save Descartes' project. Since 1960, however, French thinkers have hearkened more to the three masters of suspicion (Marx, Freud, and Nietzsche), each of whom has called the subject and consciousness itself into question. Ricoeur has typically declared that "consciousness is not a given, but a task," and Foucault has announced the death of the "subject."

The other common theme in French philosophy is the preoccupation with language. According to Michael Dummett, the Anglo-Saxon analytical tradition of philosophy arose out of a dismissal of epistemology as the principal part of philosophy. Theories of knowledge were displaced by theories of meaning and language. Moreover, language philosophy in the Anglo-Saxon tradition has been inspired largely by logic. In France, by contrast, while there has been a turn to language and away from epistemology, the discipline that has inspired most French thinkers is not logic but linguistics. A study of the actual phenomenon of language was more conducive to a tradition steeped in phenomenological analysis—the "life" of language, as it were—rather than its logic.

The Swiss linguist Ferdinand de Saussure's *Cours de linguistique générale* (1916) has had a profound influence throughout the French intellectual world, affecting disciplines as diverse as psychoanalysis, anthropology, literary criticism, and philosophy. For Saussure, language is a self-contained differential sign system in which signifiers (i.e., the signs or words) refer only to other signifiers, never to the signifieds (i.e., the concepts or things). The meaning of a sign is a function, not of its positive relation to some thing, but

---

6. Jeffrey Stout, *The Flight from Authority: Religion, Morality and the Quest for Autonomy* (Notre Dame: University of Notre Dame Press, 1981).

rather of its difference from other signs. A language is thus a structure of binary oppositions (e.g., hot/cold, good/bad, rational/irrational). The significance of Saussure's view for philosophy is that language as a structured field (*langue*) always precedes conscious thought and speech (*parole*). Language is a free-standing structure that is determined neither by thought (subjectivity) nor by things (the world).

It is somewhat ironic that French philosophy has proved to be particularly influential in disciplines other than philosophy. Literary criticism and literary theory have proven especially receptive to poststructuralism, for instance. The reasons are not hard to find. According to Derrida, philosophy itself resembles literary theory, once one deconstructs the hierarchical opposition between logic and rhetoric. Indeed, to the extent that all fields of human life and inquiry can be considered "texts," the reach of French philosophy is virtually boundless. Anglo-American philosophers like Richard Rorty share the French view that philosophy is actually a form of culture criticism.

While poststructuralism and deconstruction have produced a number of extreme and somewhat careless disciples (and caricatures), it would be a mistake to write off these movements as merely faddish, or as examples of "silly relativism." As Christopher Norris has observed, many who criticize Derrida's conclusions have never even read him. It is important to view Derrida's work in the larger context of Western philosophy and not only French thought. Derrida does not advocate an "anything goes" relativism, nor does he take a cavalier or irresponsible attitude toward the history of philosophy. On the contrary, his works are characterized by an almost fastidious attention to classical philosophical texts, which he interrogates with his own brand of analytical rigor. Deconstruction is not destruction but rather a patient "undoing" that removes the various historical and social layers that have formed a particular concept. Derrida himself claims to be pursuing Kant's question about the limits of reason.

ASPECTS OF THE FRENCH PREDICAMENT

Subjectivity

According to the French thinkers, the subject is not at all as Descartes had pictured it, knowing its own mind with clear and distinct ideas. The subject is not a sovereign but a situated consciousness. It inhabits a particular body, with a race and gender, located in a social context and using a particular language. Indeed, it may be more appropriate, in the case of certain French thinkers, to speak not of the situated but the superseded subject. Both in structuralism and poststructuralism, the subject is superseded by language systems, discursive formations, and cultural practices.

French philosophy is still coming to grips with the demise of Cartesian thought and the loss of subjectivity. Knowing the conscious self (or what the self is conscious of) now represents only a small part of the task of philosophy. The vaunted knowing subject cannot even know its own mind, for language is not a transparent but a highly selective medium, a medium, moreover, that is subject to material, sociopolitical forces. There is no such thing as "pure" reason; all reason is "always-already" context-dependent. Indeed, many poststructuralist thinkers might be said to offer critiques of "impure" reason, critiques that resemble cultural studies rather than epistemology, insofar as they highlight the unavoidable entanglement of reason in history and tradition, body and desire, cultures and practices, power and politics.

Language

Language has become the central preoccupation of French philosophy. Philosophy that resembles literary theory occupies the place traditionally reserved for metaphysics and epistemology; yet, the burning question is a transcendental rather than an analytical one. That is, French thinkers are concerned with the ways in which language is the "condition for the possibility of" intellectual, ethical, and political experience.

French thinkers have found many applications for Saussure's insights into language. Indeed, we might say that the picture of everything structured like a differential sign system has held them captive (in anthropology, psychology, literary theory). Structuralism was the search for universal unifying structures in language. Lévi-Strauss suggested, in the field of anthropology, that kinship systems are structured like a language. Similarly, Jacques Lacan challenged Freudian psychoanalysis by claiming that the unconscious is structured like a language. And in political theory, Louis Althusser amended Marxism by producing a structuralist theory of ideology.

A philosophy may be considered poststructuralist when it displays an "incredulity towards structures." Saussure had already acknowledged that the differences within differential sign systems are arbitrary. The poststructuralist expands upon this insight and suggests that any structure as a whole is also arbitrary. The poststructuralist, in other words, refuses to give a privileged position to any center that would give stability to a given structure. For the poststructuralist, structures give only the illusion of stability. Poststructuralist analysis exposes the fault lines and weak spots in systems and structures. Deconstruction in particular shows that, insofar as a structure is a differential sign system, it is inherently unstable because the play of differences is endless and never comes to rest. Deconstruction undoes the "structurality" of structure by showing that no system of signs is ever necessary or complete in itself.

World

The notion of the world also becomes an example of "textuality," for the world is viewed as an undifferentiated surface structured by language. The world as we know it is "always-already" written. Consequently, the "world itself" cannot really constrain our theories. However, what we can say is limited by constraints of other kinds. Ideology (the prestructuring that precedes conscious thought) is the condition for the possibility of thinking about the world. Nevertheless, all representations are considered suspect.

RESPONSES

French philosophers have responded to the crisis of Cartesian thought, first, by exploring other theories of subjectivity (e.g., those of Husserl and Heidegger), and second, by exploring language as the condition for the very possibility of subjectivity. French thinkers have sought creatively to appropriate past thinkers (e.g., Marx, Freud, and Nietzsche) and other disciplines (e.g., linguistics and literary theory) in their search for a kind of post-Cartesian or postmodern philosophy. The influence of Saussure's linguistics, above all, is apparent in contemporary French thought. Jean Baudrillard claims that we are now in the last of the four stages of the sign: "(1) It is the reflection of a basic reality [premodern]. (2) It masks and perverts a basic reality [modern]. (3) It masks the absence of a basic reality [structuralist]. (4) It bears no relation to any reality whatsoever; it is its own pure simulacrum [poststructuralist]."[7]

By and large, however, contemporary French thinkers have been content to *bricoler* (potter about, do odd jobs), rather than lay bricks. A *bricoleur* is a handyman who makes use of various tools and materials but is not interested in constructing his own edifice. Recent French thought is typically more deconstructive than constructive, more concerned with iconoclasm than with laying new foundations. Though France still has its revered "Grands Ecoles," the age of empire appears over. There is a systematic distrust of "metanarratives" (Lyotard), a suspicion of any account that attempts to explain everything. Instead, there is an interest in exploring particular perspectives and in ensuring that particular perspectives will not be swallowed by grand schemes. Economics may be global, but there is a resistance in the marketplace of ideas to any kind of ideological monopoly. The "one" must be sacrificed for "the many."

The ethical face of French philosophy is best seen in the work of Emmanuel Lévinas. He too feels that epistemology, in its quest for universal synthesis, tends to reduce the many to the one, the "other" to the same. The history of philosophy, he says, "can be interpreted as an attempt at universal synthesis, a reduction of all experience, of all that is reasonable, to a totality wherein consciousness embraces the world, leaves nothing other outside of itself, and thus becomes absolute thought."[8]

Lévinas calls for ethics rather than epistemology to be the "first philosophy." Instead of trying to possess objects in order to "comprehend," the

---

7. Mark Poster (ed.), *Jean Baudrillard: Selected Writings* (Cambridge: Polity Press, 1988), 170.

8. Emmanuel Lévinas, *Totality and Infinity* (Pittsburgh: Duquesne University Press, 1969), 75.

philosopher should remain open-minded to inquiries from the other. The subject is not "for itself," but "for another." Finite beings as we are, we cannot complete the task of knowledge. Insofar as we try, we coerce the Other into the category of the Same. As finite beings we must choose between epistemology and ethics.

THE PREDICAMENT IN GERMAN PHILOSOPHY

One cannot understand the scene in contemporary German philosophy without understanding certain influences on the present discussion. The influence of "classical German philosophy"—that flowering of critical and systematic philosophy between Kant's *Critique of Pure Reason* in 1781 and Hegel's death in 1843—continues to be felt across the curriculum, both by traditionalists and by rebels. Adapting the French example, we might speak of the crucial four German H's as Hegel, Husserl, Heidegger, and hermeneutics.

Hegel's Philosophy of the Absolute Subject

The serious study of Hegel's philosophy, and of German Idealism in general, which continues in Germany today, means that one often encounters a concern with rationalism—the belief that important truths can be discerned through a priori reason alone without reliance on science or direct sense experience—uncommon in the previous two traditions. Because Hegel's philosophy was dialectical, moving with rational necessity through a repeated triadic movement of thesis, its opposite (antithesis), and a synthesis of the two at a higher level of reflection, German epistemology continues to argue the merits and liabilities of dialectical thought patterns.

Husserl's Philosophy of the "Eidetic" or Essential Subject

Husserl attempted a "phenomenology" of consciousness, that is, a description aimed at uncovering the essential structures of what it is to be a conscious agent. Like Descartes (but without the reliance on God), he relied on introspection and meditation, combined with careful conceptual analysis, in order to lay out the "life-world" (*Lebenswelt*) of the human mind.

Heidegger's Philosophy of the Individual Existing Subject

Heidegger's starting point was existential not eidetic: he began with *Dasein*, the individual existing human subject, and attempted to explain what it is for *Dasein* to be always unfinished, to exist as always already thrown into a world, to have projects, concerns, and cares, and to anticipate its possible final completeness. Though radically individual, his philosophy also seeks common structures in human existence. In Heidegger's later writings he became increasingly preoccupied with language and with the Being that undergirds all individual beings. The approaches of both the early and the late Heidegger have inspired significant work by contemporary German philosophers.

Hermeneutics and the Birth of Pluralism

Arising out of Heidegger's later philosophy was the work of Hans-Georg Gadamer and other hermeneutic thinkers. Like Heidegger they criticized the alleged objectivity of science, shifting attention from objective explanation to the subjective understanding of texts and of history. We can never know the author's intended meaning; at best we can achieve a "fusion of horizons" with a past tradition. This focus on multiple traditions of interpretation obviously connects (and in many cases has influenced) movements such as pluralism, multiculturalism, poststructuralism, and cultural or historical relativism, both within and outside of German-language philosophy.

Responses to the Contemporary Situation

Some German epistemology continues to be characterized by a turning back to earlier high points in the history of Western thought: the Greeks, medieval philosophy, the ontotheological tradition in modern metaphysics (say, from Descartes to the early Kant), and, of course, classical German philosophy (especially Kant, Fichte, Schelling, and Hegel).

Other strands have become critical of these classic roots and have begun to look elsewhere for their intellectual resources. One thus finds sophisticated appropriations, *inter alia*, of Anglo-American analytical philosophy and philosophy of science (e.g., Stegmüller, Hans Albert, Rudolf Haller, and Lorenz Puntel), of Marxist thought (the Frankfurt school and its offspring: Horkheimer, Adorno, and Habermas), and of American pragmatism (e.g., Apel).

Finally, a third group has extended the trends of German thought in a more radically skeptical direction. Many of the "philosophers of suspicion" wrote in German (Schopenhauer, Feuerbach, Marx, Nietzsche, and Freud), and their followers have extended and deepened their well-known critiques of knowledge. There is, then, a highly skeptical and antitraditional movement in German philosophy today, not unlike many of the French figures considered above, although their influence within German universities today is certainly less strong than would be the case in France.

Truth, Rationality, Pluralism

Above all, the impression must not be given that there is a consensus on these subjects in German philosophy; one finds forceful disagreement. If any general observations at all can be made, they would probably include the following. First, pluralism and postmodernism have not been embraced to the extent they have been in France and the U.S. Second, the views on rationality are precisely as diverse as the individual movements and influences mentioned above. Third, despite this diversity, German thinkers do seem to see themselves as facing a specific set of options regarding the truth question. Some hold that the traditional understanding of the notion of truth emerges unscathed from contemporary critiques. New resources (e.g., those of analytical philosophy) allow us to solve once intractable problems. A major new work by Lorenz Puntel, for example, supplies a reexamination and defense of something like the classical coherence theory of truth through a careful appropriation of recent analytical thought. Other thinkers argue that we must modify the traditional view. So, for example, Habermas holds that truth is only one goal of "communicative action," and at one point he even argued that truth is just consensus among the participants in an ideal speech situation. Finally, some have argued that we must abandon altogether the traditional quest for a definition of and criteria for truth. Following Nietzsche's lead in questioning the value of truth, they advocate instead a concern with power or beauty or the transformation of society.

Again at the risk of oversimplification, many of the German positions in this debate could be located at one point along a single continuum, depending on which of the following four theses they accept and which ones they oppose. (1) There is a knowable, unified truth, and it is the goal of philosophical reflection to grasp and to formulate it (e.g., Dieter Henrich and Wolfhart Pannenberg). (2) There is a single truth, but we do not grasp it, or we grasp it only in part. We must be "epistemic pluralists," because our best efforts at knowledge do not rule out enough of the options (e.g., Hans Albert). (3) Epistemic pluralism is correct, and the goal of a final, unified truth can be no more than a "regulative idea" presupposed by the activity we call "the search for knowledge." The idea of truth, then, is merely a human construct that helps to guide our epistemic and ethical efforts. We might call this view "regulative monism" (e.g., the use of the term "Being" by Gadamer). (4) The ontological pluralists, finally, hold that there is no single Truth (e.g., Hermann Timm); such an idea should simply be abandoned by philosophers as well as by theologians.

COMMONALITIES

If we had to be careful about drawing generalizations within German, French, or Anglo-American philosophy, even more caution will be called for in the search for commonalities among all three traditions. Nevertheless, even when all necessary caveats have been expressed (and even observed!), it is still possible to identify a few common themes that run among the three traditions.

More thinkers now than in the past are asserting a *priority of ethics over epistemology*. Just as all observations of the world are theory-laden in one way or another, so too is epistemology. What we take knowledge to be expresses particular assumptions, prejudices, and values. In German it has been Marxist social theory that has emphasized the connection between Knowledge and Human Interests (as the title of Habermas's early book states it). In France philosophers have struggled with "the problem of the Other" (the other person, the other viewpoint, the "other" to language), with the social formation of "epistemes" (e.g., Foucault), and with the apparent fact that human thought is value-laden from the very beginning. In the U.S., Putnam and Goodman (among others) have argued that what we claim to know depends on evaluative judgments. Alasdair MacIntyre argues that formation in certain moral virtues is a necessary prerequisite for intellectual inquiry.

All three traditions manifest a *preoccupation with language.* Whether we examine the "linguistic turn" in analytic philosophy, hermeneutics in German philosophy, or deconstruction, linguistics, and literary theory in France, we find the same interest in the medium in which thought takes place. Language is not a medium that can be disregarded when asking about knowledge and truth, like a clear window that does not disturb the viewer. Instead, its contribution—the fact that we have to work with it and through it—is of crucial importance to the debate about knowledge and truth.

In all three traditions today one finds signs that contemporary thinkers are struck more and more deeply by the radical implications of the *role of social construction*, as opposed to "the real" in what we take to be knowledge, and with doubts about whether categories such as "the Real" or "the True" have any usefulness any longer within philosophy. For others it has motivated new efforts to provide accounts of justification that dispense with the picture of a mind-independent reality as the basis for knowledge, or with the very picture of language over-against reality; language itself is a part of reality and the means by which we encounter and engage with (nonlinguistic) reality.

Not unrelated to the previous point, all the traditions today evidence an increasing focus on anthropology, on the *theory of the subject*, as relevant to epistemology. It would not be an exaggeration to say that the French thinkers have replaced epistemology with a theory of the subject, its presence and absence, its construction and deconstruction. Since Kant, German philosophers have recognized that the categories which the human subject brings to its experience help to constitute its world. This is why one speaks of classical German idealism instead of realism. Moreover, in all three traditions doubts have been raised about the very existence of a Cartesian knowing subject, one who truly meditates in abstraction from its location within the world. Instead, attention has shifted to the role of ideology, to the "situation" or "location" of the subject, and how these affect what humans take to be knowledge. This "locatedness" includes the thinker's location in his or her own body and the effect of the body (or the physical in general) on thought. In this sense both feminist and neopragmatist critiques of knowledge are antidualistic and holistic in a way not typical of traditional philosophy. Thus, one might say either that the subject has disappeared or that the modern individualist account of the subject was mistaken; subjects emerge only within social relationships.

In each tradition we find concern with the problem of the *many and the one*, or pluralism versus universality. If I know that there are many religious traditions, how can I assert that one alone is true? If the evidence available to the scientist underdetermines his or her choice among multiple competing theories, or only slightly supports one of them above the others, should the scientist withhold assent from any? Should one employ multiple criteria in selecting one's beliefs, using different criteria in different contexts, or is there a single set of overriding criteria that determine all theory selection? Can multiple systems of belief be simultaneously true? Put differently, all three contemporary linguistic traditions are pluralistic in a new sense. Not only is there a recognition of radical diversity in all areas of human experience, there is a questioning of the possibility, and the value, of a consensus that would overarch and overcome these differences.

Connected with this trend, one finds a higher degree of *skepticism* in all three traditions than, say, forty years ago. It cannot be merely a matter of coincidence that all three are looking back on major orientations that preoccupied several generations of scholars, such as positivism, ordinary language philosophy, and the "knowledge as justified true belief" tradition in Anglo-American philosophy, structuralism and phenomenology in France, Hegel, Husserl, Heidegger, and hermeneutics in Germany, and are expressing skepticism about what these orientations have achieved and whether they are worth pursuing any longer.

Often, where contemporary thinkers do claim to have solved the problem of skepticism, they do so by means of a turn to radical *particularity*. No longer is the affirmation "All rational persons must think this way," but "I (or we) happen to think this way"; no longer "This is the right way to live," but "In our tradition we value this"; no longer "This claim meets the necessary criteria for knowledge," but "In our group (or for our particular practice) we take this to be justified."

These commonalities suggest that a more ambitious undertaking may be in order. In the next chapter we move from a geographical mapping of epistemological issues to an attempt at a more systematic analysis.

CHAPTER TWO

The State of Claims to Truth

Having described some of the regional distinctives in the theory of knowledge, we move to the more ambitious task of attempting to provide a *systematic map* of the major alternative views on pluralism, rationality, and truth.[1] At the outset, we must note a profound dispute about the very desirability of truth or rationality as goals to be sought or defended. It is appropriate to refer to a parting of the ways in Western thought as a "continental divide" because, while valuing truth and knowledge is not exclusively characteristic of Anglo-American thought, its rejection is clearly associated with Continental philosophy and literary criticism.[2] On one side of the divide is the traditional view that knowledge is a good to be sought. On the other side, dating back at least to Friedrich Nietzsche's charge that "knowledge" masks the will to power, there has been a growing tendency to call into question the value that Western thought has traditionally placed on knowledge, truth, and rationality. For example, Michel Foucault has set out to show that knowledge is not what it seems—a neutral record of what is there—but rather represents the interests of whatever group has the power to impose its will on others. Thus, he holds, knowledge is neither obviously a good thing nor morally neutral. Those who undermine or "deconstruct" accepted ways of thinking may be morally in the right over against those who attempt to maintain the grip of a "totalitarian" consensus.

---

1. It should be emphasised that such a systematic project cannot be pursued without touching on deep methodological assumptions and commitments. To come to an agreement on a taxonomy of this scale, seven specialists in the field have had to compromise at various points on their own positions and interpretations, including positions on which some of them have written extensively. There are thus points in what follows from which individual contributors to this chapter would wish to distance themselves, points which will be obvious to those familiar with the individual publications. We have, however, deemed it too cumbersome to add specific footnotes to indicate every single difference.

2. The distinction between the Continental and Anglo-American traditions in philosophy is a conventional one, used to designate different approaches to philosophy that have developed during the modern period. It is important to remember, however, that many philosophers in the U.S. and Britain contribute to the Continental tradition, while many on the Continent participate in the Anglo-American tradition.

To describe this conflict, we have divided the treatment of knowledge and rationality between those positions that continue to presuppose the desirability of knowledge and those that altogether reject it as a goal to be pursued. We have adopted the term *logocentrism*, coined by Jacques Derrida (the founder of "deconstruction"), to stand for the traditional valorization and pursuit of knowledge. We shall be speaking, then, of the former group of thinkers as "logocentrics" and those who wish to remove reason from its central place in Western values as "logoexcentrics."

In the interests of as clear a presentation as possible, the first section is subdivided into two further sections, one concerning debates about realism and truth, the other by debates about rationality. Before proceeding, however, we should note that such a separation is itself highly controversial; some insist that we cannot speak of "what is" or "what is true" apart from a given understanding of knowledge. Others insist that questions about the nature of a mind-independent reality must precede an examination of human knowing.

THE LOGOCENTRICS

CLAIMS TO TRUTH AND THE KANTIAN CRISIS

This general position within philosophy concerns itself in the first place with the question of truth—namely, what it is and whether we can possess it—and only secondarily with questions of rationality and justification. Certain primary questions are addressed by these thinkers. Is our language to be interpreted "realistically"? What does it mean to say that it is about an "externally existing reality"? Do skeptical considerations raised by epistemologists cast into doubt the very idea of concepts corresponding to a language-independent reality? Is such a correspondence with reality (*adequatio rei et intellectus*) the definition of truth? Should Truth (with a capital T) be replaced by multiple truths, such that my language might be "true for me" but not "true for you"? These ways of framing the questions have been largely inspired by Continental philosophy.[3]

According to this point of view, to stake a truth claim involves making rational claims about something. The Cartesian anxiety that we have discussed in the previous chapter—the crisis over the nature and locus of rationality—is only one aspect of the contemporary predicament. It is one thing to defend a belief's rationality, but quite another to defend its reference to the real. We have, therefore, to speak also of a *Kantian anxiety*. Do our

---

3. There are, of course, exceptions. Foundationalism, for example, has often first assumed a mind-independent reality and then begun to look for foundational propositions that correspond to reality. Some coherence theories (e.g., the position of Nicholas Rescher in his influential 1973 study, *The Coherence Theory of Truth* [cf. n. 25]) also speak of a "fit" between the set of coherent statements and reality. We should also add that analytical/Continental distinctions have become more difficult to draw in recent years.

statements and our concepts, even the rational ones, represent the real? If not, what are we to make of their claim to truth? What we have termed the contemporary predicament thus concerns not only the problem of how to make intelligible truth claims, but the perhaps even more difficult task of making the very concept of truth itself intelligible.

The "Kantian" challenge is how to make sense of the notion of truth and the relation of language to the real world. This question focuses on the predicament of the relation between language and the world in a way different from the epistemological question of the claim to rationality (discussed later). According to the thinkers to be addressed here, the truth question is irreducible to the justification question, since a claim can be rationally justified but mistaken. This debate about truth has obvious relevance for those who make Christian truth claims, since it asks them to specify just what they mean by these claims and what they think their theological statements are about. In short, the rationality question concerns the *intelligibility* and *justification* of a theological claim; truth its *reference* or *aboutness*.

THE KANTIAN PROBLEM: CAN WE TALK ABOUT THE REAL?

For many contemporary thinkers, Kant's formulation of the problem continues to be paradigmatic. Kant's problem was how to account for objectivity: specifically, the validity of Newtonian physics. His transcendental approach asked the question, what are the necessary conditions for the possibility of objective knowledge of the external world? His solution combined the empiricist and rationalist traditions and suggested that objective knowledge is produced by the mind's bringing a bundle of percepts under a concept. In other words, the world and the mind (percepts and concepts) *together* make up objective knowledge. Kant's "Copernican Revolution" reversed the traditional view of the subject-object relation. Qualities that things were once thought to have on their own came to be seen as determinations imposed by the knowing subject.

Indeed, Kant defines "world" as the product of the mind processing experience. Humans share a world because they all use the same basic categories to make sense of their experiences. The "world" is just human experience as processed by human categories. The "world" is, therefore, constructed and constituted, partially at least, by the activity of the human mind. Kant thought of our concepts and categories as carving up and ordering an undifferentiated manifold of sense experience. He accounted for objectivity by maintaining that all thinkers use the same "categories of the understanding" for making sense of experience. The categories are "transcendental": necessary conditions for the very possibility of meaningful perceptual experience. They impose distinctions upon the world. Kant, however, holds them to be objective rather than subjective, precisely because they are necessary for any thought whatsoever. On this view, objectivity becomes intersubjectivity; or, to put it another way, the world is seen not from a "God's-eye" but from a "humanity's-eye" point of view.

Kant's account of knowledge relies on a crucial distinction between "phenomena" (that which appears in the everyday world of human space-time experience) and "noumena" (the world as it is in itself). Reality as it is in itself cannot be known. It is beyond the reach of human language and concepts. Yet Newtonian reality is saved because this is precisely the world of space and time experience. For Kant, the everyday world of human experience is a construct built up of an undifferentiated reality and a differentiating mind.

The Kantian picture contributes to the epistemological predicament, for he demonstrated that there is a constructive dimension to human knowing. The mind does not simply mirror reality, but rather works reality over. While it is readily acknowledged that Kant erred in absolutizing his twelve categories, it is claimed by many that conceptual schemes get in the way of the mind's attempt to know reality. Kant could not imagine forms of logic or physics other than those of Aristotle and Newton, yet we now have to contend with alternative forms of logic, geometry, and physics. What Kant took to be universal categories of the understanding have instead turned out to be contingent and historically conditioned. The mind is not a mirror but a filter of nature. For post-Kantians, then, the predicament is that we construct the world with historically variable and culturally conditioned conceptual schemes.

The Kantian problematic amounts to the fundamental dilemma whether anything—sand in the Sahara, football games, marriages, values, God—is really there; are they "given," or is everything constructed ("graven")? Is the real begotten (by God) or made by humans? Is the world differentiated, divided up into natural kinds and natural orders, or are all these distinctions—for example, between one kind of tree and another, between trees and other kinds of vegetation, between trees and animals and animals and humans—products of a contingent system of projection, the result of our felt human need to keep our world tidy? When we stake a truth claim about the world, are we talking about the world or only about ourselves, our habits of perception, or our will to dominate? The difficulty—the Kantian problematic—is that there is no way to get behind or above our language and our conceptual schemes to check whether they fit with reality.

KINDS OF REALISM

Can we talk about the real, or is our talk really about ourselves—i.e., about the way we talk? Does the world have a determinate character regardless of our language about it, or does our language create those distinctions and features of the world we find most significant? Does language invent or discover the structure of reality?[4] Different answers have been given to these crucial questions.

---

4. There is some dispute as to whether realism is an epistemological or an ontological position. John Searle argues for a nonepistemic definition: the view that the world exists independently of our representations of it, cf. *The Construction of Social Reality* (New York: New York University Press, 1995). Moreover, realism does not say how things are, but only that there is a way things are. While there are those who hold to an ontological understanding of antirealism (e.g., Absolute Idealists, Vedantic Hinduism),

EXTERNAL REALISM

This is the view that the real exists as something over against and independent of the ways humans speak or think about it. Naive or "commonsense" realism holds that it is the world that fixes the content of our conceptual schemes. Our minds are designed in such a way as to know the world, not exhaustively, but partially (though truly). Things may be known as they really are. We might term this position "hard metaphysical realism": "hard" because it is both the most vigorous manifesto for realism and difficult for philosophers to accept after Kant.

According to the external realist, reality is differentiated independently of the mind's activities and interpretations. Reality, in other words, is not a formless mass but has a definite structure. A determinate world exists both independently of our representations of it and accessible to us. Truth is a matter of the correspondence of our language and the world. To the extent that scientific knowledge approximates reality, it approximates the mind of God, or at least a "God's-eye point of view." There is one conceptual scheme that offers the best picture of ultimate reality, one privileged perspective from which we can discern the way things really are (such a scheme was the Holy Grail of classical metaphysics).

Only a robust realism of this sort, it is urged, can give proper weight to the possibility of error. There can be mistaken descriptions and theories only because there is a right way to describe things. Most of the antirealist positions here examined direct their attacks at this version of realism rather than Searle's relatively uncontroversial thesis of nonepistemic realism. Antirealists are against the notion that there is one true and complete description of the way the world is. As we shall see, the modest or critical realist affirms that the world is indeed mind-independent but does not believe that it is necessary to say there is only one conceptual scheme that can do it justice.

CRITICAL REALISM

This view represents a more moderate and modest metaphysical realism. The world is there, mind-independent and differentiated, yet it is indescribable apart from human constructions and only partially accessible. The modest realist claims "that reality is to a very considerable degree self-structuring, but in most cases not to the degree that it imposes a unique scheme of individuation and sorting upon us."[5]

The moderate realist insists that though our knowledge of the world is partial it can be true. A true belief is an accurate representation of the world, not merely a useful fiction. Against Putnam (cf. below), objects are not constituted by conceptual schemes, but they "can emerge as determinate only

---

most of the dispute at present centers on whether or not reality can be known and whether or not our knowing is a "making" or a "finding."

5. Frank B. Farrell, *Subjectivity, Realism and Postmodernism* (Cambridge: Cambridge University Press, 1994), 167.

when we put a particular set of concepts to work in talking about reality."
Against Kant and Putnam, the world cannot be so indifferent to our various
descriptions of it that we can impose any conceptual scheme whatsoever
upon it. "It is not as if any interest at all on our part will do if we are inves-
tigating what reality is like."

There are various levels of description that complement one another.
Each gives us a partial insight into what is there. The modest realist grants
"that we need a pluralism of vocabularies in order to give an adequate
account of how matters stand."[6] Nevertheless, as Searle observes: "The
interest-relativity of our representations of reality does not show that the
reality represented is itself interest-relative."[7] Although our conceptual appa-
ratus is never turned off, it may still be the world that appears to us. Even
if the world appears in a way that accords with our conceptual scheme, it
may nevertheless be the world that is appearing, not the scheme itself. There
is an alternative between seeing the world either as an unconceptualizable
noumenon or as a construction projected by our practices.

The order of the world is exposed through our conceptual categories. But
it does not follow, from the fact that descriptions are always relative to a
conceptual scheme, that the fact or reality itself can only exist relative to the
scheme as well. Knowledge of the real world may well be mediated by language and conceptual schemes, but it does not follow that such knowledge
is divorced from a reality that exists independently of all such schemes.

The modest or critical realist believes that we can adjust our ways of con-
ceiving and speaking about the world under pressure from the world, from
the standards of rational argument and from human experience. The notion
of a God's-eye point of view is valuable, not as something that we can attain,
but as a regulative idea that stands both for the ideal and for the demand
that we conceive the world as it actually is. Truth here is more like ideal correspondence than ideal justification or assertability.

According to Donald Davidson, we know the world roughly as it is
through a process of "triangulation." This term is his shorthand for describing
the necessity of holding the world, the speaking self, and cultural practices
together. Truth is not conferred from a single source, either from the world or
from subjectivity or from cultural practices, but rather from the coordination
of all three together. There is a mutual determining of world, language, and
human behavior. On the one hand, the world is already there and somewhat
determinate, because it affects the way we use language and behave. What
appears in our language and our beliefs is, at least very roughly, the world
itself. On the other hand, the world underdetermines what we can say about
it and how we can behave in it. In short, the world both guides and underdetermines our language and our practices (Davidson, Farrell). Our practices are
neither built on Platonic foundations nor are they arbitrary, but are rather part
of a holistically adjusted process of gradually getting things right.

---

6. Ibid., 129.
7. Searle, *Construction of Social Reality*, 159.

INTERNAL REALISM

This is the view that the real connotes something over against human beings but in some ways dependent on the ways they speak or think about it. The world is determinate, but only from inside our conceptual schemes. It follows that (most of) the world's differentiations are human constructions. To the extent that there is a mind-independent reality, it is inaccessible to us. A reality of which nothing determinate can be said, however, is not much different, for all intents and purposes, from no reality at all. This may account for the resemblance of this position to some of its antirealist counterparts.

Internal realism is especially associated with Hilary Putnam, though, according to Putnam, Kant was the first "internal realist."[8] He credits Kant with the insight that all the objectivity we have is a human objectivity, one which allows for the mind's construction of the world. He agrees with Kant that we can never talk about the thing itself but that there are nevertheless experiential inputs that can affect our concepts. Putnam also wants, however, to abandon the opposition between what is *really* there and what we *project* upon it. Such a distinction evaporates when we find that we must use a certain conceptual system. If we simply have to think of the world in a certain way, it makes no sense to claim that it is not really "the way things are in themselves."[9]

Putnam's main criticism of external realism is that it leads straight to skepticism. The way God sees the world is beyond our grasp. Reality could be differentiated, but wholly indifferent to human attempts to know it. Putnam prefers to speak of "human" realism. We may continue speaking about reality and about truth, but only relative to a particular conceptual scheme.[10]

How many objects are there in the world, for example? There is no one right answer. For what counts as an object is internal to different conceptual schemes. There are no lines in nature: "Reality does not have a preference for a unique way of determining what an object is over all the others; nor does it have a preference for a unique way of describing it, such as that of the natural sciences."[11] External realism, it is argued, leads to inconsistencies because it allows inconsistent descriptions of the supposedly independently existing reality. All talk about "the way things are" is more accurately talk about "the way things are from here." Even in science we only have access to a world that already bears the mark of the organiza-

---

8. Hilary Putnam, *Reason, Truth and History* (Cambridge: Cambridge University Press, 1981), 60.

9. Hilary Putnam, *The Many Faces of Realism* (Lasalle: Open Court, 1987), 70.

10. Berkeley believed that the root of skepticism was the belief in a reality that is independent of human perception, for we could never know whether what is beyond our perception is like what we perceive (there is an interesting parallel here with Barth's resistance to the notion of a God behind or beyond the event of Jesus Christ).

11. Farrell, *Subjectivity, Realism and Postmodernism*, 166.

tional power of human beings. This is a very Kantian point: "Since all of our experiences are conceptualised, what we perceive may be just how we perceive things, and not how things are in themselves."[12]

Systems of representation, such as vocabularies and conceptual schemes, are human creations. "We cut up the world into objects, when we introduce one or another scheme of description." Putnam, together with the antirealist, seems to hold that there is no possibility of knowledge without such systems of representation, and that because these systems are conventional, they divide up the world in arbitrary fashion.

Putnam does not even believe it makes sense to ask if the facts might be different from the best possible theory. One can never get at reality except from within some conceptual scheme. The question then arises whether there is anything at all to the notion of reality that is not specifiable in terms of some given system of concepts. Whereas Putnam is inclined to think that the best possible ways of human thinking could not be false, the hard metaphysical realist, by contrast, insists that even the best conceptual net can fail to catch the fish.

Putnam nevertheless lays claim to the label "realist" by arguing that there is a fact of the matter, though it is subsequent to our choice of a particular conceptual scheme. Whereas the external realist distinguishes the way the world is from the way we know it, Putnam collapses this distinction: "the mind and the world jointly make up the mind and the world."

Internal realism is, very simply, the claim that reality is always only from our point of view. Reference to the world is only fixed by a given theory. In one conceptual scheme, "table" may refer to inanimate objects with a flat top and three or four legs, while in another scheme it may refer to inanimate objects with flat tops and four legs only. What there is thus becomes what our theories say there is.

What makes our beliefs true is not the world as it is in itself; rather, it is a matter of "internal affairs," it lies within our conceptual systems. We cannot even ask what and how many objects there are in a room except within a particular conceptual scheme that highlights certain of our interests rather than others. The external realist will complain that this is not enough. How, for example, could Putnam rule out astrology on this view? At best, Putnam's is a soft metaphysical realism. At worst, it slides into a form of idealism.

CONCEPTUAL OR TRANSCENDENTAL REALISM

This view, like the previous one, takes its starting point from Kant's notion that the mind has access only to its own ideas and representations. The world is there but undifferentiated and inaccessible. The mind imposes distinctions and connections that allow us to conceptualize the undifferentiated substratum of the world. What matters is not correspondence but rather

---

12. Joseph Runzo, *World Views and Perceiving God* (New York: St. Martin's Press, 1991), 149.

coherence in the system of ideas and representations. We might call this position soft metaphysical antirealism.

According to Nicholas Rescher, "The mind shapes . . . not nature itself, but nature as it is for us."[13] What is mind-dependent is not reality itself but as-we-conceive-it. Rescher is not an absolute idealist but rather a conceptual idealist. Correspondence is not a helpful notion on this view, for the only reality to which a statement could correspond is reality-as-we-think-it. This view stands rather close to the previous position. Searle judges Putnam's attempt to find a coherent position between external realism and antirealism a failure.[14] The two positions are so soft that they begin to melt into one another; both stress the role of human thinking in constructing objects and their relations in the world. The difference is finally one of accent or emphasis: both agree that the mind and the world make up the mind and the world, but the internal realist stresses the world's input and the antirealist focuses on the element of human construction.

NONREALISM

Whereas the soft realist and soft antirealist are trying to find a middle way between hard metaphysical realism and an "anything-goes" conceptual relativism, the nonrealist—a hard metaphysical antirealist—holds that there is nothing deep down inside us or in the world that we have not put there ourselves. Reality is only what humans make of it. The world is the product of various systems of differentiation. All structure and differentiation is a product of mental activity and linguistic practices. There is no God's-eye point of view. Instead, what shapes or differentiates the world is the plurality of human vocabularies.

The nonrealist is distinguished from his or her soft antirealist counterpart by the former's rejection of any possibility that our projections can be corrected either by the world (through correspondence) or by intersubjective rationality (coherence). On the nonrealist view, the way the world is structured is subject to the vagaries of cultural practices and political power. Reality is simply what the dominant language of the day says it is.

NEOPRAGMATIST NONREALISM

Richard Rorty acknowledges that we have deep-seated intuitions about reality. The question for Rorty, however, is whether these intuitions are valid insights into the way things actually are, or whether they are merely products of our social conventions and practices. He defines pragmatism as the view that "there are no constraints on inquiry save conversational ones."[15] To

---

13. Cited in Roger Trigg, *Reality at Risk: A Defense of Realism in Philosophy of Science* (Totowa, NJ: Noble Books, 1980), 6.

14. Searle, *Construction of Social Reality*, 164.

15. Richard Rorty, *Consequences of Pragmatism* (Minneapolis: University of Minnesota Press, 1982), 165.

modify the old adage: "It is language habits all the way down." We can never step outside our conversations or conventions to make overall claims about their status vis-à-vis the world. Truth-telling is never more than a provincial practice.

Rorty asks whether the ubiquity of language can ever really be taken seriously. Can we ever see ourselves encountering reality except under a chosen description? Rorty shares with Derrida the notion that we can never "break out of" language in order to compare our words to the world. Strictly speaking, there is no language-world relation. Philosophy, insofar as it is the attempt to say how language relates to the world, is, strictly speaking, impossible.

POSTSTRUCTURALIST NONREALISM

The poststructuralist shows us that what we think is natural or given is actually shaped by the dominant patterns of language use. Neither the world nor the self has any depth. The power of making things determinate has passed from the world and from the mind to cultural practices. In poststructuralism, neither the world nor rationality acts as authoritative constraints on cultural practices. Indeed, both the world and reason are seen as artifacts of the practice of power. Language is not only the house, but the architect, of Being. In postmodernity, "the very distinctions have broken down between reality and a simulation of it, between truth and fiction, between objectivity and rhetorical manipulation."[16] Being postmodern means facing up to conceptions and practices that have lost their metaphysical support. How we talk and think is neither grounded in nor essentially related to the way things are, except in the sense that reality just is what we say about it.

According to Foucault, objects are constituted by cultural practices, by "regimes of power/knowledge." Phenomena such as madness or homosexuality only came into being when a particular discursive practice constituted them. In Foucault's view, a discursive practice projects classification onto the world. Systems of language are projected onto an indeterminate world and so structure it. Yet Foucault is a poststructuralist because he believes there is a variety of incommensurable discursive practices: which practice happens to hold sway at any given time is less a matter of the way the world is than of who controls the most social power. For Foucault, there are no givens in reality (he is thinking particularly of social reality); all distinctions are therefore coerced. "Man" himself has no reality, but is a social or political projection.

KINDS OF FACTS

It is possible to be a realist regarding a set of beliefs or statements in one area and a nonrealist regarding those in another area. For instance, it is possible to be a realist about physical and social facts, but a nonrealist with

---

16. Farrell, *Subjectivity, Realism and Postmodernism*, 246.

regard to morality. In particular, a number of thinkers today are nonrealists about religious beliefs without being nonrealists across the board.

Few thinkers question external realism with regard to physical reality (nature). The difficulty comes only when it is a matter of what transcends the level of the sheerly physical: minds, marriages, moral values, sin, angels, God. Many philosophers are unwilling to be realists about anything other than the physical world.

John Searle maintains that there are aspects of the real world that are objective facts only by human agreement. There are things that exist—for example, national boundaries, the game of football, money—only because we believe them to exist. These things are institutional realities as opposed to brute facts, the products of culture rather than nature. What social facts have in common is that they exist relative to the intentionality of observers; they are "ontologically intersubjective."[17] A social fact is any fact that involves collective intentionality. Unlike natural facts, a social fact can be created simply by collective recognition. The President is the President because the citizens collectively acknowledge both the office and its holder.

ETHICS AND MORAL REALISM[18]

Is there a moral reality, a set of objective values, which is independent of our moral beliefs and which determines whether or not they are true or false? Is there a moral reality that resists being reduced either to physical or social facts? The difference between social and moral reality is not immediately apparent. Indeed, many would argue that moral facts *just are* social facts. A moral value has its ground in collective intentionality and recognition.

Modern philosophy after Kant made subjectivity the ground of moral determinacy. For Kant, morality is a matter of practical reason. Ethical values are human projections (albeit necessary ones) onto the world. Whereas the antirealist argues that moral values are human projections, the moral realist maintains that the world itself guides our sense of the good, thanks to our perceptions of intrinsic worth. In the latter case, we perceive the rightness or wrongness of an act. The modest moral realist argues that one's training cultivates certain moral sensibilities, including the capacity to be open to moral aspects of the world. The moral realist perceives not things or objects, but rather certain patterns that emerge when we achieve a competence at a certain level of description, sophisticated enough to make them stand out.

RELIGION: THEOLOGICAL REALISM

Is God a mind-independent reality? Is God the way God is regardless of how humans conceive God? Theologians have not been insensitive to the argu-

17. Searle, *Construction of Social Reality*, 9.

18. Cf. David McNaughton, *Moral Vision: An Introduction to Ethics* (Oxford: Blackwell, 1988).

ments against metaphysical realism. Indeed, it was largely due to the pressure of the Kantian problematic that Schleiermacher relocated theological truth claims away from the being of God toward religious feelings and Christian faith. He was thus able to defend talk about religion to its "cultured despisers," though not to talk about God as anything other than talk about religion.

The theological realist holds that God is independent of our religion and our theologies and can be indirectly observed in or "read off" the world (for example, Aquinas's cosmological proofs). Feuerbach's suggestion that God is a projection of human ideals has been modified, but not substantially improved upon, by Marx and Freud. Others have more recently suggested that God is a social fact, a projection of our cultural practices or our ways of speaking. The critical theological realist argues that God, or divine activity, is more like an emerging pattern that one sees only when one has achieved competence in a certain level of description, observation, or sensitivity.

APPROACHES TO THE TRUTH QUESTION

The fact that there are so many philosophical theories of truth already indicates that there is little agreement as to what questions any philosophical theory of truth should answer. R. Kirkham characterises the current situation as one of "four-dimensional confusion."[19] Should a theory of truth define "truth," spell out the meaning or essence of truth, develop criteria for determining what is true (and false), analyse what the phrase ". . . is true" means, or explain what a person means by saying that something is true?

Moreover, what is the nature of the things that can be true? Are the "bearers of truth" beliefs, propositions, sentences, or, perhaps, other kinds of things? To complicate matters further, theories of truth are often embedded in larger philosophical programs in the field of epistemology, linguistics, logic, or metaphysics. The wider aims of these programs determine the kind of problems the theory of truth in question is supposed to solve.[20]

It should be emphasised that in spite of many differences, the various theories of truth do not necessarily exclude or contradict one another. It is important at least to distinguish between *definitions* of (the meaning of) truth and *criteria* for determining or recognizing whether particular beliefs (propositions or sentences) in a certain context are true. For instance, it is not inconsistent to hold that the nature of truth consists essentially in a kind of correspondence, whereas coherence is the criterion of truth (N. Rescher).

19. R.L. Kirkham, *Theories of Truth: A Critical Introduction* (Cambridge, MA: MIT Press, 1992), 1ff.

20. For this reason, the existentialist account of truth (K. Jaspers) and the phenomenological–hermeneutical accounts of M. Heidegger and H.-G. Gadamer will not be summarized here. As Puntel points out, what these philosophers have to say about truth is so tightly woven with all sorts of other philosophical insights and intuitions that it is virtually impossible to render them sufficiently precise for the present purposes. Cf. L.B. Puntel, *Wahrheitstheorien in der neueren Philosophie. Eine kritisch-systematische Darstellung* (Darmstadt: Wissenschaftliche Buchgesellschaft, 1978), 15ff.

Or, from a holistic perspective, coherence may be taken both as the nature of truth and its mark (B. Blanshard).

Bearing in mind this perplexing diversity, we will try to outline as clearly as possible the main features of the traditional theories and contemporary proposals which are still relevant to the current epistemological predicament. The central insight of *the correspondence theory* is that a belief (or statement) is true if it corresponds to reality, the world, the facts, or how things are (for example, Aristotle, J. L. Austin, and A. White).[21] Depending on how the relation of correspondence is construed, two versions of the theory can be distinguished. The relation can be understood as a *correlation* between what is said or stated and the world (weak sense) or as *congruence* (strong sense).[22] In this latter case the theory claims that if a statement is true, there is an isomorphism, a one-to-one correspondence, or a relation of mirroring or picturing, between that statement and the state of affairs with which it corresponds.

The congruence interpretation of correspondence (B. Russell, the earlier Wittgenstein) faced such serious difficulties regarding the precise nature of the mirroring relation that it was virtually abandoned. This does not mean, however, that *all* correspondence theories should be seen as obsolete. We cannot compare a belief or statement with how things really are "out there," because what is "out there" independent of the mind cannot be assessed apart from the totality of the skills, beliefs, and expectations that make up our way of doing and seeing things.

Nevertheless, although correspondence theorists may well agree that we have no access to uninterpreted reality, yet they still hold, without contradiction, that truth consists in an agreement or fit with the facts or with how things are.[23] The correspondence definition of truth, understood as a correlation between what we believe or say and the world, does not, as such, provide us with a criterion for determining whether a particular belief in a given context is, in fact, true.

Like the correspondence theory, *the coherence theory* has a long and venerable history.[24] According to the coherence theory, a belief is true (or false)

---

21. Cf. Aristotle, *Metaphysics* 1011b, 26ff.; J.L. Austin, "Truth" in *Proc. Arist. Soc.* 24 (1950); A.R. White, *Truth* (London: Macmillan, 1971), 109, 129. Note that the nature of that to which language is supposed to correspond ("what is," "reality," "world," "state of affairs," "fact," "how things are") is itself a matter of controversy between correspondence theorists.

22. Cf. G. Pitcher, "Introduction," in G. Pitcher (ed.), *Truth* (Englewood Cliffs, NJ: Prentice-Hall, 1964), 10.

23. Consequently, a supporter of the correspondence theory need not necessarily be committed to realism; cf. Kirkham, *Theories of Truth*, 133ff. Nevertheless, many correspondence theorists are realists, for instance, M.Devitt, *Realism and Truth* (Oxford: Blackwell, 1991).

24. Cf. R.C.S. Walker, *The Coherence Theory of Truth: Realism, Anti-realism, Idealism* (New York: Routledge, 1989). On Walker's account, Spinoza, Hegel, Bradley, and to a certain extent also Kant and Fichte are coherentists. Modern supporters are B. Blanshard, the later Wittgenstein, D. Davidson, and to some degree also W. Quine.

if it coheres (or fails to cohere) with a particular system or set of beliefs. For example, Otto Neurath, a logical positivist proponent of the theory, held that each belief of the system should logically imply every other belief. For him, the one system with which all true beliefs must cohere is science. Less scientistically inclined supporters of the theory, however, say that a belief is true only if it coheres with, or fits into, a larger system of beliefs about the universe. That system need not be known or worked out fully at the present time. It may be a metaphysical system that comprises everything upon which humankind will, in the long term, agree.

Since coherence theorists give varying accounts of the nature of the system with which our beliefs should cohere, views about the nature of "coherence" differ widely. Nicholas Rescher contributed greatly to a revival of the coherence theory by giving a logically more precise account of "coherence," explicating it as comprehensiveness, consistency, and cohesiveness or unity.[25]

Obviously, the coherence theory, especially if it is taken as criteriological, is attractive to those who have abandoned the correspondence theory and its idea of a world independent of mind and language. The best test of the truth of a belief, in the light of our incomplete knowledge of the world, is to see whether it fits coherently into the web of our beliefs.

The pragmatic theory of truth originated from the work of the philosophers C.S. Peirce, W. James, and J. Dewey. According to Peirce, truth is what the community of inquirers would ultimately agree upon after a long and possibly endless process of investigation. Due to our fallibility, ultimate consensus cannot be guaranteed, but experience and scientific inquiry are still the most effective guides to achieving it.

According to James, an idea (belief, statement, or theory) is true if it "works" and false if it doesn't. This does not mean that he rejects the traditional definition of truth as agreement with reality. Rather, James attempts to explicate "agreement" in terms of certain ways of satisfactory working.[26]

An idea "works" when it guides us to "beneficial interaction" with the world, or when it is satisfactory or useful (that is, when it helps us to manipulate the objects of the world, allow for successful communication, lead to accurate predictions, or explain other occurrences). Thus each time an idea or belief proves immediately useful in these ways, it is evidence of its truth and of its being useful in the long run or on the whole.[27] In short, the pragmatic theory concentrates more on the practical problem of how to arrive at, or how to test, what we take to be true in concrete situations, and less on the problem of the meaning of truth.

---

25. Cf. N. Rescher, *The Coherence Theory of Truth* (Oxford: Clarendon Press, 1973), 169ff., where a criteriological coherence theory is defended; L.B. Puntel, *Wahrheitstheorien*, 200.

26. Cf. W. James, *The Meaning of Truth: A Sequel to Pragmatism* (Cambridge, MA: Harvard University Press, 1975), 283.

27. Cf. Kirkham, *Theories of Truth*, 100ff. Kirkham classifies James's theory as an instrumental theory of truth which equates, but does not reduce, truth to other values. Dewey too may be taken as an advocate of the instrumental theory; cf. White, *Truth*, 124.

The redundancy theory of truth arises in the insight, according to some philosophers of logical positivist inclination (for example, F. P. Ramsey, A. J. Ayer), that the so-called problem of truth is just a linguistic muddle. The central assumption of their "no-truth theory of truth," as it is called, is that to say that *p* is true is *logically* equivalent to saying that *p*. Hence, "truth" is redundant.

The crucial objection to this view is that it mistakenly assumes that logical equivalence is the same as equivalence in meaning. Though "*p*" and "it is true that *p*" are logically equivalent, they clearly do not have the same meaning.[28] The point of the redundancy theory is very limited, for it fails to answer the question of the meaning of truth.

The semantic theory of truth was proposed by the logician A. Tarski.[29] His aim was to give an adequate and formally correct definition of truth that would be part of a scientific semantics, avoid certain logical paradoxes, and tally with our intuitions of what it means to say that something is true. Such a definition should be in accordance with a formula that entails all possible equivalences of the form "X is true if and only if *p*" ("X" denotes, or is the name of, any given declarative sentence and "*p*" stands for the content of that sentence). This so-called T-convention makes it possible to define truth for certain restricted (formalized) languages as a particular conjunction of two sentences, such as "'Sugar is sweet' is true if and only if sugar is sweet."

Precisely because the semantic conception of truth is applicable only to formalized (or semantically open) languages, it has been criticized for being vacuous. Tarski's theory does not give an adequate definition of truth for natural languages and it does not contradict any of the other theories of truth. Another frequently made objection is that it is philosophically inadequate because it only defines truth for artificial languages but leaves us in the dark as to the meaning of extralinguistic truth.[30]

The performative theory is sometimes called the "nondescriptive" theory of truth. It takes its starting point in the by now familiar idea that by saying things people also do things: for instance, they give orders, make requests or promises, or take oaths. According to the performative theory, "true" or "false" are not used to describe the property of a statement but rather to appraise that statement (so, P. Strawson and M. Polanyi). To say that it is true (or false) that the cat is on the mat is to express one's (dis)agreement with the belief or statement that the cat is on the mat. Thus "true" (or "false") functions as an assertive device that expresses a person's assent to (or rejection of) the content of an assertive utterance.

No doubt the performative theory makes an important point about one of the uses of "true" and "false." The theory leaves largely unanswered, how-

---

28. White, *Truth*, 92.

29. Cf. A.Tarski, "The Semantic Conception of Truth," in *Philosophical and Phenomenological Research* 4 (1944): 341–75.

30. For an extensive discussion of Tarski's theory, cf. Kirkham, *Theories of Truth*, chapters 5 and 6; also, White, *Truth*, 95ff.

ever, the question as to whether this is a wholly adequate answer to the meaning of truth (and falsity). To say that *p* is true may well be to express agreement with *p*. But, at the same time, why could it not also say something about *p*? As White points out, what we *do* when we say that something is true is not the same as what we *say* when we say that something is true.[31]

The consensus theory of truth contains elements both of Strawson's performative theory and C.S. Peirce's pragmatist theory. Its main proponent, the German philosopher Jürgen Habermas, gives an account of truth as part of a pragmatic theory of communicative action. According to Habermas, the bearers of truth are not sentences but assertive speech acts. In saying that something is true we make a validity claim. In communicative action, an assertion or statement "that *p*" conveys to the hearer the information that *p* is the case, while its character as a truth claim is tacitly presupposed. On the theoretical metalevel of discourse, by contrast, a validity claim can be made good by being warrantedly assertable. The warrant in question can only be achieved through intersubjective communication—specifically through a process of argumentation leading to rational consensus. Truth, according to Habermas, means *warranted assertability*.[32]

In order to safeguard the possibility of achieving a rational consensus rather than a mere actual or irrational one, Habermas develops both a pragmatics of rational argumentation and a conception of an "ideal speech situation" in which communication is wholly free from distorting influences. This ideal situation is, of course, counterfactual, but it is also a constitutive condition of communicative discourse. Ultimately, then, there is a link between truth and "the intention of the good and true life."[33] In brief, the consensus theory is not so much an answer to the question of what "truth" means as an attempt to answer the question of the criteria for truth by accounting for the general conditions under which a claim to truth is rationally justified.

One can see from the detail and complexity of the theories of truth just sketched that it will be no easy manner to determine their relevance for a missiology of the twenty-first century. To do so, one would need to consider the implications of these general theories of truth in specific contexts, such as theology, science, and morality. At this less general level, certain characteristics of religious conceptions of truth and falsity—characteristics that we have not developed here[34]—will have to be brought into the picture too.

---

31. White, *Truth*, 100ff.

32. Cf. J. Habermas, "Wahrheitstheorien," in Helmut Fahrenbach (ed.), *Wirklichkeit und Reflexion* (Pfullingen: Neske, 1973), 240 (cited in L.B. Puntel, *Wahrheitstheorien*, 153).

33. Cf. Thomas McCarthy, *The Critical Theory of Jürgen Habermas* (Cambridge, MA: MIT Press, 1978), 307.

34. For an excellent collection of essays on precisely this topic, see Daniel Guerrière (ed.), *Phenomenology of the Truth Proper to Religion* (Albany, NY: SUNY Press, 1990), especially Louis Dupre, "Truth in Religion and Truth of Religion" and Philip Clayton, "Religious Truth and Scientific Truth."

These might include, for instance, the element of authentic human subjectivity involved in the discovery of, or the commitment to, truths which are central to the views and actions of human beings. To undertake this task is like attempting to bridge a deep chasm. But then, it is precisely this chasm between philosophical accounts of truth and religious conceptions of truth which is a central feature of the current epistemological predicament in the first place.

CHAPTER THREE

The State of Claims to Rationality

A growing number of philosophers today, especially in the Anglo-American tradition, take a different approach to questions of knowledge from those represented above. Richard Rorty, for example, writes: "It is pictures rather than propositions, metaphors rather than statements, which determine most of our philosophical convictions."[1]

Two such pictures have gripped the modern philosophical imagination. One Rorty describes as "mind as the mirror of nature." This image goes back to the ancient Greeks. In early modern philosophy it led to conceptions of knowledge that Wallace Matson describes as "inside out."[2] That is, accounts of knowledge begin with some sort of inner representations (such as ideas and sense data) which are taken to provide knowledge of whatever is outside the mind. The question then arises, how can one know that these representations are accurate portrayals of reality, or indeed if there is a real world for them to represent? Later versions of this representational view of knowledge included Kant's critical realism (described above). Most recently, the question is couched in terms of language: do our categories, concepts, and theories accurately depict a real world?

Rorty, Matson, and a number of other contemporary philosophers—most of them following the thought of Ludwig Wittgenstein—argue that the image of knowledge (or language or conceptual schemes) as a picture *over against reality* is the source of many unnecessary philosophical problems, such as skepticism and worries about the existence of a real world. It would be better, they argue, to begin with our ordinary recognition that we are in contact with a real world, and then ask ourselves how it is best to describe that world. Thus, for many, the central epistemological question is how to arbitrate among competing accounts of reality: i.e., what is the justification for accepting one description of reality as the *true* one? Or, more modestly, how can we judge the relative *adequacy* of the various accounts?

---

1. Richard Rorty, *Philosophy and the Mirror of Nature* (Princeton, NJ: Princeton University Press, 1979), 12.

2. Wallace Matson, *A New History of Philosophy*, 2 vols. (San Diego, CA: Harcourt Brace Jovanovich, 1987), 275–76.

Discussions of the justification of knowledge claims in the modern period have themselves been much influenced by a picture of knowledge "as a building." As a consequence, a particular approach to the justification of knowledge claims has assumed a high priority. Since a building cannot stand without a solid *foundation*, knowledge claims cannot stand if they cannot be traced back to "foundational" beliefs that are not themselves in need of justification. Or, to summarize the foundationalist argument without metaphor: the justification of beliefs in terms of other beliefs must neither be circular nor result in an infinite regress; justification must stop with beliefs that, for one reason or another, need no further justification.

Early modern foundationalists turned to "clear and distinct intuitions" or to the immediate deliverances of sense experience. Not surprisingly, one group of contemporary epistemologists consists of the successors of these early foundationalists. These thinkers believe that the building metaphor is still sound, and that whatever problems have arisen in attempting to think of knowledge in foundational terms can be overcome.

A growing number of philosophers, however, has judged the foundationalist metaphor itself to be the *source* of modern perplexities regarding knowledge. Some pursue the traditional epistemological questions of justification or truth in the light of a new "holist" metaphor: i.e., a system of knowledge is more like a web or net than like a building. Others believe that once liberated from misleading pictures of knowledge, the problems of epistemology dissolve. In the following sections we examine these options in turn.

CHASTENED FOUNDATIONALISM

There are contemporary epistemologists who hold that, contrary to the widespread opinion that foundationalism has collapsed, it is still the best theory of justification available. Prominent among them are the so-called "Reformed Epistemologist" Alvin Plantinga and a variety of philosophers, of which the best known is Susan Haack, who has put forward "foundherentism" as a theory that can fill the gap between a (weak) foundationalism and a (moderate) coherentism. Weak or "chastened" foundationalists agree that classic foundationalism is faulty and its search for ultimate and certain foundations misconceived. They also hold, however, that there are no serious problems for weaker versions of the theory. Leaving aside much technical detail, it should be pointed out that there are important differences between weak foundationalists (of which Plantinga can be seen as the main representative) and the classic foundationalists such as Descartes, Leibniz, Locke, Hume, and their followers.

According to classical foundationalists, the foundation which is needed for justifying our beliefs should consist only of beliefs that are self-evident or evident to the senses. Since these basic beliefs are not themselves based on other beliefs, classical foundationalists bestow on them a privileged status of being certain, indubitable, incorrigible, or even infallible. The underlying idea is that these privileged beliefs are not justified by the support of other beliefs but by a person's direct sensory and/or introspective experience. Not only should they be strong enough to deal with the threatening infinite regress of justifications, but other beliefs should only be accepted on the basis of them. That is to say, every other justified belief must be evidentially supported by the foundational beliefs—preferably by way of deduction, but otherwise inductively or abductively.

Thus, foundationalism comes in different degrees. Requiring *infallible* beliefs as the foundation for knowledge and a *deductive* support relation for all beliefs based upon them yields a much stricter (and more restrictive) kind of foundationalism than versions which take basic beliefs to be fallible and allow the support relation to be inductive (or weaker still, abductive). What is unsatisfactory about the stronger versions? Is it just that they are excessively strict and even arbitrary, or are there "internal" difficulties as well? First of all, as Plantinga points out, strong foundationalism fails to satisfy its own requirements: clearly, it is neither self-evident nor evident to the senses. Also, the class of self-evident beliefs (relatively simple logical and arithmetical truths) is so small that preciously few beliefs could in fact be justified on this basis.[3]

Perhaps certain beliefs which are "evident to the senses," those that appear to be immediately about my own experience, might be indubitable: for example, the belief that I seem to see a tree in front of me. Such beliefs are so devoid of substantial content, however, that they could hardly make up the foundation of the edifice of human knowledge. Even scientific beliefs cannot be properly basic, precisely because they are characteristically revisable and thus not incorrigible, indubitable, or infallible.

If there is any truth in these objections to strong foundationalism, then hardly any of our beliefs may count as knowledge. The result would be a rather unwelcome dilemma between skepticism (the view that justified belief is unattainable) and relativism (the view that all true beliefs are equally justified). Weak foundationalism can thus be seen as one of the attempts to steer a middle course between these extremes.

A further criticism of classical foundationalism is that it requires a specific relation of evidential support (deductive, inductive, or abductive) between the experiential content of basic beliefs and the nonbasic beliefs they support. According to the classical view, a person is justified in believing only if the belief is held on the basis of evidence (construed as experiential propositions), if those propositions are believed and if they do in fact support the belief.

Plantinga's weak foundationalism rejects each of these three requirements. A person is justified in believing if that person has the experience cor-

---

3. Plantinga uses the word "warrant" rather than "justification," because in his view the epistemological tradition in which the latter notion is embedded is fundamentally flawed. Cf. *Warrant: The Current Debate* (New York: Oxford University Press, 1993), 43ff.

responding to that belief,[4] the cognitive capacities are functioning properly in an appropriate environment, and the aim is to acquire true beliefs. Apart from naturalizing his account, Plantinga also allows many kinds of beliefs as candidates for inclusion in the foundation of a person's system of beliefs. Memory beliefs, perceptual beliefs, beliefs about the mental states of other persons, inductive beliefs, and testimonial beliefs can all be properly basic, as well as certain moral beliefs and the belief in God.[5]

In this reconstrual of classical foundationalism, little remains of the firm and ultimate "foundation." Once the impossible requirements—Cartesian certainty, indubitability, and incorrigibility—are laid on one side and replaced by weaker ones, a new position emerges. We have called this "chastened" foundationalism. In some respects it is closer to its main rivals in the field, namely, coherentism and contextualism.[6] Since the relative merits of these general theories of justification are hotly debated in current epistemology, definite findings cannot be presented here. In completion of this sketch of weak foundationalism we will summarize the main diferences between them.

Coherentism is a theory in general epistemology which says that beliefs are justified only by relations of mutual support between beliefs within a system, network, or weblike structure (e.g., N. Rescher, K. Lehrer, L. BonJour). Pure coherentism differs from weak foundationalism in at least two respects. First, the latter, but not the former, allows the input of experience which, in whatever way it is characterized, is at least partly of a nonbelief nature. Second, whereas weak foundationalists construe the support relation between beliefs as one-directional (from basic to nonbasic beliefs), pure coherentists require justification to be a matter of mutual support relations among beliefs (which, they insist, need not imply vicious circularity).

The main issue between the rivals concerns roughly the role of experience in justification. According to weak foundationalists that role is crucial: the regress of justification can only be brought to a halt by a set of basic beliefs which is justified for a person by experience (which, they insist, need not imply that these beliefs are infallible or even epistemically privileged). By contrast, pure coherentists hold that a belief is justified if and only if it belongs to a coherent set of beliefs, a view which seems to imply that all beliefs in a coherent set are exactly on a par with respect to their justification.[7]

Like foundationalism, however, coherentism comes in degrees also. Moderate coherentists may lend some beliefs a more privileged or central status in virtue of their role in the support relations or by their being more

---

4. Cf. A. Plantinga, *Warrant and Proper Function* (New York: Oxford University Press, 1993), 184. In fairness to Plantinga, it should be noted that this is a paraphrase of the rather technical notion of "being appropriately appeared to."

5. Ibid., 183ff.

6. Cf. Susan Haack, *Evidence and Inquiry: Towards Reconstruction in Epistemology* (Oxford: Oxford University Press, 1993). Another option is reliabilism (A. Goldman, F. Dretske, D. Armstrong), which says that a belief is justified if it has been formed by a reliable belief-forming mechanism, process, or faculty.

7. Ibid., 17ff.

deeply embedded in the set than others. They may allow for coherence not just between beliefs but between beliefs and the content of experience. Against weak foundationalists they argue that, in order to find out which beliefs are properly basic, sometimes beliefs higher up the system will have to be invoked. Adopting holism (see below), they may also wish to stress that to specify any properly basic belief presupposes having concepts and a language. To this weak foundationalists can reply that sometimes beliefs may be justified in virtue of their cohering with other beliefs. As Plantinga admits, the weak foundationalist denies that coherence is the only source of warrant, not that it is not a source of warrant at all.[8]

At this point, weak foundationalism and moderate coherentism appear to become overlapping positions. Steering a middle course between these two rivals, Susan Haack proposes "foundherentism," which, unlike pure coherentism, allows the relevance of experience to the justification of empirical beliefs, but, unlike foundationalism, does not require a class of properly basic beliefs justified exclusively by the support of experience. Moreover, like coherentism, it does not construe justification as exclusively one-directional (as does foundationalism), but as involving relations of mutual support.[9] Foundherentism is, however, by no means the only alternative.

Contextualism is another theory of justification. According to contextualist accounts (e.g., R. Rorty and S.P. Stitch), a belief is justified in terms of conformity to the current standards of some epistemic community. These standards may still count as "basic," but only in the sense that they do not stand in need of justification by the community in question. Thus, contextualists can be seen to address the question of how to account for the conditions under which people can justify their belief vis-à-vis the members of some community, rather than the problem of how they are justified in their belief.

Since contextualism does not seem to acknowledge even the possibility of a community whose standards are more indicative of truth than those of others, one of the serious problems arising in connection with it is relativism. We will return to contextualism below when we discuss the views of those philosophers who believe that, with the collapse of classic foundationalism, epistemology itself has come to an end.

POSTFOUNDATIONALIST EPISTEMOLOGISTS

The decisive break with foundationalism came with the works of W. V. O. Quine. In an article "Two Dogmas of Empiricism," he argued against the empiricist "dogma" that each meaningful statement is equivalent to (or can be reduced to) terms that refer to immediate experience. The other "dogma" that came under his attack was the analytic-synthetic distinction, which had provided justification for a sharp differentiation between the sciences as empirical disciplines and philosophy as purely conceptual.

8. Cf. Plantinga, *Warrant: The Current Debate*, 83ff.; *Warrant and Proper Function*, 180.
9. Cf. Haack, *Evidence and Inquiry*, 19.

Quine's most important contribution, however, was the new picture or metaphor of knowledge as a web or net:

> The totality of our so-called knowledge or beliefs, from the most causal matters of geography and history to the profoundest laws of atomic physics or even of pure mathematics and logic, is a man-made fabric which impinges on experience only along the edges. Or, to change the figure, total science is like a field whose boundary conditions are experience. A conflict with experience at the periphery occasions readjustments in the interior of the field. Truth values have to be redistributed over some of our statements, re-evaluation of some statements entails re-evaluation of others, because of their logical interconnections—the logical laws being in turn simply certain further statements of the system. . . . Yet the total field is so underdetermined by its boundary conditions, experience, that much latitude of choice remains as to what statements to reevaluate in the light of any single contrary experience. No particular experiences are linked with any particular statements in the interior of the field of our beliefs, except indirectly through considerations of equilibrium affecting the field as a whole.[10]

In addition to the picture we have just described, Quine's "holist" theory of knowledge differs in several important respects from foundationalism. First, there are no indubitable (or unrevisable) beliefs; nor are there any sharp distinctions among types of belief, but only degrees of difference about how far a belief is from the experiential boundary.

Second, for foundationalists, reasoning (construction) goes in only one direction—*up* from the foundation. For holists there is no preferred direction. The kinds of connections among beliefs in the web are many: strict logical implication, weaker probabilistic arguments, arguments *forward* to further conclusions, arguments *backward* to presuppositions. In general, what "holism" means is that each belief is supported by its ties to its neighboring beliefs and, ultimately, to the whole. This view differs from earlier coherentist accounts of knowledge because it recognizes that empirical constraints are transmitted throughout the web by means of these connections.

Quine's holism removes the foundationalists' uneasiness: because there is no place in the web of beliefs for a foundation, its absence does not lead to skepticism. Unfortunately, Quine's picture almost inevitably produces the new epistemological worry of relativism. Quine himself is not a relativist, however, for in his scheme the web of beliefs is understood to comprise the whole of knowledge. It is possible gradually to alter the whole (as in Neurath's image of having to repair a ship at sea, without all the advantages of a dry dock), but it is impossible to imagine replacing the whole at once.

---

10. W.V.O. Quine, "Two Dogmas of Empiricism," in *From a Logical Point of View* (Cambridge, MA: Harvard University Press, 1953), 42–43.

The trouble is that Quine has a fairly circumscribed view of what counts as knowledge: science, logic, and everyday knowledge of the sensible world. If we apply the holist model to other realms of thought, such as the social sciences or religion, we encounter a larger number of competitors. At the same time, the arbiter between them, experience, becomes more difficult to apply.

So, justification of belief now involves two sorts of questions. Not only is there the question whether a particular belief is justifiable within a particular web to which it belongs—and here, of course, we know how to proceed—but whether this web of beliefs is justified over against its competitors—and here it is not at all clear how we are to proceed. The fact that logic and philosophy for Quine are themselves but part of the web intensifies relativist worries: if rational principles as basic as the laws of logic are subject to the same vicissitudes as common theory, how can one stand outside of competing webs and use criteria such as consistency and logical coherence to evaluate them? So, if Quine is not worried about relativism, perhaps he should be! Whether he intended it or not, Thomas Kuhn has provided powerful arguments for relativism in the philosophy of science.[11] The language in the philosophy of science may be somewhat different from that of Quine's, and the unit of analysis also different (paradigms in place of total webs of belief), but most of the claims cause the same worries: namely, that data are theory-laden and hence are underdetermined by experience, that theory is underdetermined by data, and that radically different theories are supported by different domains of data, or at least by differently interpreted data.

In addition, in Kuhn's survey of paradigm changes, we have compelling evidence of radical conceptual changes in science. We also find some support for the claim that scientific worldviews employing these different concepts are incommensurable. The most significant contribution Kuhn makes to the relativist's resources, however, is his claim that standards of rationality are "paradigm dependent."

A variety of thinkers have taken up the challenges posed by Kuhn. We look at two of the most important: Imre Lakatos in the philosophy of science, and Alasdair MacIntyre, whose epistemological concerns grew out of his work in philosophical ethics.

Lakatos[12] set out to respond to Kuhn's claim that paradigms involve their own standards of success by fashioning Kuhn's assorted "maxims" (such as empirical fit and fruitfulness) into a single criterion that would provide a clear answer to the question of which competing paradigm or research program is the more acceptable. Lakatos's criterion has been much criticised; yet, whether it works or not as he intended, he has nonetheless made two important contributions toward responding to relativism. The first is his

---

11. Cf. Thomas Kuhn, *The Structure of Scientific Revolutions*, 2d ed. (Chicago: University of Chicago Press, 1970).

12. Cf. Imre Lakatos, "Falsification and the Methodology of Scientific Research Programmes," in John Worrall and Gregory Currie (eds.), *The Methodology of Scientific Research Programmes* (Cambridge: Cambridge University Press, 1978), 8–101.

claim that research programs need to be evaluated on the basis of how they change over time. That is, consideration of the data supporting a research program or its degree of coherence at any single point in its history will not reveal the qualities that ought to be considered in evaluating it. Empirical progress, in other words, is an intrinsically historical concept. Thus the temporal dimension is an important ingredient in epistemologies that begin with a holist account of knowledge and then attempt to answer the second-order question of how one justifies an entire web of beliefs (or a paradigm, or a research program).

Lakatos's second lasting contribution to postfoundationalist epistemology is his strategy for justifying his own methodology. Lakatos described the structure of science in terms of competing research programs. Each research program consists of a succession of theories, each of which is a modification of its predecessor. In the case of a progressive program, each new theory is better than its predecessor in that it has more empirical content.

Lakatos made a point in describing his own methodology as but a minor modification of Karl Popper's. Thus, he cast his own methodology of scientific research programs not as a single theory, but as the most recent reformulation of a *research program* in the history and philosophy of science—as a progressive problem shift relative to Popper's. So, in effect, Lakatos viewed the history of the philosophy of science as *isomorphic* with the history of science itself. The justification of his methodology in this manner assumes a metaphilosophical methodology—a theory about the justification of philosophical theories, which is identical in structure to the theory it is used to justify.

The importance of this move can be seen by contrasting Lakatos's work with his predecessors in the philosophy of science. The logical positivists' "verification criterion" (a sentence is meaningful only if it can be empirically verified) was rejected in part because, when applied self-referentially, the criterion also showed itself to be meaningless. Analogously, Lakatos argued that most of the major theories about science, if considered as theories about scientific rationality, *failed to measure up to their own standards*. In particular, Popper's insistence on strict and decisive falsifications of scientific theories is falsified by the history of science: scientists simply do not operate that way! Paul Feyerabend suggests that Lakatos was the first to develop a theory of rationality "sly and sophisticated enough" to apply to science. Lakatos might respond that his real achievement was to develop a theory of rationality sly and sophisticated enough to apply to itself.

MacIntyre's work in ethics and epistemology reveals a similar complex structure. In his book *After Virtue*,[13] he concluded that the justification of an ethical position requires locating the position within a specific tradition of moral enquiry. In order to avoid moral relativism, he grants that one needs a way to arbitrate among competing moral traditions. But moral tradi-

---

13. Alasdair MacIntyre, *After Virtue*, 2d ed. (Notre Dame: University of Notre Dame Press, 1984). Cf. especially the Postscript.

tions—and this could be true of religious traditions as well—are embedded in larger traditions that incorporate their own standards of rationality. What we have here is an analogue to Thomas Kuhn's problem of the paradigm dependency of standards of rationality. The core of MacIntyre's epistemological position is acceptance of the tradition-ladenness of justification: "to be outside of all traditions," he says, "is to be a stranger to enquiry; it is to be in a state of intellectual and moral destitution."[14]

We can most easily describe MacIntyre's many-layered epistemology by tracing its development through several works. In an early article, he argued that justification of theories in science depends on our being able to construct a historical narrative that makes the transition from the old to the new theory intelligible:

> What the scientific genius, such as Galileo, achieves in the transition to his new theory is not only a new way of understanding nature, but also (and inseparably) a new way of understanding the old science's way of understanding nature. It is because one can only characterize the inadequacy of the old science *from the standpoint of the new science* that the new science is taken to be more adequate than the old. It is from the standpoint of the new science, in other words, that the continuities of narrative history are re-established.[15]

Thus, MacIntyre claims, *scientific reason turns out to be subordinate to and intelligible only in terms of historical reason.* This conclusion is closely related to Lakatos's insistence on the historical character of justification in science. Let us call this aspect of justification the *diachronic* dimension. With this move to the diachronic dimension, MacIntyre is answering the question how one justifies a modification of a given tradition. A second question, however, is how one justifies the tradition as a whole over against its rivals.[16] One aspect of the adjudication between competing traditions is to construct a narrative account of each tradition—of the crises it has encountered (for example, its incoherence or new experiences it has been unable to explain) and how it has or has not been able to overcome these crises. Has it been possible to reformulate the tradition in such a way that it overcomes its crises without losing its identity? Comparison of these narratives may show that one tradition is clearly superior to another; that is, it may become apparent that one tradition is making progress, while its rival is sterile.

---

14. Alasdair MacIntyre, *Whose Justice? Which Rationality?* (Notre Dame: University of Notre Dame Press, 1989), 367.

15. Alasdair MacIntyre, "Epistemological Crises, Dramatic Narrative and the Philosophy of Science," in Gary Gutting (ed.), *Paradigms and Revolutions* (Notre Dame: University of Notre Dame Press, 1980), 69.

16. He takes up this issue in *Whose Justice*, and again in *Three Rival Versions of Moral Enquiry: Encyclopaedia, Genealogy and Tradition* (Notre Dame: University of Notre Dame Press, 1988).

In addition, if there are participants within the traditions with enough empathy and imagination to understand the rival's point of view in its own terms, then protagonists of each tradition, having considered in what ways their own tradition has *by its own standards of achievement* in enquiry found it difficult to develop its enquiries beyond a certain point, or how it has produced insoluble antinomies in some area, may ask whether an alternative and rival tradition has done a better job. Might it be that the rival tradition has found resources to characterize and explain the failings and defects of its own tradition more adequately than we, using the resources of our tradition, have been able to do?[17] Let us refer to this aspect of justifying a tradition as the *synchronic*, noticing, at the same time, that it involves the diachronic evaluation of each tradition as an intrinsic element.

We come again to the self-referential twist. MacIntyre's own account of tradition-constituted enquiry is itself a theory and, as such, is subject to evaluation by some narrative method (in both its diachronic and synchronic aspects). In *Whose Justice? Which Rationality?* he both uses his narrative method to justify his own reformulation of the moral tradition in which the concept of virtue plays a central role and, simultaneously, argues for the narrative method itself by placing it within a large-scale intellectual tradition— The Aristotelian-Thomist. Consistent with his own method, he then compares this tradition to its major rival, the Enlightenment approach to rationality.

To make a successful case MacIntyre must show three things: first, that the Enlightenment tradition of "traditionless reason" is incapable of solving its own most pressing intellectual problems, in particular the problem of the tradition-ladenness of standards of rationality; second, that his own version of the Aristotelian-Thomist tradition has a good chance of solving the problem; third, that we can explain why we could have been so misled by a tradition that claimed to reject all tradition.

Put differently, MacIntyre makes his argument by assuming the standpoint of tradition-constituted reason and then, by using that perspective, to diagnose the mistakes of his predecessors. The Enlightenment tradition cannot tell its own story intelligibly because its own standards of rationality require such standards to be universal and not historically conditioned. This is not the case, however. His own account is vindicated to the extent to which it sheds light on this aspect of intellectual history.

So, MacIntyre claims that his own reformulation of the virtue theory is justified because it solves the problems which its predecessors in the virtue tradition of moral reasoning could not solve; furthermore, it explains why they could not solve them. This approach to the justification of an ethical position is in fact an instantiation of a broader theory of rationality. According to this new theory, a tradition is vindicated both by the fact that it has managed to solve its own major problems while its competitors have failed to do so and because it can give a better account of its rival's failures than the

---

17. MacIntyre, *Whose Justice?* 166–67.

rival can itself. This theory of rationality, in its turn, needs to be justified by showing that it is part of a large-scale epistemological tradition (the Aristotelian-Thomist), and that this tradition is justified. Consistent with the narrative theory of rationality, it is justified by the narrative which shows both how it has overcome its problems and its main contemporary competitor, modern Enlightenment reason, has not.

The foregoing account of epistemological developments in the wake of Quine's "Two Dogmas" allows us to construct a typology of holist positions. These fall along a spectrum ranging from relativism to a form of universalism. At the extreme relativist end is what we call *insular* holism. This is the view that data and standards of rationality are internal to webs or traditions, and that there is no possibility of rational adjudication among competitors. Within this type, we can distinguish between those who admit the existence of a mind-independent reality, while seeing it as irrelevant for discriminating between worldviews, and those who deny the very existence of such a reality.

At the opposite end of the spectrum is the position according to which standards of rationality are internal to the web of belief, and yet, as a matter of contingent historical fact, these standards are seen to be held universally. Thus, although relativism is a logical possibility, it is not an actuality. We take this latter to be Quine's view.

In between are the positions which take seriously the paradigm-dependence or tradition-dependence of standards of rationality, yet argue that it is nonetheless (sometimes) possible to make rational judgements among competitors. Lakatos and MacIntyre can be classified as belonging to this group.

POSTEPISTEMOLOGISTS

Rorty has been one of the most significant critics of foundationalism. He does not count foundationalism as a "modern" view, however, but rather indicts the entire Western philosophical tradition for being captivated by the notion of knowledge as a picture—the picture of mind as the "mirror of nature" and knowledge as a reflection of reality. Rorty argues that we need to think of knowledge more along pragmatist lines, as that which is good for us to believe. Once we wean ourselves from the long-standing habit of thinking of knowledge as mirroring or picturing reality, then all of the traditional problems of epistemology disappear. Rorty claims that epistemology as a discipline needs to be abandoned, and in its place one needs to consider the conditions under which discussion, in pursuit of consensus, can proceed in an open manner.

A closely related search for a successor discipline for epistemology is the turn to hermeneutics. Richard Bernstein argues that the distinction between the *Naturwissenschaften*, which proceeds on the basis of a rational method, and the hermeneutical disciplines that comprise the *Geisteswissenschaften* has broken down. All understanding, being mediated by human concepts, involves interpretation.[18] In this move, and in the related use of the German philosopher Jürgen Habermas by the Cambridge philosopher of science Mary Hesse,[19] we find a breakdown of the old opposition between Anglo-American and Continental thinkers. With their new focus on problems of interpretation and praxis, these thinkers have drawn much closer to German philosophers such as Heidegger and Gadamer who subordinate questions of knowledge to those of understanding.

Yet another attack on the hegemony of epistemology comes from the sociology of knowledge, especially from the denial of the distinction between scientific and other disciplines. Proponents of the "strong program" in the sociology of scientific knowledge argue that all communities' theories of rationality or truth ought to be treated as on a par by the sociologist. It is not necessary first to discriminate between true and false theories or world-views, and then to explain the origin and acceptance of true theories along different lines from the false ones. All such developments are equally open to sociological analysis.[20]

In myriad ways the antiepistemological moves mentioned here owe a debt to the work of Ludwig Wittgenstein. In his later work Wittgenstein was antifoundationalist, claiming that when we seek for ultimate justification we come at last to a point where nothing can be said except "this is what we do." In other words, the justification of our justificatory procedures themselves is social convention. Wittgenstein's later work is antiepistemological in the sense that it is generally antitheoretical. He came to believe that, because of the dependence of language and knowledge on local practices, there could be no grand philosophical theories about knowledge or truth. The meaning of language lies in its use. If you want to know whether a sentence is "true" or "known," you have to see whether it is being used consistently with the conventions that govern the "language game" out of which it arises.[21]

THE LOGOEXCENTRICS

For an increasing number of philosophers, the crisis in epistemology—which might go by the name of the "Cartesian anxiety"—is more than shaking the foundations. They maintain that it is not only foundationalism, but subjectivity and rationality in general, that have been discredited by the new "masters of suspicion." These are the thinkers who are concerned with deepening the Cartesian anxiety. We have already referred to them as logoexcentrics.

The so-called Cartesian anxiety refers to philosophy's traditional preoccupation with finding a stable home for meaning, truth, and knowledge.

---

18. Cf. Richard Bernstein, *Beyond Objectivism and Relativism* (Philadelphia: University of Pennsylvania Press, 1983).

19. Cf. Mary Hesse, *Revolutions and Reconstructions in the Philosophy of Science* (Bloomington: Indiana University Press, 1980).

20. Cf. David Bloor, *Knowledge and Social Imagery* (London: Routledge, 1976).

21. Cf. Ludwig Wittgenstein, *Philosophical Investigations* (New York: Macmillan, 1953).

Whereas Descartes located this home in consciousness, many contemporary philosophers have *relocated* rationality, most often into intersubjective practices and procedures. The question is whether this change in locale solves, or only changes the location of, the problem of rationality: namely, how to ensure that one holds not only opinions but justified true beliefs.

"Logocentrism" is Jacques Derrida's term for the belief, typical of Western philosophy, that the meaning and truth of words and ideas is guaranteed by an authoritative source or "center" (for example, Reason, subjectivity, the *cogito*). Thanks to the *logos* (thinking), a thing is "present" to the mind as an idea. Descartes is a good example of such logocentrism, insofar as he gives pride of place to self-consciousness. What the knowing subject knows first and foremost is his own mind. But the so-called "masters of suspicion" (Freud, Marx, and Nietzsche) called into question the ability of consciousness to know its own mind, by arguing that consciousness is constituted by something prior (such as ideologies, unconscious drives and desires, or by the historical tradition of which it is a part).

Derrida's term "logocentrism" embraces more than foundationalism. He argues that the Western philosophical tradition has privileged "speech" over "writing," because speech enjoys an immediacy, a "presence" of consciousness to its words and ideas. The speech to which philosophers accord epistemological privilege is the voice of reason, the voice of self-consciousness— in short the voice that says, "I think, therefore I am."

Similarly, as we saw, Richard Rorty has argued that Western philosophy, at least since the seventeenth century, has been working with a false picture of the mind as a mirror of the world. For Rorty, the whole history of philosophy is the story of numerous searches for a kind of philosopher's stone which would allow the knower to transcend the limitations of time and place, the merely conventional and contingent aspects of one's life, in order to see the world as it truly is. Both thinkers maintain that epistemology, the concern about true beliefs, is the anxious and allergic response to the human condition, namely, the condition of having only a human point of view on things. We have called those who dismiss the project of logocentrism the *logoexcentrics*. They contend that not only the subject but rationality itself has been "decentred." Both have now been removed from their privileged places in philosophy and Western culture. More radically, the logoexcentrics argue that philosophy itself has been decentred by poetry, by other human practices, and by politics. Philosophy should no longer be accorded the privilege of regulating the discourse of other practices by judging them "rational" or "irrational."

Whereas traditional logocentric philosophers privilege "speech" (a shorthand for the coincidence of language, mind, and world), Derrida has suggested that "writing" is more fundamental. "Writing" should not, however, be taken literally. Derrida is speaking metaphorically about the priority of the language system to the subject. Consciousness is preceded by what he calls *langue*, i.e., the linguistic unconscious or differential sign system which is the condition for thought, but which thought can never master. "Writing" serves as Derrida's metaphor for the always decentred and deferred exchange of signs. "Its operations are precisely those which escape the self-consciousness of speech and its deluded sense of mastery of concept over language."[22] If Derrida is right, the logos or word is cut off from the knowing subject. The home of meaning is not the *cogito* but the linguistic code itself, the site of a differential sign system. Prior to logos is writing, for the condition of being a speaker or thinker depends on something that is *extrinsic* to consciousness.

The categories with which reason works are always-already contaminated by language. Postmodernism is thus a sustained polemic against modernity's belief that reality informs thought and thought informs language. Poststructuralists argue that all speech and thought is governed by variable codes that serve as the condition of their existence, and these codes are themselves subject to change (contra Kant). There is no such thing for Rorty as nonlinguistic knowledge. Rather, knowledge is always-already situated in language systems that are themselves subject to the vicissitudes of history, culture, and politics.

The *logos* as the home of reason is not in a spiritual realm of its own, but is rather enmeshed and entangled in concrete forms of life. Kant's notion of a "pure" reason, it turns out, was a convenient fiction. What passes for rationality is instead situated, immanent, and impure. The attempt to get behind or above language to something that grounds thought has failed. In the Western logocentric tradition, the body was repeatedly treated as the lower member of the binary opposition mind/body. It was thought to be the seat of passions, desire, and unreason. The logoexcentrics have a more positive view of the body as an indispensable condition for humanity's negotiation with the world. Propositional knowledge is not foundational but rather is grounded in our dealings with the world.

What exactly is extrinsic to the logos of epistemology? Emmanuel Lévinas's short but massive answer is the "Other." The Other is the "other than reason." Lévinas reads the history of Western epistemology as the progressive colonization of the Other. Anything that does not fit into our rational schemes has been tabled "irrational" and systematically excluded from all positions of privilege and respect:

> This history (of philosophy) can be interpreted as an attempt at an universal synthesis, a reduction of all experience, of all that is reasonable, to a totality wherein consciousness embraces the world, leaves nothing other outside of itself, and thus becomes absolute thought.[23]

Knowledge is a matter of bringing reality under our conceptual schemes and categories. In subsuming the "other" to the "same," however, the French

---

22. Christopher Norris, *Deconstruction: Theory and Practice* (London: Methuen, 1982), 28–29.

23. Emmanuel Lévinas, *Totality and Infinity* (Pittsburgh: Dusquesne University Press, 1969), 75.

thinker argues, epistemology inevitably wreaks violence on things. All objects are made to conform to our concepts. Lévinas argues that an ethical philosophy will abandon epistemology's aggressive desire for unification (the final solution) and totality. The purpose of ethics is to unsettle "essences" and "certainties." The purpose of ethics, in short, is to undo epistemology.

What, then, are the consequences of this recognition of the impurity of reason and of the decentering of epistemology? What specific alternatives have been proposed to rationality and epistemology? Briefly, we can consider four: practice, poetry, play, and power.

PRACTICE

Pragmatism is one alternative. One may concede the impossibility of the Enlightenment project of discovering *universal* criteria of rationality, without giving up altogether on criteria for knowledge. These criteria will be contingent conventions that operate at some times and places rather than at others. It is commonplace to appeal to Wittgenstein's idea of a language game as an example. What counts as knowledge depends on the particular language game being played. Some interpret Wittgenstein as saying that there exists a plurality of incommensurable language/knowledge games, so that what passes for knowledge or justification varies from context to context.

Richard Rorty urges philosophers to abandon altogether the search for accurate representations of the world on the basis of reliable starting points, and to recognize instead that language and knowledge are human tools for coping with reality, tools that are relative to contingent circumstances and human interests. Instead of asking what conceptual scheme "gets it right," philosophers ought to be comparing various vocabularies in search of better ways of talking and acting. Philosophy in this view becomes an "edifying" discourse concerned with helping people with their own local tasks rather than an epistemological discourse striving for universal consensus.

POETRY

Heidegger shares with other logoexcentrics the belief that the human subject is not set over against the world but in it. Western philosophy has wrongly encouraged an "us–it" mentality, in which reason is construed instrumentally as allowing us to manipulate and control objects. Heidegger sought a kind of thinking other than the calculative. He believed that instrumental rationality could not think the question of Being itself. Instead of the "natural light" of the mind that human knowing shines on objects (beings), Heidegger proposed that Being itself comes to light in noninstrumental language and thought. To the thing as scientific object Heidegger opposed the thing as the place where the truth of Being happens. To the kind of thinking that seeks to grasp things Heidegger opposed poetry, the kind of thinking that receives things.

Truth for Heidegger is a matter of "unveiling." Language does not correspond to Being; rather, Being shows itself in and through language. Truth is an event where Being comes to light in language. The task of the thinker is not to assimilate beings to some conceptual scheme or other, but rather to receive Being. Propositional language and thought, however, objectify Being and force it under some concept. Such a grasping is the opposite of the letting-go which Heidegger associates with truth. It is not propositions but poetry that permits Being to show itself, for poetry transcends the subject–object distinction and projects a world in which subjects are always-already rooted. "Art then is the becoming and happening of truth."[24]

PLAY

Deconstruction is the attempt to undo the privilege of logocentric concepts by exposing how they are rhetorical constructs rather than natural givens. All conceptual schemes are unstable structures that mistakenly claim the stability of a center. This desire for a stabilizing center is precisely the logocentric desire. Logocentrism—the privileging of rationality—is "nothing but the most original and powerful ethnocentrism."[25] Instead of a center, argue the deconstructionists, there is language: endless, empty and infinitely changing. Instead of stability, there is only the endless play of signifiers—signs that refer only to other signs, never never to a signified and never to reality.

Derrida both reveals the underlying play and seems to revel in it. Yet this is play with a purpose. He claims to stand in the Kantian tradition of inquiring into the limits of reason. Indeed, deconstruction may be likened to a critique of impure reason, a study of the conditions of the *impossibility* of knowledge. "Writing" is the most important condition for the impossibility of knowledge, insofar as it stands for the system of differences that forever forestalls language or thought ever coming to rest in a nonlinguistic reality. There simply is no anchor by which signifiers are "earthed" or attain being.

It is only because Western philosophy has been successful in repressing the disruptive effects of language that it was able to maintain the illusion of the superiority of rational discourse. Philosophy is the discourse that, at least traditionally, privileges logic over rhetoric, the intelligible over the sensible, the literal over the figurative, and metanarratives over narratives. Such privileging is, however, itself a rhetorical move, not something that mirrors the natural order of things. Philosophy is only able to maintain these hierarchies by means of strategies of exclusion and repression. The task of deconstruc-

---

24. Martin Heidegger, "The Origin of the Work of Art," in David Krell (ed.), *Martin Heidegger: Basic Writings* (New York: Harper and Row, 1977), 183. Ultimately, Heidegger may be a logocentric, to the extent that he views Being as self-presencing and insofar as he too seeks "origins" and "truth." This, at least, is Derrida's judgement. Yet this form of logocentrism is one that is in discontinuity with much of the Western tradition, as it seeks ultimate origins in what is other than Reason.

25. Jacques Derrida, *Of Grammatology* (Baltimore: John Hopkins University Press, 1976), 3.

tion is to expose these rhetorical strategies and so to undo the hierarchies which they support. The logocentric concern for rationality and a privileged access to knowledge is, for Derrida, a symptom of philosophy's inability to acknowledge its kinship to literature.

POWER

Foucault's critique of rationality stems from his detailed analyses ("genealogies") of the ways in which various social practices and institutions come to distinguish the true from the false, the rational from the irrational, and the healthy from the sick. Contra Plato, Foucault believes that truth does not come "from above" but is manufactured "from below." What counts as knowledge or truth depends not on eternal Forms, but on the sociopolitical situation of the day.

Foucault's genealogy of prisons and asylums analyzes fields of knowledge in terms of the power relations that ground and support them. For instance, "insanity" only exists as something about which true and false statements can be made because it has been constituted as an object by a set of discursive practices. The thesis that emerges is that the criteria for knowledge and truth are laid down by the institutional authority of the day. In Foucault's opinion, the will to truth is inseparable from the will to power. He can thus speak of *la régime du savoir* (the regime of knowledge).

A "discourse" is a domain of language use subject to rules of formation and transformation. Theoretical discourses are often formed by nondiscursive practices. What counts as knowledge is often the result of a struggle for power or a political decision: "Power and knowledge directly imply one another . . . there is no power relation without the correlative constitution of a field of knowledge, nor any knowledge that does not presuppose and constitute at the same time power relations."[26] A "discourse," therefore, is a matrix of power/knowledge.

An *episteme*, acording to Foucault, is a knowledge/power situation that determines what is considered knowledge or truth at a particular time. Foucault's celebrated announcement of the "death of man" signalled the transition from the modern episteme, which enshrined self-consciousness, to the current episteme, in which language is acknowledged to be constitutive of subjectivity and knowledge alike. Foucault concludes that knowers move from one regime of knowledge and truth into another. No one stands outside some system of knowledge/power: "Truth is of this world; it is the product of multiple constraints. And it induces regular effects of power. Each society has its regime of truth, its 'general politics of truth.'"[27] The writing on the wall for traditional epistemology is, again, "writing": the discursive practices that inevitably intrude between the mind and the world.

---

26. Michel Foucault, *Discipline and Punish: The Birth of the Prison* (New York: Vintage Books, 1979), 27.

27. Michel Foucault, *Power/Knowledge: Selected Interviews*, Colin Gordon (ed.) (New York: Pantheon Books, 1980), 131.

SUMMARY

In the all too short summary given in these first chapters, we have sided neither with the critics of reason nor with its defenders. It has been our goal instead to *describe* what is being widely heralded as the epistemological predicament in the Academy and in Western society at the end of the second millennium. In order to convey the fullest possible picture of this crucial debate, we have treated the discussion about justification and realism each on its own. We have also provided in the previous chapter brief sketches of the major schools within three Western linguistic traditions, the Anglo-American, French, and German, both isolating distinctive features and looking for important overarching themes.

It will have been clear again and again to the reader with an interest in missiology that these debates have everything to do with the study of mission. In what way does a theologian's analysis of the epistemological situation influence thinking about mission? When the "truth" of theology is spoken about, what is meant? Do Christians need to speak of their tradition as true? Can they call their beliefs "knowledge"? How will their decision on this matter affect those with whom they speak? Finally, what should the study of mission look like as a discipline? For example, the attack on logocentrism is of course also an attack on the "ology" in missiology. Do the epistemological worries cast doubt on the very foundations of missiology as a discipline? Or, do they open up exciting new horizons, helping to free the participants further from the "Christendom" model and to foster dialogue and open conversation between Christians and their secular or religious counterparts? These are some of the central questions that must preoccupy us as we turn now to more explicitly Christian themes.

PART TWO

The Epistemological Predicament
and Missiology

CHAPTER FOUR

Missiology, Epistemology, and Intratraditional Dialogue

ANDY F. SANDERS

INTRODUCTION

What has epistemology to do with a missiology of Western culture? The reply to this question will have to be unfolded as we go along, but a first step would be to draw up a list of the main features of contemporary Western culture. Such a list would almost certainly include characteristics like pluralist, individualist, secular, (post)modernist, and scientistic. Others could easily be added, such as liberal, economized, technocratic, bureaucratic, ecologically damaging, manipulative and exploitative of human beings, relentless consumerism.[1]

Focusing on the intellectual side, the plurality of modern culture is exhibited in a vast diversity of legal, moral, political, philosophical, and religious traditions that partly overlap, partly interconnect, partly oppose each other, and partly are just different. We find ourselves confronted with large-scale diversity in virtually all areas of social life: fragmentation and disagreement, rather than unity and consensus, are characteristics of the situation in which the Christian religion finds itself essentially contested by other worldviews, both secular and religious.

Western culture is also individualistic, in the sense that it protects and cherishes the autonomy of the individual. Technology enables the individual to take notice of, and even to participate in, different traditions located in distant areas of the globe. At the same time, the mass media exerts an enormous influence. The young especially are exposed to a host of conflicting images, values, life-styles, and views of life with which they are largely left to grapple by themselves. The shift to postmodernism is obvious here too.

---

1. Cf. D.J. Bosch, *Believing in the Future: Toward a Missiology of Western Culture* (Valley Forge, PA: Trinity Press International, 1995), 3.

As the social psychologist Kenneth Gergen puts it, even the humanistic conception of an authentic self is in the process of being dismantled:

> Under postmodern conditions, persons exist in a state of continuous construction and reconstruction; it is a world where anything goes that can be negotiated. Each reality of self gives way to reflexive questioning, irony and ultimately the playful probing of another reality. The center fails to hold.[2]

Rapidly receding from view, the humanistic "authentic self" seems to follow the same course as the Christian conception of the self as becoming authentic in relation to God.

Western culture is secularized in that it shows, on the whole, a decrease in the number of people affiliated to institutionalized religion, an increased indifference to religious teachings, and a loss of the moral, social, and political influence of Christianity in general.

Further, Western culture may still be called modernist in the sense that it remains deeply influenced by the Enlightenment ideals of freedom, autonomy, and progress. But the Enlightenment's ideal of attaining universality and certainty on the basis of secure foundations of knowledge is thoroughly compromised. As a consequence of the postmodern critique of modernism, all grand narratives of orientation and salvation appear to have fallen into disrepute. Not only Euro-American Christianity, but the great ideologies of the nineteenth and twentieth centuries (Marxism and Humanism) have also lost their authority and power to unite and inspire large groups of people.

Each community or group has its own traditions, histories, practices, narratives, and truths, but there is no longer any recourse to a universal theory of the true and the good. According to postmodernists, there is no way of adjudicating between the opposing claims of differing traditions. The upshot is that we are left with a plurality of heterogeneous traditions, each of which is the sole determinant of its adherents' ways of knowing and acting. The predicament is that we have to live with this plurality and we can only speak to and converse with others from within our own traditional practices.

Finally, Western culture may be called scientistic in the sense that modern culture as we know it would be unthinkable without the all-pervasive influence of science, its methods, and its successes. The deep impact of science on culture has led to forms of scientism which are in direct conflict with religious worldviews and which are at least partly responsible for culture's secular and modernist features.

As the Christian religion is itself part of Western culture, it is only to be expected that it exhibits similar characteristics. Western culture is deeply rooted in the mind of Christian believers, no matter how alienated or dis-

---

2. K. Gergen, *The Saturated Self: Dilemmas of Identity in Contemporary Life* (New York: Basic Books 1991), 7.

tanced they may feel themselves from it. This is the culture in which they were born and educated, learned its languages and histories, and in which they live and work. Plurality in the culture at large has its parallel in the vast denominational diversity within institutionalized Christianity. But diversity is not only a domestic matter: within the larger culture, Christian faith has various other religious and nonreligious worldviews to compete with. In the eyes of detached onlookers and religious pluralists it is no longer the one and only true path to salvation. Further, the individualism of modern culture has an obvious parallel in the growing number of people who are not religiously affiliated but who nevertheless consider themselves believers in the divine, the sacred, or transcendence. Finally, the undeniable loss of Christianity's intellectual respectability among the educated, combined with the large-scale indifference toward it in the culture at large, makes the status of theology over against the other scientific and scholarly disciplines deeply problematic. How does one account for the epistemic credentials of the central narratives of faith in a culture in which reality is commonly believed to be identical with what can be established empirically or, even more restricted, with what the empirical sciences may discover or explain?

If this sketch of the current situation is anywhere near correct, the question of how to communicate, in speech, writing, or action, the Christian message to Western culture is a truly formidable one. Obviously, a missiological account of the intellectual, moral, and religious predicament in the West will have to depend primarily on requirements internal to the Christian tradition itself. Yet, precisely because it is also part of Western culture, a careful assessment of the relations between the Christian tradition and the larger culture is called for.

Against this background, my epistemological contribution to the missiological endeavour will proceed on the assumption that the collapse of foundationalism is not some distant calamity to be left only to philosophers to deal with. On the contrary, as it has far-reaching consequences for theology, it is crucially important that this is fully understood. Thus my aim will be to clarify the implications for theology of some of the main epistemological beliefs that are involved in the current debate concerning how and where to find reliable and reasonable bearings in our pluralist culture.

Apart from the task of clarification, I will also try to outline a postfoundational position in religious epistemology that may commend itself to theologians as a reasonable epistemological stand to take and from which they may engage confidently in dialogue with people who have different views of the world and life. Such dialogue, I take it, will always be *intertraditional* in the sense that the theologian will engage from within the Christian tradition with participants in other large-scale traditions, whether religious, secular, Western, or non-Western.

I call my position *traditionalism*, which I believe is epistemologically consonant with Christian faith itself. So, no capitulation to, or assimilation of, alien standards will be involved. Even if no audience or conversation partner were found, it need not be theology that is responsible for the breakdown in communication. Although the message may in itself be "scandalous," at least the messengers themselves will not have to give offense.

FOUNDATIONALISM AND DOGMATISM

What are the implications of the collapse of foundationalism for theology? Let us, first, be clear about the meaning of the term. According to Susan Haack, three different senses of foundationalism should carefully be distinguished. First, we have *a theory of justification* which postulates basic beliefs justified by experience as the foundation of knowledge (F1). Next, we have two meta-epistemological uses of the term: *a conception of epistemology* which regards epistemology as an a priori discipline founding the sciences (F2), and *a thesis* that "criteria of justification are not purely conventional but stand in need of objective grounding" because they are only satisfactory if they are truth-indicative (F3).[3]

Like Haack, I uphold (F3) and reject both (F1) and (F2). Contrary to what might appear to be the case, there is no contradiction involved, for (F3) does not imply or include either (F2) or (F1). (F2), of which logical positivism would be a good example, need not be considered in this context any further. And since I will return to (F3) later, for the moment we will concentrate on (F1), foundationalism as a theory of justification with its long and venerable history. The story of its collapse, I think, is in part also the story of what goes under the name of dogmatism.

The word "dogmatism" is often used negatively to refer to "a way of thinking based upon principles which have not been tested by reflection" (*Shorter Oxford English Dictionary*) and "to dogmatize" means to make positive assertions without the backing of sufficient argument or evidence. The term has also been used, notably by Sir Karl Popper, for the attitude of holding on to one's beliefs in a "come what may" fashion. Thus, even when counterevidence is persistent and overwhelming, and better alternatives are available, dogmatists hold on to their beliefs. To keep out as much recalcitrant evidence and criticism as possible, all kinds of immunizing strategies are employed.

Dogmatists are convinced that some of their beliefs are immune, or at least nearly immune, from error and thus universally or absolutely true. They may have come to accept these truths either on "faith" or on the deliverances of reason. In the former case the dogmatist turns out to be a fideist who holds that what is believed, although contrary to or at least beyond reason, is nevertheless securely grounded. In the latter case, he or she often turns out to be a foundationalist: in the final run, the beliefs are founded on a stock of basic beliefs, not supported by any other beliefs.

The following definition brings us to the epistemological core of the dogmatist's position: "there are certain propositions such that it follows from

---

3. Cf. S. Haack, *Evidence and Inquiry: Towards Reconstruction in Epistemology* (Oxford: Blackwell, 1993), 186.

our believing them that they are true and which are such that we can't fail to believe them."[4] Asking what these privileged beliefs might be leads us directly into foundationalist territory: they are basic in that they make up the foundation of our knowledge. Basic beliefs support or justify other (derived) beliefs but are themselves not supported by any other beliefs. As they are justified directly by experience or introspection, they block the threat of an infinite regress of justifications. Traditionally, basic beliefs are held to be either (1) self-evident (e.g., simple logical and mathematical truths, like "2 + 3 = 5"), or (2) about one's own current mental states (beliefs, sensations, images, feelings, and thoughts, e.g., "I seem to see something red," "I had breakfast this morning," or "I feel that God is giving me the strength"), or (3) the result of reliable belief-forming processes (e.g., perception, memory, and inference). As such, they satisfy the immunity conditions of being incorrigible, indubitable, and even infallible.

The main and probably fatal objection to the stronger versions of foundationalist dogmatism is that they require basic beliefs to be both justified independently of the support of any other beliefs and rich enough to be capable of supporting all other (nonbasic, derived) beliefs. As Haack points out, the more privileged basic beliefs are held to be, the more plausible it is that these requirements are in competition and cannot be met at the same time. The richer the content of basic beliefs, the less secure they are; the more secure, the poorer their content.[5]

What about weaker forms of foundationalism? Its adherents do not embrace the immunity conditions and they take basic beliefs as only prima facie or, to some degree, justified, but not indefeasibly so. Against this position, Haack argues convincingly that weak foundationalists cannot allow a person to be more or better justified in holding a belief because of her current experience (say, her seeing a dog), when some of her other beliefs (say, that her eyes are in working order, that she is not dreaming, etc.) clearly support it. Weak foundationalists cannot allow this because basic beliefs are exclusively justified by something other than beliefs.

In sum, as the foundational dogmatist account of justification meets with insurmountable difficulties and as dogmatists are strongly inclined toward absolutizing their basic beliefs and immunizing them from critique, their position becomes untenable. Also, their preoccupation with the old skeptical worry about certainty and their hankering after ultimate justification as the solvent of that worry clearly shows that they still belong fairly and squarely within the parameters of the foundationalist enterprise of the Enlightenment.

What does all of this add up to for theology? First, a familiar response has to be dealt with. It is sometimes pointed out that, if dogmatism is applicable at all in a theological context, it is because faith is conceived as a system of propositions to which people are committed. It might then be objected,

---

4. Cf. S. Haack, "Fallibilism and Necessity," *Synthese* 41(1979): 52f.
5. Cf. Haack, *Evidence and Inquiry*, 30.

however, that this is actually a misconstrual of faith. So, if faith is not a matter of holding beliefs, we need not worry too much about dogmatism. This line of reasoning will not do, however. As W.L. Sessions shows convincingly in his recent analysis of six major models of religious faith, propositional belief is central in at least one (the belief model) and required by at least two (the personal relationship and the hope model). In one model (the devotion model), propositional belief is permitted and to some extent useful, whereas in the attitude model it is at least permitted. Only in one model (called by Sessions the confidence model of faith) is propositional belief excluded.[6] For this model faith is a nonrelational conscious state, exemplified by S.B. Park's *choshin* concept of faith in Korean Buddhism; it is not typically Christian.[7] So, in Sessions's analysis, the particulars of which cannot be elaborated here, propositional belief, although never primary, is always to a greater or lesser degree involved in faith, not least in Christian faith.

Furthermore, it seems clear that especially where communication with the larger culture is concerned, both language and action are essential. Rather than employing the well-worn distinction between theory and practice, we have to take account of the fact that both presuppose a vast background of intentional states (beliefs, desires, purposes), stances, and preintentional skills and capacities. It is in terms of that background knowledge, and in reliance on it, that people act, speak, and think. Such knowledge may properly be characterized as knowing how to do things and knowing what things are for, rather than as either "objective" or impersonal descriptive knowledge or as propositional knowledge that so-and-so is the case. Hence, no matter the primacy of living faith and granting that beliefs as such are not what living faith is about or directed at, at least on the level of theological reflection about language and action belief cannot be discarded, either in the sense of a (mental) attitude or in the sense of content.

So what about theology? In view of the serious objections to foundational dogmatism, it should be clear that it is not the position to adopt. I see no good reason to withdraw, intellectually, morally, or otherwise, from communication with the wider culture, especially from dialogue with participants in other cultural practices such as science, morality, law, art, and politics. Withdrawal may lead, to paraphrase Bloom, to a "closing of the Christian mind," surely a serious impediment to any Christian sense of mission. If more or less consciously opted for, the result would be a self-professed tribalism.

But closure, retreat from the marketplace, flight from the academy, is neither necessary nor called for. On the contrary, as the Princeton theologian Wentzel van Huyssteen argues, the primary locus of a postfoundational theology is in its engagement in interdisciplinary dialogue.[8] Moreover, viable

---

6. Cf. W.L. Sessions, *The Concept of Faith: A Philosophical Investigation* (Ithaca and London: Cornell University Press, 1994), 134ff.

7. Ibid., 227ff.

8. Cf. J.W. van Huyssteen, *Essays in Postfoundationalist Theology* (Grand Rapids, MI: Eerdmans, 1997), 3f.

and challenging alternatives to foundationalism are available, and to one of them I will now turn.

FROM DOGMATISM TO TRADITIONALISM

Perhaps the most serious theological worry about taking leave of foundational dogmatism is whether the essential element of personal commitment that is at the heart of the Christian faith can still be adequately accounted for. As faith is both a gift and a response to God's revelation in Christ, surely that revelation is the foundation of the Christian tradition. When this foundation is universal, in the sense of being the one and only measure of the meaning of liberation for humankind, wouldn't the rejection of foundationalism imperil or even discard it?[9] As I hope to make clear in the subsequent sections, because the answer is no, we don't have to take this worry too seriously.

At this stage, it is worth pointing out that we should not be led astray by the foundation metaphor. To talk about the Christ event as the foundation of the Christian tradition is to talk about its essence, core, or originating event. It need not be construed as a thesis in the epistemology of the Christian religion at all. To do so is not so much a theological as a philosophical move, one deeply indebted to Enlightenment philosophy.

The crucial element of religious commitment can be accounted for in a nonfoundational way by drawing on developments in epistemology and philosophy of science during the second half of this century. Briefly, the story is now that even in science the adoption of a healthy measure of dogmatism is not only quite rational, but even necessary for progress. For instance, Imre Lakatos's conception of a scientific research programme explicitly lets the so-called hard core of such a programme go unquestioned, protected by a belt of auxiliary theories, at least for as long as there is no imminent danger of its being superseded by a competitor in the field.

This kind of dogmatism is significantly different, however, from the fideist or foundationalist brand. It may be called *methodological dogmatism* and be described positively in terms of a thesis which in the course of inquiry allows us to hold on to our beliefs and theories, as long as this is reasonable and no better alternative is available. A methodological or heuristic principle of tenacity is involved which says that we should not give up our theories or stories in the face of adverse evidence too soon, because doing so would deprive us of the opportunity to find out their strength, fruitfulness, and significance.

---

9. This worry seems to underlie Andrew Kirk's suggestion that the Christian story "is the measure of all other stories" and that all other stories are therefore "ultimately defective." Employing the law of excluded middle, Kirk then argues that if this is not conceded, truth claims based on the singularity of the Christian message "have nowhere to go" and relativism and inconsistency will follow. In what follows I hope to make clear that radical relativism is by no means the one and only alternative to foundationalism.

Where precisely to draw the line beyond which holding on to our theories or stories becomes irrational cannot be specified in advance. It will depend to a large extent on the relevant context, the beliefs in question, their relation to the other beliefs of the person involved, the strength of the counterevidence, and, of course, the question whether a better alternative is available. In any case, the decision will always have to be made with care and competence, both in the light of prevailing standards of inquiry and of what the inquirer takes to be the truth of the matter.

Of course, foundational and methodological dogmatisms are not totally different. The connection between them, I suggest, is one of implication or inclusion. It seems entirely plausible to assume that the former includes the latter but that the reverse need not hold: one can be a methodological dogmatist without being a foundational dogmatist.

A further worry need not arise either. Giving up the ideal of unshakable foundations for knowledge does not imply that theology must fall prey to skepticism. The very idea that there are only two options, either certainty and secure foundations (dogmatism) or no substantial knowledge at all (skepticism), is itself part of the Enlightenment project. As soon as the metaphor of founding is jettisoned, skepticism loses much of its force: the point of denying the possibility of completely justified and totally secure foundations is lost. Indeed, the founding and grounding metaphor would be better replaced by Neurath's picture of the ship that can only be rebuilt on the open sea, because the option of dismantling it in dry dock and reconstructing it there out of the best materials is not available.[10] The boat we sail in stands for the tradition in which we participate.

Taking leave of foundationalism does not mean that no reasons could or should be given for or against religious beliefs and values whenever this is called for. But the aim of giving these reasons to the best of our knowledge and experience is not to construct foundations that could withstand critique from all quarters. Surely, the easiest way to achieve this would simply be to evade any encounter with adherents of non-Christian or even nonreligious views of life that might challenge the Christian tradition. Instead of admonishing us to isolate ourselves from the wider culture, that tradition calls us to be ready "always to give an answer to everyone that asks you a reason for the hope that is in you" (1 Peter 3:15). This exhortation confidently presupposes that there are reasons for that hope that are communicable and intelligible.

A further characteristic of methodological dogmatism is that it will not focus on questions of how beliefs stand up to experience in isolation, but rather on how the totality of the beliefs that make up a theory or worldview

---

10. The logical positivist Otto Neurath already attacked foundationalism by denying the possibility of taking conclusively established pure protocol sentences as the starting points of science: "We are like sailors who must rebuild their ship on the open sea, never able to dismantle it in dry dock and to reconstruct it there out of the best materials."; Cf. his "Protocol Sentences," in A.J. Ayer (ed.), *Logical Positivism* (New York: The Free Press, 1959), 201.

do so. Here the methodological dogmatist adheres to Quine's holist thesis that "any statement can be held true come what may, if we make drastic enough adjustments elsewhere in the system. . . . Conversely, by the same token, no statement is immune from revision."[11] Of course, this is not to say that all beliefs are on a par. Some beliefs will be held as more central and, in that sense, as more distinguished than more peripheral ones. As the latter are nearer to experience, it is by their revision that changes are distributed throughout the system.

At this point the question may be raised whether the metaphor of "central beliefs" might not be letting (F1) foundationalism in through the backdoor. However, as Michael Williams put it, identifying certain beliefs as central says nothing more than that, at any one time, we must have some stock of well-entrenched beliefs which set the bounds within which current inquiry proceeds and which provide the touchstone for empirical justification.[12] Though this point refers to empirical knowledge in general, I don't see why it could not analogously be applied to theological inquiry as well. (F1) foundationalism is not involved, as long as it is not claimed that central beliefs are *only* justified by something (experience, introspection) other than the support of other beliefs.

Enlarging the perspective a bit further, the methodological dogmatist emphasizes the importance of the tradition(s) to which people adhere. People are born and educated into communal traditions and practices which provide for them the starting points from which their inquiries into meaning and truth have to be undertaken. But as starting points need not be foundations (in the foundationalist sense), people may nevertheless be wholly rational in relying confidently on their traditions. Mikael Stenmark's distinction between "full acceptance" and "dogmatic acceptance" bears out this point nicely. Dogmatic acceptance disregards "future counter-evidence of what is believed," whereas full acceptance "is compatible with an openness to criticism."[13] That does not mean, of course, that full acceptance of a belief should lead consciously to testing it to check whether any counterevidence might be found. In fact, the believer may be quite confident that no such evidence will ever turn up. Full acceptance of a belief is rational, says Stenmark, "unless there are good reasons to cease from accepting it, or, at least, cease from accepting it fully, and there is no better alternative available."[14]

---

11. W.V.O. Quine, *From a Logical Point of View: Logico-Philosophical Essays* (New York: Harper and Row, 1963), 43. A similar version of this thesis was put forward by Michael Polanyi in the context of his "invitation to dogmatism" as a way out of objectivism. Cf. A.F. Sanders, *Michael Polanyi's Post-critical Epistemology* (Amsterdam: Rodopi, 1988), 195f.

12. M. Williams, *Groundless Belief: An Essay on the Possibility of Epistemology* (New Haven: Yale University Press, 1977), 84.

13. M. Stenmark, *Rationality in Science, Religion and Everyday Life: A Critical Evaluation of Four Models of Rationality* (Notre Dame: University of Notre Dame Press, 1995), 295.

14. Ibid., 293f.

Finally, methodological dogmatism also bears on the broader context of inquiry. Following Polanyi, I suggest we envisage this context as a communal one in which responsible problem solving is undertaken from within the fiduciary framework that any particular tradition of inquiry provides. Referring to St. Augustine's biblical maxim *nisi credideritis, nisi intelligitis,* Polanyi characterizes such a framework as follows:

> tacit assent and intellectual passions, the sharing of an idiom and of a cultural heritage, affiliation to a like-minded community: such are the impulses which shape our vision of the nature of things on which we rely for our mastery of things. No intelligence, however critical or original, can operate outside such a fiduciary framework.[15]

Polanyi's notion of a fiduciary framework as a living tradition embedded in the practice that transmits it points to a recovery of the tradition. *Traditionalism* holds that persons possess a fund of pretheoretical acceptances and anticipations which are not merely taken for granted, but in an important sense are relied upon in processes of belief formation, learning, inquiry, and action. The tacit knowledge embedded in a tradition need not, and indeed cannot, first be argued before we embark on its application or on our attempts to discover its significance. On the contrary, it is a precondition for any serious arguing or explicating of the beliefs that are central to that tradition.

This is, then, my explication so far of methodological dogmatism as an essential ingredient of traditionalism. Traditionalists fully acknowledge that we are crucially dependent on the cultural practices in which we participate and the religious (sub)tradition to which we belong. The standards, values, and ideals inherent in them constitute the only point of view available to us. As it is implicitly a limited and fallible one, it goes without saying that we should attempt to understand, and learn from, other religious or secular traditions. As these values and ideals are both essentially contested and held by us with universal intent, the ongoing endeavour of reinterpreting them in various contexts makes this attempt all the more necessary.

Furthermore, and in contrast to foundational dogmatists, traditionalists fully accept that we lack an Archimedean point, a God's-eye point of view, indeed, that we lack some eternal, unchangeable foundation from which we could judge, evaluate, or compare traditions as a whole vis-à-vis the available evidence. We are finite and fallible humans and our knowledge is always partial. What we do have are the vast resources of the tradition on which we may rely confidently. That we as veracious inquirers are fallible

---

15. M. Polanyi, *Personal Knowledge: Towards a Post-Critical Philosophy* (London: Routledge and Kegan Paul, 1958), 266. The same point was recently made by Alasdair MacIntyre: "We, whoever we are, can only begin enquiry from the vantage point afforded by our relationship to some specific social and intellectual past through which we have affiliated ourselves to some particular tradition of enquiry. . . ." *Whose Justice? Which Rationality?* (Notre Dame: University of Notre Dame Press, 1988), 401.

may seem evident and at most only worth mentioning in passing. Still, it is an essential component of my traditionalism that has important epistemological implications for the Christian dialogue with other religious or non-religious traditions.

FALLIBILIST TRADITIONALISM

Fallibilism is the rationale underlying methodological dogmatism. It may be characterized as an epistemological thesis which says that our human cognitive powers are fallible in the sense that we are liable to hold false beliefs. As Haack points out, it is also a methodological recommendation, namely, that we should always be willing to revise our beliefs in the light of new evidence and experience.[16] Thus, fallibilism is diametrically opposed to foundational dogmatism on the issue of openness to criticism, for it takes the adoption of the critical stance as an epistemic virtue. Its point is the simple idea that, as C.S. Peirce put it, "the first step towards *finding out* is to acknowledge you do not satisfactorily know already. . . ."[17]

As a component of traditionalism, fallibilism and methodological dogmatism form a viable alternative to either foundationalist dogmatism or skepticism, while they do not imply any form of radical relativism. Admittedly, it shares with skepticism the thesis of the possibility of error, and it concedes to foundationalism that we may be holding true beliefs. But it denies the thesis that to know is to know that one knows; rather, it affirms that we may be mistaken in determining which of our beliefs are in fact true.

Another feature of fallibilism is that it comes in degrees. For example, it can be characterized as the thesis that we are nowhere entirely immune from the possibility of error.[18] But it can also be given a more radical interpretation. According to Lehrer, "Men often believe what is false, and, when what they believe happens to be true, there was a chance that they might have erred."[19] Still, from this it certainly does not follow that our beliefs are on the whole or largely false, let alone that we may not be justified or confident in holding any particular belief.

Fallibilism should not be confused with the idea of falsification, whether in its naive (Popper) or more sophisticated form (Lakatos). Falsification, whether of scientific theories or of a series of such theories (research programmes), is a methodological rule that presupposes the general thesis of the fallibility of our cognitive powers. Fallibilism has a clear educational ally in the idea that people may learn from their mistakes. But it certainly does not imply that, for instance, religious forms of inquiry should be submitted to experimental testing as if they were hypotheses of empirical science. In

---

16. Cf. Haack, "Fallibilism and Necessity," 41.

17. Charles Hartshorne and Paul Weiss (eds.) Vol. I–VI. The Collected Papers of Charles Sanders Pierce (Cambridge: Harvard University Press, 1931–1956), I.13–14.

18. Cf. J. Dancy, *Introduction to Contemporary Epistemology* (Oxford: Blackwell, 1985), 58.

19. K. Lehrer, *Knowledge* (Oxford: Oxford University Press, 1974), 237.

fact, when applied to a particular field of inquiry, fallibilism is perfectly consistent with the further thesis that the standards, aims, and subject matter of the tradition in question will largely, though not exclusively, determine what constitutes error, misunderstanding, and the like.

Fallibilism might be false, but if it is true it applies to all domains of human inquiry, including philosophy of religion and theology. Not surprisingly, dogmatist theologians, whether foundationalists or fideists, will disagree. Consider only one example from postliberal theology, namely, George Lindbeck's claim that really competent speakers of religious language are to be found in mainstream traditions and that "the reliability of their agreement in doctrinal matters may not improperly be called infallible."[20] Surely, if "infallibility" is used here in its epistemic sense, Lindbeck's position boils down to a version of theological absolutism. In that case we would have to agree with D.Z. Phillips, who characterizes Lindbeck's claim as "staggering," and who rightly criticizes it for identifying agreement in procedures, or what in fact proves acceptable, with religious truth.[21]

In defence of Lindbeck it might be suggested that he is using "infallible" in a rather special sense. The claims that certain propositions within Christian language games should be regarded as "intra-systematically infallible" in the sense that they cannot be denied, or held to be false, without "destroying or gravely damaging the identity or integrity" of the forms of life in question. This is confusing the issue, however. What Lindbeck seems to be referring to are beliefs constitutive of the Christian tradition as a whole.

On the other hand, many philosophical theologians and philosophers of religion seem to have committed themselves to some form of fallibilism. A good example is the philosopher of religion Basil Mitchell, who, in accounting for the openness to criticism of the Christian faith, argues that if it were demonstrated conclusively that the concept of God is self-contradictory, we could be sure that a person was mistaken in supposing that he or she was conscious of being in the presence of God.[22] As an extreme case of the role of counterevidence he suggests that

> if good historical evidence were to accumulate tending strongly to show that the gospels were forgeries and that Jesus was a fictitious

---

20. G.A. Lindbeck, *The Nature of Doctrine: Religion and Theology in a Postliberal Age* (Philadelphia, PA: Westminster Press, 1984), 100. For his underlying theological and ecclesiastical concerns, see also his *Infallibility* (Milwaukee: Marquette University Press, 1972), 49f., and his "The Reformation and the Infallibility Debate," in P.C. Empie, T.A. Murphy, and J.A. Burgess (eds.), *Teaching Authority and Infallibility in the Church* (Minneapolis: Augsburg Publishing House, 1978), 101–19.

21. Cf. D.Z. Phillips, *Faith after Foundationalism* (London and New York: Routledge, 1988), 220f. It would be interesting, though, to know why Phillips finds this so staggering. Note also that his assertion that what turns out to be acceptable in some religious contexts should not be confused with religious truth presupposes a general conception of truth which is *not* relative to that context.

22. Cf. B. Mitchell, *The Justification of Religious Belief* (London: Macmillan, 1974), 115.

character, there must come a point at which it would no longer be possible to accept the doctrine of Incarnation.[23]

Whether or not these examples are live options is not the point here. What counts is the willingness to modify our beliefs in the face of new and possibly even contrary evidence. This is not to say that theologians, let alone ordinary believers, should be out to test, let alone to falsify, their beliefs as if they were like hypotheses advanced in the context of experimental physics. Rather, it implies both the willingness to acquire new and hopefully deeper insights into the still undisclosed meanings of what we believe and to state a condition for open dialogue with the larger culture.

The issue of the revisability of belief is not merely a matter of logical relations between propositions. Mitchell rightly points out that, although there is a Christian duty to trust in God, this does not imply a duty, let alone an unconditional one, to go on believing that there is a God if the arguments against God's existence were to become cumulatively overwhelming. The requirement of unconditional faith has its place *within* the system of Christian belief but cannot properly be interpreted as an obligation to continue to embrace the system itself.[24]

The point of this remark, however, would be misunderstood if it were seen as an attempt to raise the problem of how to decide when that moment might have been reached. Rather, the point is to acknowledge openly that both theology and the living faith of which it speaks are amenable to criticism and revision. To deny this, in theory or in practice, is to deprive oneself of the opportunity of coming to know better and seeing more clearly. It will also fuel the deep suspicion among the more cultured despisers of the Christian religion that an open discussion with its participants is senseless to begin with. If Christians know already, surely there is no need for such discussion. And if, as C. van Til puts it, "The Christian knows the truth about the non-Christian," it shouldn't come as a surprise that non-Christians will not be particularly eager to join in that discussion.[25]

This, of course, does not mean either that any old criticism will be acceptable, or even has to be taken seriously, or that the Christian believer may not be critical of his or her opponent as well. I am only suggesting that the external critique of particular Christian beliefs may be justified: for instance, in the case of young children who are not vaccinated against certain diseases because some Christians think it is up to God alone to decide whether they will walk or get polio. Behavior like this will not only harm the children in question, it may also harm the credibility of the Christian case in modern society in a way that years of mission will not be able to undo.

---

23. Ibid., 150.
24. Ibid., 140.
25. C. van Til, *A Christian Theory of Knowledge* (Phillipsburg, NJ: Presbyterian and Reformed Publishing Co., 1969), 13. I agree with D.Z. Phillips that this claim is extremely ambitious and untenable. Cf. Phillips, *Faith after Foundationalism*, 102ff., from which this quotation is taken.

Still other worries regarding theological fallibilism might crop up. Is it coherent to be committed wholeheartedly to the truth of a certain belief while at the same time admitting that it may be false? Would it not be incoherent to say, "I am convinced that p, though I admit that p might be false"? The answer depends on a number of factors; for instance, on the place my belief has within the whole network of my beliefs (whether it is central or peripheral, or whether the support relations to more central beliefs are strong), on how "conviction" is defined, on the force of the evidence, and so on.

If being convinced means that a person S will remain committed to what S is convinced of, no matter what counterevidence exists, S will be irrational by definition. If the counterevidence is strong and my belief only peripheral, I should probably discard the belief. But other cases may well be much more difficult and the decision will be a matter of personal and responsible judgement.

The same goes for certainty. Can I say, without implicitly contradicting myself, "I am certain that p, yet I may be mistaken"? According to Ruth Weintraub, this statement is incoherent if there is an epistemological possibility that p is false. Weintraub holds that "the possibility of error allowed by the second conjunct undermines the confidence affirmed by the first."[26] But again, this only holds insofar as it is assumed that being certain or sure means being certain that no evidence shall ever be acquired that will make it rational to revoke my confidence. But to assume this is to be in the grip of a foundationalist epistemology. Why think that this assumption is an uncontrovertible truth? For all I know now, I can be certain that p, but it is easy to imagine situations in which I might start to wonder whether p, or even to doubt that p. Similarly, being confident of something or trusting a person does not mean that it is impossible that my confidence or trust may not be undermined or, worse, may have been misplaced. Admitting this does not imply that my confidence or trust is only provisional or tentative.

In this connection, Stenmark gives a good example to show that being convinced or confident or certain is not necessarily at odds with the possibility of a prevailing counterargument or evidence turning up. Regarding his belief that his wife loves him, he points out that

> A full acceptance of that belief does allow that it is nevertheless possible that she does not love me and that if there are special reasons to doubt this, I would start an inquiry. Does this mean that I am less convinced of my wife's love? By no means, since realizing that I could be wrong does not mean that I am less convinced that I am right![27]

---

26. R. Weintraub, "Fallibilism and Rational Belief," *Brit. J. Phil. Sci.* 44 (1993): 258.
27. Stenmark, *Rationality in Science*, 297; cf. also 322f.

The obvious analogy here is faith in the sense of trusting reliance on God. In this sense, Stenmark rightly concludes, I think, that "belief in the sacred . . . is not threatened by the fact that it is possible that it is wrong."

These, then, are the main elements of my proposal for fallibilist traditionalism. The story is not yet complete, however. On a traditionalist account, a person may be rational in holding on to his or her religious tradition even in the face of contrary evidence, whether in the form of moral or natural evil, paradoxes, incongruities, or rival worldviews. The further question now is whether a person is also justified in maintaining his or her beliefs in this way. After all, one might be tempted to think that now secure foundations cannot be found anywhere, everything everywhere must be equally unfounded. If this were the case, what about truth?

Surely, this is not just an abstract philosophical worry. We do not even have to accept the classical definition of knowledge as "justified true belief" in order to acknowledge the relevance of the issue of justification for the truth question. Holding a particular belief as true but not having a clue as to what may be said either in support of or against it is not what we are inclined to value highly. After all, my true belief might be the result of a mere guess, a wild fantasy, or just hearsay. Clearly, in that case something important and valuable is missing: I am not justified in holding that belief. The connection between a person being justified in her belief and the truth of her belief is brought to light by Haack, who points out that standards of justification are the criteria "by which we judge the likelihood that a belief is true; they are what we take to be indications of truth."[28] So how does the traditionalist deal with the issues of justification and truth?

TRADITIONALISM AND JUSTIFICATION

It is often suggested that the demise of foundationalism saddles us with relativism as the only alternative. Postfoundationalists try to get beyond this alleged dilemma by working out a viable position somewhere in between. In this sense, traditionalism is thoroughly postfoundational. According to Haack's map of rival theories of justification, foundationalism has two important competitors in the field, coherentism and contextualism. What choice should the traditionalist make?

First, *coherentism* as a theory of (empirical) justification says that a belief is justified if and only if it belongs to a coherent set of beliefs. The important point is that it requires justification to be exclusively a matter of relations among beliefs. According to some versions of coherentism, no belief within the coherent set has a distinguished status. Moderate versions take it that some beliefs have a distinguished initial status (e.g., perceptual beliefs) and that justification depends on weighted mutual support. Other moderate versions maintain that some beliefs have a distinguished status because they

---

28. Haack, *Evidence and Inquiry*, 12.

are more deeply embedded in the coherent set than others. This suggests that the moderate versions allow the possibility of degrees of justification.

Coherentism has some tough problems to deal with, however.[29] As coherentists often take consistency as a necessary condition of coherence, the first objection is that this is just too much to ask. Most human beings will have some sort of inconsistency lurking in the network of beliefs they are holding. But a minor inconsistency shouldn't imply that one's belief, say, that snow is white, is not justified. To meet this objection, the coherentist might specify some subset of beliefs as the one to which beliefs will have to cohere in order to be justified. Yet, even if this is successful, there is the further objection that the consistency of that set of beliefs is insufficient to be an indication of their truth. Invoking "comprehensiveness" or "explanatory coherence" as further requirements may help, but as the meaning of these terms is hard to spell out, it is not clear how or whether this will solve the problem.

An even stronger objection to coherentism, no matter what sophisticated account of "coherence" may be given, is that it cannot be satisfactory because it does not allow nonbelief input (experience). Of course, the coherentist will admit that experiences (my hearing a voice) may cause beliefs (that someone is speaking in my vicinity), but will also insist that causal relations are not logical ones and thus should not play a role in justification. Moderate coherentists may try to solve this problem by appeal to a set of distinguished beliefs which are more basic or central than others. To avoid the charge of arbitrariness they should be able to give an account of how or where these beliefs get their distinguished status. If the coherentist were to distinguish simple perceptual beliefs as being closer to experience than others, the central thesis that justification is solely a matter of relations between beliefs, and nothing else, would have to be dropped.

For the traditionalist, the prospects of coherentism don't look too good. So, what about *contextualism?* According to this theory of justification, whether a person is justified in believing something depends wholly and solely on the prevailing standards of that person's epistemic community. Contextualists may identify certain beliefs as "contextually basic" in the sense that they do not stand in need of justification within their community.[30] As there are in fact many different epistemic communities, contextualism seems to imply a pluralism of differing standards of justification. For example, I may be justified in believing that *p*, according to the criteria of my community, while you may well be justified in believing that not-*p*, in respect to the standards of yours. Moreover, contextualism may easily lead to what Haack calls "conventionalism," the meta-epistemological thesis that epistemic standards are entirely conventional rather than objective, intertraditional, or truth-indicative.

---

29. On the whole I follow Haack's preliminary account of the credentials of coherentism (cf. ibid., 25ff.). For her critique of the coherentists L. Bonjour and D. Davidson, cf. ibid., chapter 3, 52ff.

30. Cf. ibid., 190.

Clearly, contextualism is strongly relativist. It presupposes, first, that different communities have different epistemic standards (why else be a contextualist?) and, second, that "there is no distinguished epistemic community, C*, such that the standards of C* are, while those of others are not, truth-indicative" (otherwise it would have to be admitted that, to be truly justified, one would need to meet the standards of C*).[31] According to the contextualist, then, our standards of justification are merely ours and those of others are just theirs, and that is all there is to it. Of course people do justify their beliefs, but since this is always done by appeal to the standards of their community, justification is only a particular social practice. So the contextualist story boils down to the thesis that the epistemic standards of every community are on a par and that justification and truth are purely local commodities.

In view of this rather bleak picture, the traditionalist can only conclude that contextualism isn't the right path to go either. Fortunately, Haack has yet another alternative in the offing, namely, *foundherentism*.[32] Roughly, foundherentism subscribes to three theses. First, a subject's experience is relevant to the justification of his or her empirical beliefs (unlike coherentism, but like foundationalism). Second, there need be no privileged class of empirical beliefs justified exclusively by the support of experience, independently of the support of other beliefs (like coherentism but unlike strong foundationalism). Third, justification is not exclusively one-directional, but involves pervasive relations of mutual support (unlike weak foundationalism but like coherentism).

Moreover, Haackean foundherentism is relative to persons rather than being impersonal, it allows of degrees of justification over time and depends on how good the evidence is—which in turn depends both on what a person believes and what it is that makes him or her believe it. Leaving out most of the details, the important point to note is that on a foundherentist account "explanatory integration" and "experiential anchoring" are the main standards of justification. That is to say, a person S is the more justified in believing that *p* is the case "the better this belief is anchored in experience and supported by other beliefs by being integrated into an explanatory story the components of which are also anchored in experience and supported by other beliefs. . . ."[33]

Foundherentism also includes the (meta-epistemological) thesis that adequate standards of justification are more or less truth-indicative. At this point the traditionalist has again to make a choice. For the thesis has an important and influential rival called *conventionalism*. According to Haack, conventionalism is a natural ally of contextualism. Local epistemic standards depend on, or just are, what the locals currently think is best. She especially criticizes Richard Rorty for advocating conventionalism (and con-

---

31. Ibid., 191.
32. Ibid., 19.
33. Ibid., 212. For a detailed analysis of the foundherentists' criteria cf. ibid., chapter 4.

textualism). According to Rorty, the demise of foundationalism really means the end of epistemology itself. Epistemology has been an altogether unsuccessful attempt to discover the essence of reality, truth, objectivity, reason, and the like. Thus it had better be discarded.

Philosophy should become hermeneutics aiming at "edification" (*Bildung*), the chief idea being that "from the educational, as opposed to the epistemological or the technological, point of view, the way things are said is more important than the possession of truths."[34] Edifying philosophy, Rorty tells us, "aims at continuing a conversation rather than at discovering truth."[35] In striving for that aim, edifying philosophy attempts to perform the social function of "breaking the crust of convention" (Dewey) in the hope of averting the danger of the freezing-over of culture. Lacking any overarching criteria for rational inquiry, truth is just the normal result of normal discourse: "objective truth is no more and no less than the best idea we currently have about how to explain what is going on."[36]

What should one think of this stance? The traditionalist, I would urge, sides with Haack in rejecting conventionalism and in holding that standards of justification should be truth-indicative if they are to be adequate. Like contextualism, conventionalism easily collapses into relativism with regard to truth: what is true for us may well not be what is true for them and there is no way to adjudicate between the two positions. This severe restriction of the meaning of truth values seems wholly counter intuitive, however. Haack shows that relativism with regard to truth simply can't be true: a person S who asserts that truth is always and everywhere relative (to some language, conceptual scheme, tradition, etc.) appeals to a notion of truth that is itself either relative or nonrelative. In the first case S's assertion is wholly vacuous, in the second self-referentially incoherent.[37]

This argument may be rather formal, but I think it is completely successful against the radical form of relativism that is lurking in the background of conventionalism. Following Haack, the traditionalist rejects conventionalism because it denies the perfectly sound idea that there may be objectively better or worse evidence for holding a belief as true across communities and traditions. Justification may, as a matter of fact, take place by appeal to local standards, but there is no reason to suppose, as the conventionalist does, that a second-order inquiry into that practice cannot be launched, the more so because such an inquiry need not be undertaken on foundationalist terms at all. Also, as Haack puts it, conventionalism is cynical, for it argues its

---

34. R. Rorty, *The Mirror of Nature* (Oxford: Blackwell, 1980), 359.
35. Ibid., 373.
36. Ibid., 385.
37. Cf. J. Margolis, *The Truth about Relativism* (Oxford: Blackwell, 1991), 11. Margolis, who defends a form of modest relativism, agrees with Haack that Rorty is a radical relativist. He also thinks Rorty's position is incoherent (cf. ibid., 210). In view of the sheer complexity of the problem and the fact that many philosophers advocate stronger or weaker versions of relativism while maintaining that they are not relativists at all, I do not wish to say that contextualism entails radical relativism of truth.

own case by appeal to the "conventional" standards of the conventionalist's community. Clearly, these standards cannot be taken to be truth-indicative on their own terms. But that means that the conventionalist "must . . . be abiding by those standards only as a ploy to persuade others less enlightened than himself by playing the game by their rules."[38]

In sum, for the traditionalist this is enough to conclude that for a viable theory of justification, *foundherentism* is the best option. It offers a more adequate alternative to foundationalism than its rivals, coherentism and contextualism. It is superior to conventionalism because it holds on to the thesis that adequate standards of justification are indicative of truth and in doing so discards cynicism and the incoherence of a radical relativism concerning truth. A final step has yet to be made: if Western culture exhibits a plurality of competing large-scale traditions, how does traditionalism deal with the question of truth in this context?

TRUTH AND INTRATRADITIONAL DIALOGUE

Recall the relativist claim that the bankruptcy of foundationalism has deprived us of the possibility of adjudicating between incompatible claims made from within rival traditions. This claim can be interpreted in many ways: for instance, that it was modernist hubris in the first place to think that philosophy (or epistemology or theology, for that matter) could provide a unique yardstick or set of ready-made (universal, unchanging) criteria for choosing between large-scale worldviews or traditions. Or it could be read as a claim that often such traditions are incommensurable or untranslatable, or that, notwithstanding the law of the excluded middle, certain oppositions between rival traditions are undecidable, at least for now. Although all these interpretations may yield weaker or stronger versions of relativism, they certainly need not all be radically or completely relativist. For the traditionalist this is not really problematic: only radical relativism, whether explicit or implicit, would be unacceptable.

As traditionalists fully accept the plurality and diversity of Western culture as the current condition of their "way of being" in that culture, how do they deal with the problem of adjudicating between rival traditions? Suppose a person is confronted with a competing worldview which is apparently as coherent as his or her own and also supported by a great mass of evidence? Could traditionalism be of any help here?

Briefly, the traditionalist's affirmative reply would run as follows. First, the question itself is somewhat puzzling. What exactly is the choice about? Analogies between scientific paradigms and large-scale metaphysical worldviews or traditions of inquiry may be illuminating, but the two are, in important respects, also quite different. Who is confronted with the choice? Is the person a participant in a large-scale tradition of inquiry? If not, the issue of choice between rival traditions will hardly be a live option

---

38. Haack, *Evidence and Inquiry*, 193.

in the first place. If he or she is a participant, there need not be a problem either.

If the person is a Christian, he or she may be well aware that his or her tradition has been confronted with competing worldviews, both religious and secular, for ages. A confrontation with, say, humanism or Islam may give rise to all sorts of puzzles and worries about incongruities, perplexities, unresolved difficulties, and the like. But that seems quite normal and certainly not an occasion for questioning the viability of the Christian tradition as a whole. Thus it seems to me that Nancey Murphy's question of what to do when faced with competing, equally coherent wholes only makes sense in a situation of internal crisis. The perplexities and incongruities have become so overwhelming that the tradition loses its authority over its adherents. Pervasive doubt may take over, the search for an alternative sets in, and the result might be a change in allegiance.

The traditionalist cannot rule out this possibility, in spite of advocating the principle of tenacity and the foundherentist criteria of experiential anchoring and integrative coherence. It seems to me, however, that unless we are to believe both that the Christian tradition is itself in a state of deep crisis and that there are on the whole good reasons to suppose there is at least one better alternative available, the problem of choice between the Christian tradition as a whole and any non-Christian tradition is simply not a live issue. People adhere to large-scale traditions, participate in the practices that embody them, and believe certain things are true. On my traditionalist account, this means that they can only speak from within the fiduciary framework of their tradition, if they are to speak truthfully or authentically at all.

The issue of truth within the current pluralist predicament is, I think, best phrased by Philip Clayton's observation that "the logic of pluralism" is reminiscent of three-valued logic.[39] As no large-scale tradition is in the possession of the whole truth and nothing but the truth, the principle of bivalence and the law of excluded middle are not always applicable in all domains of inquiry. Hence, our only recourse is to enter into dialogue with other traditions within the larger culture in order to find out what their adherents may have discovered and experienced in areas of mutual concern, and to integrate the findings into our view of life.

The question of how to communicate the Christian message in the context of pluralism is obviously too large to be dealt with here. From a traditionalist point of view I only want to address some aspects of the openness

---

39. A similar view is defended by the "robust" (moderate) relativist J. Margolis, who urges that the logical principles of bivalence and *tertium non daretur* should be replaced by "some set of many-valued truth-values or truth-like values." In his view, in some sectors of inquiry "the intelligible world can coherently support truth-claims that on a bivalent model would yield inconsistency and self-contradiction." He goes on to suggest that the interpretation of artworks, human history, and the appraisal of high-order theories in physics and metaphysics may be such fields of inquiry. Cf. Margolis, *The Truth about Relativism*, 10ff.

of the tradition to the views and voices of others. Clearly, it is a matter of intellectual honesty that the way in which the message is communicated must be consonant with its content. The "how" and the "what" should be in accord, and this may not always be easy to determine. Here we may envisage an "ethics of dialogue" that might replace or amplify the more familiar topic of the "ethics of belief." It means at least sincerity, intellectual honesty, openness, fairness, and respect.

A parallel with interreligious dialogue may be illuminating. Pointing out that conflicts and disagreement cannot always be avoided, D'Costa suggests that interreligious dialogue "requires intellectual, imaginative and sympathetic qualities" and that "one of its basic aims is understanding the partner and his or her religion."[40] I wholly agree and would like to add that the aim of dialogue with adherents of secular worldviews should not be different. If one of the ways of being respectful to non-Christian religious believers is trying to understand them, surely the same respect is due to the adherents of secular worldviews. Of course, interreligious dialogue takes place on a common ground of a shared sense or intimation of the transcendent, and no such ground exists with the nonbelievers. Still, there may be other common ground as, for instance, in concern for the environment, fair distribution of wealth and goods, a just political order, and so on. The "otherness" of nonbelievers should not be made so great that dialogue with them is impossible to begin with.

Of course, communicating the Christian message need not be verbal, and if it is verbal it need not be dialogical. Sometimes the most appropriate way of communicating is by action or by refraining from action. Sometimes the church, as well as the individual believer, may be called upon to protest, to warn, to denounce, and even to prophesy. Granted this, some features of the way in which communication with the larger culture is traditionally conceived may warrant some comment.

Consider, for example, "proclaiming." According to my *Shorter Oxford English Dictionary*, to proclaim is "to make official announcement of something . . . in some public place," "to announce publicly." Then, consider "evangelizing," which is more specific because it is "to proclaim as good tidings." "Preaching" also contains the element of proclaiming: "to set forth or teach (anything) in the way of exhortation," "to exhort people (to some act or practice)." As a speech act, to proclaim the Christian message is an assertive utterance, the point of which is to say how things really are. It is *eo ipso* also a truth claim. The element of "exhorting," "to admonish earnestly," or "to urge . . . to laudable conduct," comes near to commanding and ordering and may therefore be classified as a directive, the point of which is to get people to do something. I certainly do not deny that in certain contexts proclaiming and admonishing have their due place in Christian speech. Still, they are significantly different from dialogical discourse because the element of reciprocity is lacking. In view of the logic of pluralism, I think

---

40. G. D'Costa, *Theology and Religious Pluralism* (Oxford: Blackwell, 1986), 124.

the latter element is crucial in communicating with other large-scale traditions within contemporary culture and should be given its due place in any Christian ethics of dialogue.

Intertraditional dialogue with other traditions, if and when entered into, may happen in many contexts: interreligious dialogue, the "science and religion" debate, the dialogue with non-Christians, engaging in Christian politics, and so on. Such dialogue may be a mere exchange of information. But, depending on the context, it may also take the form of argument and discussion, if the conversation partners wish to solve an acknowledged difference of opinion by those means. If, in the course of the dialogue, a Christian needs to take a stand, it will follow the form of a confession. A confession is a kind of truth claim: it asserts what we believe to be true and demonstrates that we sincerely and responsibly believe how things are and what things ought to be done.

Truth, then, is at the heart of the intertraditional dialogue into which the Christian tradition has to enter. Not primarily in the sense of arguing the truth of this or that belief to the exclusion of others, but simply in the sense that to believe is also always to believe as true. Whenever we as veracious inquirers stake a claim, truth is at stake because the claim is uttered with the *intention* of saying what in that context is true for all. This is also the point of the foundherentist claim that standards of justification are only adequate if they are truth-indicative: the hope of truth itself is not abandoned. A fallibilist traditionalism will of course not claim that experiential anchoring and explanatory integration are guarantees of truth, but it does claim that if anything is indicative of it, they are, on the whole, the best indications of it.

Fallibilism allows full acceptance of one's beliefs, because it does not say, as skepticism does, that knowledge or truth is unattainable. Nevertheless, in spite of the vast resources of the Christian tradition—the biblical stories, the theological and religious literature, the rituals, liturgies, creeds, and forms of art—we don't see the whole of the picture. This is why our religious knowledge is partial and why the truth can only be known in part. As we know only aspects of the inexhaustible divine reality, truth is inexhaustive as well. Theologically this would be to say that, although we are convinced of the truth that Jesus Christ is "the knowability of God," this truth is nevertheless partial because its full and true meaning has yet to be disclosed.

CONCLUDING REMARKS

What I have argued provisionally is that traditionalism allows firm adherence to what we believe to be true and good (methodological dogmatism), while acknowledging that our knowledge is fallible, partial, and corrigible (fallibilism). As long as no cumulatively overwhelming contrary evidence is met, and no better alternative is available, we are rational in fully accepting what we believe. In order to be justified, Christian beliefs should be both experientially anchored and explanatorily integrated (foundherentism). There is no compelling reason to think that the Christian faith cannot be justified in that way (of course, the actual argument for such a justification is a wholly different project, a long way beyond the scope of this essay). Finally, fallibilist traditionalism helps the theologian who engages in inter-traditional conversation with non-Christian others not to forget that, like them, we do not see the whole of the picture. In terms of truth that means that what we may now firmly believe as true will yet have to become more fully known as the dialogue with the larger culture develops. If we can grasp the whole truth, and nothing but the truth, that will be in the future or not at all. Here epistemology fuses with eschatology. In the meantime, we can only proceed confidently with our inquiry from where we stand.

CHAPTER FIVE

Missiology between
Monologue and Cacophony

PHILIP CLAYTON

INTRODUCTION

This book as a whole rests on the premise that the oft-cited crisis in mission today can be helped, at least in part, by missiological reflection, i.e., reflection on the nature of what it means to engage in mission. It also assumes that such a study of mission must be responsive to the "crisis of knowledge" in the West today. The following essay is an attempt to restate that crisis and to offer a constructive theory of mission in response to it.

What is the "epistemological context" in which we in the West reflect on mission today? It has become common to use the word "modernity" to designate an epistemic framework in which truth claims were made without regard for context or motivation. According to the standard view, the "modern" speaker held his beliefs to be objectively true on the basis of purely rational considerations. There was no need for broader dialogue with others because his own personal context played no role (at least as he saw it) in what he believed, why he believed it, or how he justified it. Nor was it necessary for him to nuance his claims to truth. Insofar as his reasons were taken to be purely objective, they were ipso facto sufficient to guarantee the truth of his beliefs.

From this definition of modern, "postmodern" is easy to define: it represents in each case the opposite of the claims and assumptions just listed. In the place of objectivity, it offers stress on the subjective; in place of context-free beliefs, it emphasises the context-bound; in place of timeless truth, the historically rooted, and in place of white, European monologues, worldwide acceptance and dialogue.

Drawing a neat conceptual dichotomy, however, is not yet to have solved any real problems. Were the situation as simple as the modern/postmodern dichotomy suggests, there would be no need for a book such as the present one, nor for countless conferences, articles, and books devoted to the various aspects of "the crisis of modernity" and the problems of postmodernism.

The title of Part One of this book refers to "the epistemological *predicament*" because the collapse of claims to context-free rationality has ended a secure structure and left only a maze of rubble and confusion. The following is one example of this situation: American students at many universities are offered an (allegedly) "value-free" education, the only explicitly stated value being that of "multiculturalism."[1] Now the stress placed on multiple cultures, life-styles, and "voices" has indeed provided a fruitful corrective against white European ethnocentrism and male sexism, weakening the hold of myths that were constitutive of the elite intellectual class of bygone generations.

For students with clear ethnic identities of their own, this is a tremendous advantage. In the best cases they are now able to construct a (more or less) consistent structure of their own out of the components of their own traditions. Nonetheless, many other students now find themselves presented with a cacophony of voices, with the claim that they are all of equal value, and with the exhortation to select the ones that are "true for you." What has been the result? For many, this "postmodern" emphasis on context and on the individual's (or group's) constructive activity has given rise to a sense of the arbitrariness and randomness of *all* beliefs they hold (or contemplate holding). Once people recognise the constructive nature of their own system of beliefs, claims for the *truth* of those beliefs seem arbitrary at best.

Especially in the West, developments such as these have had an immense impact on Christianity. One is now "entitled" to believe, in contrast to the time, only a few decades ago, when talk of secularism, positivism, and the "death of God" created an atmosphere much more hostile to religious belief. Yet, the burgeoning of new religious movements and the openness to religious belief of all kinds means that the church often becomes just another special interest group, just another way of "naming your own particularity." Interestingly enough, not just those on the outside but many within the church as well hold this view of the arbitrariness of their own belief and practice.

At the same time that the religious options have increased dramatically, the climate has become more hostile than ever to giving reasons for one's particular set of beliefs. Perhaps many believers still suppose there are good reasons for believing in *some* sort of divine purpose behind the universe; they imagine that neither cosmic chance nor Darwinian evolution has the last word. The only reasons most can imagine for practicing the Christian rather than the Jewish or Muslim faith, however, have to do with the happenstances of their own particular history.

Religious experience, either one's own or that of the subculture or church group with which one identifies, now does the lion's share of the work. But

---

1. For a good manifesto see Amy Gutmann (ed.), *Multiculturalism: Examining the Politics of Recognition* (Princeton: Princeton University Press, 1994).

these experiences would, of course, have been different had one been raised within another culture or tradition. If the most we can say about our own religious practice is "this we believe" or "it works for me," is it any wonder that we are hesitant about evangelism? Indeed, the framework of multiculturalism makes it positively questionable, even morally suspect, to proclaim the truth of *our* tradition to those who belong to other cultural traditions.

Herein lies the predicament facing talk of mission today. Like many of my coessayists, I do not find it difficult to name the extremes. On the one side lie objectivist or absolutist claims that dismiss or disregard the other; on the other side looms an unbounded relativism that does not allow for the making of any truth claims at all. Neither represents, in my opinion, an acceptable approach. The challenge, then, is to formulate an epistemology that lies between the two extremes, and then to work out its implications for missiology today. This will be my task in the remaining pages.

THE STATUS OF REVELATION

I assume that any viable Christian theology is one that appeals to divine revelation. Revelation, naturally, concerns the nature of God; but it also concerns the nature of human beings, those who are the listeners.[2] A Christianity that consisted merely of the values of a particular culture or the discoveries of human reason and human moral instincts might be a successor religion to Christianity, but it would not be the Christian faith.

Immediately, however, reservations arise: how can the revelation of an infinite God be fully comprehended by human beings? How can even a revelation about "the true nature of human beings" be universally comprehended? Would not the terms in which revelation was expressed inevitably reflect the assumptions and happenstances of one particular culture, whether by divine choice or human necessity? Surely the core of God's self-revelation would have to pertain to all human beings at all times. But, would not most (or all) of the concrete expressions of that revelation, the teachings and the doctrines, necessarily be culture-bound?

Once one acknowledges the strength of these questions, do not these teachings either lose their authoritative status or stand in need of continual transformation in the light of later centuries and radically different cultures? Such conclusions challenge one all the more urgently if one does not find it credible that God would "baptize" one particular culture, thereby negating all others as non-Christian, or that Christianity would require conversion to a particular culture, say, to the English language, to Western dress and social mores, and to one particular type of piety.

If that is the cultural argument, there is a theological one as well. The infinity and majesty of God give us reason to believe that the actual moment of divine inbreaking into the human realm would be a moment of such tran-

---

2. On the content of revelation as both theological and anthropological, see Lesslie Newbigin, *The Gospel in a Pluralist Society* (Grand Rapids, MI: Eerdmans, 1989).

scendent power and meaning that it would not be fully describable in *any* human language. For the purposes of this essay I will presuppose that such a moment or moments of divine impact do take place and that they are revelatory of divine reality.

The *meaning* of the revelatory event or events, however, comes to us always already mediated through history, the interpretations of eyewitnesses or later interpreters, careful reflection and study, and the presence of the Holy Spirit to later believers. If this is the case, one might suspect, for example, that the New Testament consists of multiple narratives of the resurrection event precisely because the event itself transcends all interpretations and languages.

Try to imagine, for example, what would have been recorded had video cameras been present at the moment of Jesus' resurrection. Any description one tries to give of what the camera would have recorded tends to sound like a Hollywood "B" movie of some sort: the camera pans from a curtain being ripped from top to bottom, out to a field of rocks being split open, and finally rests on the huge boulder as it first trembles and then rolls slowly away from the mouth of the cave, revealing a shining individual in white clothes whose face is so bright that its features wave and blur in the camera lens. Now it may well be that some interpretations of the mysterious moment of divine inbreaking are more adequate than others (more on this below), but none, so it seems to me, can fully capture the event itself.

The same inevitable inadequacy pertains to all interpretations of divine revelation as this has been recorded in the Christian scriptures and theological traditions. The traditions represent, at best, a series of approximations to the actual divine communicative event. We have, for example, the various scriptural reports, theological reconstructions of them, interpretations of the theologians, competing religious traditions, and the like. If there exists a concrete set of religious truths (not just a noumenal "x" refracted into countless forms in the world's religious traditions,[3] or just a "truth as constructed reality," about which it is incorrect to ask, "Is it really true?"),[4] then it is possible, indeed necessary, to say that some approximations are closer than others. Our constructive (cultural, creative) contributions in formulating the beliefs that we hold does not invalidate talk of their closeness or distance from (in this case) the nature of God and God's action. Some religious beliefs are more true, and some are less true; yet, none can overcome the inevitable chains of finitude in order to *be* The Truth.

In this sense, the doctrine of revelation represents a sort of analogue to Jacques Derrida's notion of *différence*:[5] any interpretation of the essential nature of the revelatory event is always *different from* the intended essence

---

3. This is the view of many today, perhaps most powerfully expressed in John Hick's *An Interpretation of Religion* (New Haven: Yale University Press, 1989) (cf. below).

4. This latter position is known in the literature as "internal realism." See esp. Hilary Putnam, *Reason, Truth and History* (New York: Cambridge University Press, 1981).

5. See, for example, Jacques Derrida, *Of Grammatology* (Baltimore: Johns Hopkins University Press, 1974); *Writing and Difference* (Chicago: University of Chicago Press, 1978).

of the communication, and at the same time its ultimate meaning is, for us in the present, always *deferred* (presumably until the eschaton). Theologically, the argument is that God's thoughts are not our thoughts, that humans can never fully comprehend the divine mind, and certainly not humans embedded in a particular culture, time, and place.

Epistemically, I have to begin with the undeniable fact of a pluralism of views and perspectives that surround us. No means are available to resolve all disagreements or to conform our particular path to the one set of true propositions or the one admissable interpretation of scripture. We can and must employ some procedures for making decisions, but none of them represents infallible and sufficient criteria of the sort that are needed to settle on one particular set of truths.

THE ROLE OF MISSIOLOGY WITHIN THEOLOGY

I have argued that two extremes must be avoided: on the one hand, a "proclamation without listening," a monologue in which Christian truth is imparted to needy and lost listeners without a contribution on their part; and on the other hand, a relativism in which one proclaims opinions without making any truth claims on their behalf ("they are true for me, but it does not matter if they are true for anyone else"). In response to both extremes, I have defended the possibility of believing that God has acted in and spoken through Jesus Christ, while at the same time abandoning claims to epistemic certainty that can no longer be justified in the contemporary setting.

Missiology has traditionally been concerned with the *crosscultural* proclamation of the gospel.[6] For this reason missiology (or at least the theoretical perspective that it represents) plays a very central role in the conception I am defending. The missiological question offers a continual reminder of this double truth: we believe in God, and hence we are trying to obtain true beliefs about God and God's action; yet every belief we (and others) formulate is always already a cultural project. Because we take culture seriously, we are reticent to claim that our particular formulation corresponds to the ultimate fact of divine revelation. Yet because we believe that God has revealed something important about God's nature and purpose

---

6. Some of the stages of coming to recognize and respond to the pervasiveness of culture within missiology were blindness to culture (other cultures simply did not exist), cultural dominance (other cultures simply did not count), strategic approaches to culture (using the cultural specifics to proclaim essentially the same gospel), integration, or form vs. content (some inexpressible form is universal to Christianity, but whenever given expression it comes out in the form of a particular culture). There was also the hidden universal response: that which never appears but underlies all appearances is the crucial moment, the "absoluteness" basic to religious belief.

There is also the Feuerbachian response to the truth question in religion. Like Laplace's famous answer to Napoleon when asked about God, some respond, "I have no need of that hypothesis." All that is left in this case is relativism: the multiple lifestyles and cultures themselves. Each has its own truth and each can enter as a voice in the discourse; but that is as far as it goes.

in the life and activity of Jesus Christ, we cannot give culture (or cultural relativism) the last word.

This, then, is my interpretation of the predicament presented in the first part of this book. It stems from the set of factors we have been examining: believing in revelation, looking to the life and teaching of Jesus Christ for the content of that revelation, having some procedures for sifting out more or less adequate interpretations, yet not possessing a set of criteria sufficient for settling on the *one* transcultural expression of Christian truth.

It also allows that the "logic" of missiology is central for the doctrine of the church. Bosch, Shenk, Kirk, and Hoedemaker have all argued that church and mission, ecclesiology and missiology, are inseparable; as Brunner wrote, "the church exists by mission, just as a fire exists by burning."[7] My reading of the predicament suggests a particular interpretation of the connection between church and mission. On the present view, the church's concern with the crosscultural communication of what it believes provides an important key to ecclesiology because, *in confronting the phenomena of culture and crosscultural communication, the church confronts the essential mystery and inaccessibility of the primary revelatory event.* "Culture" becomes a shorthand way of saying that claims about Christianity are always already incarnated in a particular language, set of symbols, collection of practices, and interpretative framework.

Culture means difference. A multicultural perspective is one in which the sameness that is largely instinctive for "me and those like me" is confronted by a dramatic *difference*, a difference which first opens my eyes to the sorts of limitations that constituted our sameness in the first place. Difference is not perceived when everyone shares the same perspective. This was, of course, the fatal danger of the Christendom model: one that either mistook divergent (non-European) forms of belief as merely alternative expressions of one's own cultural perspective, or that dismissed them as subhuman (like the Greek notion of "barbarians"), or that felt compelled to conquer the other forcibly (either by military might or, more recently, by sheer Western cultural domination), in order to make others utilize one's own vocabulary and concepts.

By contrast, the strength of the multicultural perspective is that it repudiates all strategies which rest on a forceful colonization of other ideas, languages, and cultures by the West. An immediate corollary of this position is that it helps one to realize, perhaps for the first time, the limited and often arbitrary nature of *one's own* perspective. Behind this Gestalt shift in the approach to missiology, or to theologizing in general, lies a fundamentally

---

7. See Wilbert Shenk, *Write the Vision: The Church Renewed* (Valley Forge, PA: Trinity Press International, 1995); David Bosch, *Believing in the Future: Towards a Missiology of Western Culture* (Valley Forge, PA: Trinity Press International, 1995); J. Andrew Kirk, *The Mission of Theology and Theology as Mission* (Valley Forge, PA: Trinity Press International, 1997); and Bert Hoedemaker, *Secularization and Mission: A Theological Essay* (Valley Forge, PA: Trinity Press International, 1998). The passage from Brunner is taken from Bosch, *Believing in the Future*, 32.

religious intuition that all human action and thought is finite, and *all* human formulations are limited in nature. We could almost make this conclusion a guiding principle for theological reflection: formulation does not reach to theological fact.

JUSTIFICATION AND PROCEDURES FOR DECISION MAKING

What justification is there, then, for turning to Jesus Christ as the locus of revelation? How can one be warranted in continuing to hold any concrete beliefs about divine intentions or actions in light of the pervasive effects of culture? Even if one can be justified "by one's own lights," how can one, given the predicament we have been describing, engage in any sort of missionary proclamation that presupposes that the beliefs of others are mistaken?

Even the more moderate positions described in the first part of this volume make clear that an *a priori* defense is not necessary to Christian belief. This is what we call the switch from evidentialist to fallibilist theories of rationality.[8] We now recognize that it is not necessary to begin by justifying knowledge claims *ab initio*. Even ideally rational procedures, such as those of the sciences, begin only by formulating and testing hypotheses, and many beliefs that humans hold are rational according to far lower standards than these.

But this sort of epistemic latitudinarianism raises a significant problem of its own. Is it now the case that one can believe whatever one wants about the content of divine revelation? Even if we assume the context of Christianity for understanding divine revelation, does it then become an arbitrary matter which branch of Christian thought and belief one selects? Is it irrelevant whether I believe that God intervened supernaturally to resurrect Jesus' body from death, or whether I take the "resurrection myth" as a symbol of human beings' eternal hopefulness that the future will be better than the past? If the content of my Christian beliefs matters, are there any criteria for adjudicating between more or less adequate types of belief? The question is of some urgency for theologians and missiologists alike, for if there are *no* criteria, then every formulation of any person in any culture stands an equal chance of correctly reflecting the meaning of the original revelatory act (at least insofar as *any* human formulation can adequately reflect divine purpose).

Consider the case of Christian beliefs in particular. In the previous section we looked at the picture of moving back through multiple interpretations of the original event toward the revelatory event itself. Under the model that I am defending, Christian believers must remain focused on the divine revelation (philosophers might speak of it as an intentionality or directionality that is basic to Christian belief), even though they may know

---

8. See P. Clayton, *Explanation from Physics to Theology: An Essay in Rationality and Religion* (New Haven: Yale University Press, 1989), esp. 49ff.

that the criteria of selection will always underdetermine the decision among the various possible interpretations. This means that pluralism will remain insurmountable until the final eschaton.

Nevertheless, it is important to note that one can be pluralistic about Christian theologies without concluding that "just anything goes." For there exist a number of *markers of adequacy* which help Christian thinkers decide among the multiple options available to them at any given point. The tradition has identified a number of guiding indices: the Hebrew and Christian scriptures, the church's progressive understanding of its faith through the centuries, individual religious experience, corporate "discernment" under the guidance of the Holy Spirit,[9] human reflection (the "natural light" of divine leading built into each human being), widely shared ethical and moral intuitions, the shared experience of worship and Christian obedience within the life of the church,[10] and careful argumentation aimed at coherently *thinking together* the results of those various indices with other sources of knowledge.

It may be impossible to specify in advance which criteria will be useful and in which combination, which will override which others, and what the final outcome will be. To be deeply aware of cultural diversity is to recognize that plurality will be with us until the end of time. It does not, however, follow from the fact that the criteria do not pick out only one theology or set of beliefs (given that the answers are always underdetermined) that no evaluations of better or worse can be made.

Let us pause for a moment to consider the richness of the procedures for decision making that are an established part of the Christian tradition. For example, the church has often sought to supplement the more systematic (and thus abstract) reflections of theologians within the academy. Fearful that they will lose touch with the life and worship of the church, mystics and "practical" theologians have emphasized the discernment available in and through the life of the church. One can think, for example, of the powerful impact that Brother Lawrence's "practicing the presence of God" has had, and continues to have, on believers. George Lindbeck also relies on a similar criterion when he emphasizes the importance of the "person in the pew" in assessing theological adequacy.[11] David Tracy urges the use of all three "publics" as criteria: the Church, the Academy, and Society.[12] One does not need to give preeminent place to communal discernment in order to grasp that the community of Christians must have an important role.

---

9. See Nancey Murphy, *Theology in the Age of Scientific Reasoning* (Ithaca: Cornell University Press, 1990).

10. William Alston makes the context of communal religious practice in his own defense of religious practice in *Perceiving God: The Epistemology of Religious Experience* (Ithaca: Cornell University Press, 1991).

11. George Lindbeck, *The Nature of Doctrine: Religion and Theology in a Post-Liberal Age* (Philadelphia: Westminster Press, 1984). See also the use of this notion in Nancey Murphy, *Theology in the Age of Scientific Reasoning*.

12. David Tracy, *The Analogical Imagination: Christian Theology and the Culture of Pluralism* (London: SCM Press, 1981).

Let us consider another example: theories of scriptural authority. Even if one concedes a very large influence of first-century culture on (say) Pauline theology, it can still be maintained that the scriptures provide significant parameters for adjudicating between different theological answers. Christians will still diverge in the particular biblical strands that they weave into the fabric of their theology: some advocate a prophetic return to traditional biblical modes of obedience to the original texts, while others discern a progression moving from the words of those texts via the fundamental principles that underlie them to new interpretations available to the church today. The former group may forbid remarriage or defend a subordinate role for women, whereas the latter group holds views on these topics based on what it takes to be more basic theological principles in the texts. Nevertheless, in both cases the biblical documents continue to provide guidance in theologizing. Neither group in this example advocates an "anything goes" approach to Christian ethics.

A variation on John Rawls's famous notion of "reflective equilibrium" is helpful for picturing what it means to apply these various procedures for decision making.[13] The believer who is engaged in the sort of process I have been describing moves between the procedures, on the one hand, the texts, theological sources, communal traditions, and personal religious belief and practice and, on the other, an ongoing experience of the world. As new inputs are received—from other religious traditions, new ideas, anomalies within the tradition, and new moral and ethical dilemmas—they are brought into dialogue with already-existing beliefs and procedures for decision making.

In an honest dialogue of this sort, neither side will exist in unquestioned authority; there will be movement on both sides. Sometimes existing religious beliefs and criteria will be modified or rejected to incorporate new experiences and inputs; at other times, even attractive claims that come from the "outside" will be resisted or rejected. Sometimes the procedure proceeds smoothly, with only mild shifts from full equilibrium. At other times, beliefs may vacillate wildly as the believer struggles to create a balance between strongly opposed tendencies (say, a secular mindset and religious practice, or divine providence and apparently random suffering in the world).

Of course, what applies to the individual in this picture applies to the community as well. A congregation, denomination, or even an entire theological tradition may sometimes sail smoothly through the waters of its cultural and historical context, while at other times it is knocked about by storms of uncertainty and confusion and pushed toward rocky counterexamples that threaten its very existence. One hardly needs to be reminded that theological traditions and forms of Christian practice, even self-understandings that at one time seemed fundamental to people's Christian beliefs, such as the return of the Lord in one generation, are sometimes abandoned and left permanently behind.

---

13. John Rawls, *A Theory of Justice* (Cambridge: Harvard University Press, 1971).

The logic of pluralism as presented here is analogous to what logicians call three-valued logics. Such logics allow, in addition to the classic judgments of "true" or "false," a third value, often labeled "undecided." Applying this structure to the field of missiology, we could say that it is not a matter merely of asserting one religious view and thereby proclaiming all others false. Instead, in belief and practice, one inhabits and explores one particular viewpoint (or collection of viewpoints), which then leads one into dialogue with other viewpoints in the attempt to decide which one (or which subgroup) is the most adequate resting place. This is not a relativism that dispenses with all truth claims, for when I believe something, ipso facto I believe that it is true. Nevertheless, in abandoning exclusivism I also abandon the more robust epistemic claims, namely, that I know all alternative positions are false. For this reason, the epistemic credentials that I must possess in order to hold the belief in a justified manner are reduced.

In conclusion, I have argued that this type of pluralism should breed epistemological humility. The openness of the procedures for decision making points toward a fundamentally dialogical understanding of missiology, not an absolutist or "monarchical" model. It is impossible to ignore the principles and beliefs that characterize one's own belief commitment within Christianity. At the same time, it is inadvisable to hold that one's own beliefs are so certain ("absolute") that one does not need to engage in dialogue, listening to the viewpoints of others (both religious and nonreligious persons) and carefully weighing the strengths of their positions. For difference is undeniable and culture is here to stay. In such a world, dogmatisms that disregard the real merits of other positions have become untenable. Mission, it appears, must mean both to proclaim and to listen; it must include all the facets of evangelization, in the broad sense of the word—dialogue and service, as well as proclamation.[14] But how are we to conceptualize such a view of mission? What sort of model can do it justice?

THE APPLICATION TO MISSIOLOGY TODAY

In the light of these epistemological conclusions, I suggest that we must define mission more broadly than has often been done in the past, as *sharing that which the church is fundamentally about*. The church is called to incarnate and represent God in the world, following the model of its founder. It is a community in process, *apostolic* in the sense of being spawned by the work of Christ and the apostles, yet *eschatological* in the sense of living in openness to the continuing work of God in the world and its culmination at the end of time. The church is "called out" to be *holy*, sharing the purity of the One who called it. But it is also called to be *catholic* including all who are called and reaching out to embrace rather than exclude all humanity.[15]

---

14. The missiological presentation that perhaps best incorporates the various elements in a balanced fashion is David J. Bosch, *Transforming Mission: Paradigm Shifts in Theology of Mission* (Maryknoll, NY: Orbis Books, 1991).

15. See Miroslav Volf, *Exclusion and Embrace: A Theological Exploration of Identity, Otherness and Reconciliation* (Nashville: Abingdon Press, 1996).

If mission is defined broadly as sharing what the church is fundamentally about, it will include careful attention to propositions and doctrines, but also to social action, inner experience, religious art, and all the other facets of the Christian life. Sharing serves well as the primary metaphor because it encompasses, alongside preaching or proclamation, actions such as dialogue, performance, service, and listening (with or without verbal response).

Let us note some of the ways in which this understanding of mission would guide the practice of mission. First, it is not necessary that one begin a priori with a complete ecclesiology, a full definition in advance of what it means to be the church of Jesus Christ, even though the *process* of answering this question is ultimately what mission is all about. If one knew ahead exactly what it meant to be the church in the world, there would be no need for the movement toward equilibrium as described above; one would simply proclaim rather than also needing to listen.

If one returns from a powerful concert, an overseas trip, or an overwhelming personal experience, it may take some time and reflection before one can find words to explain to others what it is that one has just experienced and why it has moved one so deeply. Indeed, if the experience was profound enough, it may take extensive discussions with friends and like-minded persons before one can speak to a general audience at all about why the experience was so fundamental and how it transformed one. In a similar manner it may take serious reflection before believers can find the words to express even to themselves the significance of their experience of Jesus Christ and their belief in the truth of his message. And it may take long conversations and study with other Christians, as well as broader dialogue with those of other faith (and nonfaith) traditions, before they begin to be able to say what their belief "really means" and what is distinctive about it.

Second, it also follows from a missiology of sharing that one cannot understand (or engage in) missions without at the same time being concerned with the question of ecclesiology, struggling toward a fuller account of what it means to be the church in the world. That is as it should be. Missiology is about the church's mission or "calling" to be a suffering and redemptive presence in the image of its founder. Hence, deep missiological questions raise equally deep questions about what it means to be the *koinonia* of the body of Christ in the world.

Third, a missiology of sharing stands opposed to all construals of the church that would reduce the need for a broader sharing outside the walls of church buildings or that claim the impossibility in principle of overcoming cultural barriers. There is no church without *some* mission, some vocation, even if that mission looks vastly different from that which missiologists described only a century (or less) ago. Thus, I have my doubts whether epistemologies based exclusively on the work of more extreme French thinkers (Derrida, Foucault, poststructuralists) will be able adequately to enunciate what it is to be a group of followers of Jesus Christ, representing his life within the world today. If contact and understanding between persons never really occurs, then the church can neither understand itself nor fulfil its mission.

In summary, sharing is like proclaiming, except that it stresses mutuality. Because one shares *something*, it is to be distinguished from mere chatting or from those instances of interreligious dialogue in which the participants do not really come as representatives of any particular belief tradition, but only as advocates of the dialogue itself. Sharing may include testifying as long as the dimension of two-sided communication is not neglected. Given the gist of the argument so far, there is no way around the problem of returning once again to the ticklish question of the truth content of Christian belief.

FACING THE TRUTH QUESTION

By interpreting missiology and proclamation in terms of sharing, I have defended a view that avoids absolutist claims and dismissive strategies, attitudes that are often deeply embedded within religious epistemologies that locate truth completely in one tradition to the exclusion of others.[16] The acceptance of the other (the other discussion partner, the member of another religion)[17] as having a perspective and set of practices that are not to be dismissed, but rather listened to, plays an indispensable part in this approach to dealing with other religions.

At the level of practice, I do not believe the framework I have defended raises any fundamental paradoxes. It is common human experience to say, "This seems to me to be true and I want to share it." Does doing so mean that all others are wrong? When I share, I can put that question in parenthesis: "I am not sure what to say about your beliefs, but I do wish to testify to what I have seen, heard and experienced. I do not know yet whether our beliefs stand in contradiction to one another, or whether they may be compatible in some deep sense."

Paraphrasing Newbigin, one might understand proclamation in this fashion: "I believe this is true because it speaks to the human condition in a way that is more illuminative than any other option I have yet encountered. It tells me about my situation in a way that no other explanation I know does." Such an attitude allows one to avoid dismissive claims about other religions that turn them into mere "objects." I do not need to maintain that others have access to God only through *my* savior, or that there is no other means to God beside this one. I can honor the insights of other traditions, while sharing freely (even proclaiming) what I have experienced from a Christian perspective and how this experience has been redemptive for me. One might say that this strategy meets the key requirement of Kantian moral philosophy: always treat the other not merely as a means but always also as an end.

---

16. My thanks go to Norris Palmer of the Graduate Theological Union for a discussion that was helpful in formulating this section.

17. Crucial recent resources on the philosophy of otherness include Edward W. Said, *Orientalism* (New York: Vintage Books, 1994); Clifford Geertz, *The Interpretation of Cultures: Selected Essays* (New York: Basic Books, 1973); and Emmanuel Lévinas, *Totality and Infinity: An Essay on Exteriority* (Pittsburgh: Duquesne University Press, 1969).

It appears, however, that the comfortable nature of this practical synthesis, with its place for both tolerance and proclamation, is shattered when one thematizes the truth question as such: are the competing beliefs of others true, or not? In what follows I shall argue that there is no easy solution to this difficulty. Neither postmodernism, "internalism," pragmatism, metaphor, or narrative dissolves the fundamental tensions that are raised by believing that a religious claim is true. We must now see why the truth question raises the stakes and how it poses a dilemma that does not arise at the practical level.

One might imagine *practice* as the normal mode of religious existence and the truth question as arising on a *metalevel*. Moving from tolerant sharing with members of other traditions (as described above) to this metalevel forces one to respond to a question that does not (usually) arise in religious practice today. The question is, "are your religious beliefs true? Are they *more true* than the beliefs of other traditions?" The dilemma is contained in whichever answer one gives, for if one says, "Yes, they are more true," one seems to be making an exclusivist claim, dismissing the beliefs of the other, and if one says no, then the natural interpretation is that religious beliefs become more like matters of taste and less like truth claims. In the latter case, I may speak enthusiastically about my love for chocolate mousse, preaching passionately about its virtues while at the same time acknowledging that this preference does not invalidate someone else's love of banana splits. It would be rather troubling, however, to say that my belief that God suffered and died on behalf of humanity and for the sake of human salvation is similar to my enthusiastic description of the pleasures of eating chocolate mousse.

A more sophisticated response, which at first sight seems to offer hope, in fact leads to the same difficulties in the end. Numerous thinkers, going back at least to Nicholas of Cusa in the fifteenth century, have argued that each religion reflects the truth of God in its own terms and from its own particular perspective. Cusa's metaphor of the one divine face seen differently from the left or right side, or the oft-repeated metaphor of the blind men describing what an elephant as a whole looks like by touching only small portions of it, are often appealed to in defending this view.

The most sophisticated version, and the one that most clearly and unambiguously reveals its implications, is found in John Hick's book, *An Interpretation of Religion*. Hick, making use of a basically Kantian perspective, argues that each religion is a "phenomenal" expression of one religious reality, which he calls the Real. Like Kant's phenomenal world, no religious formulations reflect the Real in itself, which lies necessarily beyond all formulation. We should not, therefore, be bothered by contradictions between religious beliefs, he argues, since the truth lies not in but beyond all distinctions. Hick raises the stakes to the highest possible level when he concludes that even the distinction between viewing the Real as personal and as impersonal, between the existence and nonexistence of God in the Jewish and Christian sense, is transcended from the standpoint of the Real.

What, then, is the status of the religious belief we hold? Hick fails to specify any correspondence between these religious beliefs and the Real to which they (supposedly) refer. This means that Hick's generous willingness to call them true is actually vacuous; no single claim is more or less true than any other. If no correspondence exists and no statement is really truer than any other, then it does not make sense to call them "true" at all. We might just as well call them all false! Ultimately, Hick's position implies that religious beliefs are *neither* true nor false. They become matters of taste, things about which we can speak with passion but to which the predicate "true" simply does not apply.

Such a conclusion is, to my mind, finally inadequate. It is basic to the nature of the religious beliefs I hold that I hold them to be true. I do not wish to do this in an exclusivist fashion, but I must also be honest about the logic of my belief. What framework can be found to help me to accomplish this task?

COMPARING VARIOUS SUBSETS OF THE TRUTH

We do not need (or expect to find) a procedure for decision making sufficient for establishing which religion is true and which false. But we do need a conceptual framework that allows us to specify what we are doing when we hold certain beliefs to be true.

David Ray Griffin once suggested in a lecture that we use the metaphor of subsets of the alphabet. In this metaphor the alphabet stands for the collection of truths about God. Imagine that one religion may grasp F, M, P, and V; another M, B, I, and Y; and yet another A, B, C, X, Y, and Z. No religion grasps the entire alphabet, hence none is fully true. Yet all (*ex hypothesi*) grasp some portion of the truth, and thus none is wholly false.

What is attractive about this metaphor is that it allows for comparative judgments in principle. I recognize that certain theological traditions contain that notion of legal substitution whereby the sacrifice of the Son propitiates the wrath of the angry Father, and that this sort of belief expresses less adequately the justice and compassion of God than do, for example, central parts of Judaism and Buddhism (call it "not-L"). By contrast, I find that the notion of divine grace and God's willingness to sacrifice self for humanity offer a clearer picture of divine compassion than do some other religions (call it C). Also, Christianity emphasizes the personal nature of the divine more fully than do a number of other religious traditions. Even if every individual collection of letters is only a *subset* of the whole, one can still draw useful comparative judgments between various subsets.

A number of readers may be reminded of the game of Scrabble when they hear the analogy of letters.[18] In this game some letters have a high value (usually the ones that are harder to incorporate into meaningful combina-

---

18. I owe the extension of the analogy to the missiologist Stan Skreslet of Union Theological Seminary in Richmond, VA.

tions, like X, Z, and J), while others are given lesser worth, for they are easier to incorporate. In addition, although there are better or worse hands that one might receive, there is no alternative to starting with the letters one has and seeking to improve on the combinations as much as possible. The words that can be made with a more limited initial set of letters are less, although almost always some moves can be made. Some hands are inherently more difficult to play, but their potential value is much greater. The analogies to sets of religious beliefs are obvious.

Of course, one might argue for a counteranalogy: in Scrabble, one must play with the letters received, whereas in religion conversion is always possible. I suspect, however, that the religious choices one makes, and the nature of the postconversion practices one engages in, are rather more Scrabble-like, that is, they are more constrained by one's religious (or nonreligious) background, than the objection admits. There is a subtle balance between the constraints of one's starting points and the ongoing quest for truth that emerges out of interreligious interactions. No one stands completely above the game.

The framework that I have proposed not only allows for comparative judgments with regard to specific features of religious traditions; it also enables one to introduce a broader concept: the degree to which a religious tradition reflects the divine nature. In practice, perhaps none of us is in the position to be able to make (and defend) a quantitative judgment about the degree of truth of a religious tradition. Short of death, no one is certain of the final score. Nonetheless, the notion of *the truth content of a religious tradition* is not in itself a contradictory notion. I take it as a sort of regulative principle that guides the practice of interreligious dialogue, since it helps to explain what it is to hold religious belief and engage in religious practices.

Clearly, judgments of truth must be made, in practice, with great care, caution, and (often) careful caveats. Cultural factors will influence one's judgments on such matters. No universal formulation of the selection criteria has yet been forthcoming, and may never be. Even if it were, we would differ concerning our application of the criteria in concrete cases. Nevertheless, the *intentionality of truth* is preserved in this account. It remains basic to religious belief and practice. According to this model, it makes sense to say that portions of religious traditions are more true than others and to make comparative judgments between traditions.

Even if we were unable to bring comparative discussions to a final conclusion (a fact that should definitely influence the manner in which we engage in such discussions), the attempt itself is a meaningful one. Our age, with its acute sensitivity to differences in culture, epoch, and perspective has found reasons to approach the topic of truth with a large dose of humility, and hence with tolerance and acceptance of divergent viewpoints. But it has not invalidated the truth question itself. The predicament covered in the opening chapter thus turns out to be fundamentally epistemological, not alethic. We know much less than we once thought and, as religious believers, we make our truth claims with much more fear and trembling than was typical of earlier centuries. But what it *means* to believe that a claim is true remains as it always did.

MISSIOLOGICAL IMPLICATIONS

Having dealt with the hard question of what it means to believe that something is true, we now return to the level of actual practice in proclamation, crosscultural dialogue, and ministry. In one sense, at the practical level, nothing is changed by this brief excursus on truth. Individual believers still share what they have found most effective and powerful for themselves. They still do it in such a way that the different experiences of those with whom they speak are acknowledged. They still recognize that truth is not an exclusive possession, for at best they understand (in a limited fashion) some subset of the truth, whilst others understand other portions as well or better.

The foregoing reflections do, however, answer the criticism that one's tolerance of other traditions reduces one's own religious belief to the level of liking chocolate mousse. Tolerance does not entail a relativism according to which whatever one believes is true simply in virtue of one's believing it. Indeed, in our sense our analysis has *raised* the stakes in crosscultural discussions of religious belief, in the sharing of one's faith, for we have found that even partial expressions of divine truth can be more or less adequate to their intention in comparison to alternative formulations. Even where crosscultural discussions become murky or their outcome unclear, what is at stake is still the most adequate and the most comprehensive formulation of that truth of which we humans are capable.

This is not the place to write a treatise on the practice of mission. Nevertheless, certain basic implications can be noted. The primary calling in mission contexts is still, I believe, to reflect the love of God in Christ. A life-style of compassion speaks more loudly than any sort of strategic intervention. There is never a substitute for "speaking in love." Any time that one tries to do the work of compassion by manipulation one has fallen below the standards required by the gospel of Jesus. Such love not only reflects the nature of the one we call our savior, but also recognizes that truth lies within other traditions as well.

Put differently, the ubiquitous role of culture described in the opening section of this chapter entails a "fuzzy logic,"[19] that is, one that acknowledges that the boundaries between traditions are more fluid than fixed. African Christians will practice their religion in ways different from Asian or French Christians. Within broader cultures, subcultural differences will also lead to further divergencies. One only has to think of the radical differences in style

---

19. On the theory of fuzzy logic see, among many others, Hans Bandemer, *Fuzzy Sets, Fuzzy Logic, Fuzzy Methods with Applications* (New York: J. Wiley, 1995); J.F. Baldwin (ed.), *Fuzzy Logic* (New York: J. Wiley, 1996); George J. Klir, *Fuzzy Sets and Fuzzy Logic: Theory and Applications* (Upper Saddle River, NJ: Prentice Hall, 1995).

and practice of white and black, rich and poor congregations in the United States.

Still, fuzzy lines do not mean that there are no lines at all. Something more than the happenstance of cultural plurality is at stake in the religious differences that we encounter. Fundamental differences of belief remind one that truth claims are being made in the religious beliefs one espouses. First and foremost, Christian actions must reflect compassion rather than manipulation. Thus some missionaries in Muslim countries observe the month of Ramadan as a sign of respect for those who visit their homes. Others offer food prohibited to practising Muslims in the hopes of pulling the children away from their family's observance and thereby creating the first cracks that will lead the entire edifice of Islam to collapse.[20]

At the same time, acts of compassion must also be supplemented by inter-religious discussion of divergent belief contents. One cannot pretend that all parties really hold identical beliefs when differences are clearly presented. Some differences, of course, reflect nothing more than cultural preference or taste. Others cannot be explained so easily. Nevertheless, difference does not justify disdain. One can still have fellowship with and respect for those whose beliefs are different. Indeed, in a sense one respects others *more* when differences are out in the open rather than hidden or papered over.

We may note what happens when one applies this perspective to the question underlying the particular project of this book, the missiology of Western culture. Worldviews such as materialism and secularism that dominate much of Western culture now appear analogous to the other religous traditions treated above. Broad orientations such as positivism, scientism, humanism, New Age spirituality, and the like reflect alternative worldview perspectives, not totally dissimilar to the differences among the world's major religious traditions. As in the case of the other religions, then, we must first acknowledge the subset of truth that lies within these schools of thought. At the same time, we recognize that more is at stake in these differences than matters of taste, as if no important differences separated us. Reductive materialism and Christian theology are not equally true.

Thus, from the standpoint of a missiology of sharing, the principles of interreligious dialogue and of Christianity's encounter with contemporary Western culture remain the same. In both cases, we wish to know where our discussion partners have insights that are part of the truth, so that we can incorporate them into our system of beliefs, and where they have seen other parts of the whole less clearly than the Christian tradition has.[21]

If we are to return to our own culture as a context for mission, we must extend the same respect and honor to our discussion partners in the West that we need to extend to the representatives of other great religious traditions. At the same time, we must preserve the sense that we have something

---

20. I am grateful to Norris Palmer for this example.

21. As a number of us in the religion–science dialogue have argued, Christian theology can learn important lessons from the openness of science to empirical input, criticism, hypothetical thinking, revision, and rational progress.

to share with the Western culture and worldviews of the day. This presupposes that we believe that our disagreements with our colleagues are not just a matter of taste.

Too often religious traditions in the developed West function merely as special interest groups, as clubs of like-minded individuals within a liberal society who meet to engage in the practices of their club and to complain bitterly about those whose life-styles are less civilized than their own. But surely much more is at stake in the missiology of Western culture than the fact that our tastes differ from the tastes of other special-interest groups around us.

To defenders of absolute truths, the conclusions reached here may be somewhat disappointing. I have not found grounds for a triumphant proclamation of Christian truth to all comers, be they other religious traditions or the secularism of Western society today. On the other hand, I have been able to defend an epistemology of mission that allows for context-sensitive, sharing-based proclamation. In that delicate equilibrium between monologue and cacophony which is our epistemic lot we can still speak with confidence and joy of what we have seen and heard, using the light that is reflected back to us from other religious and secular traditions as an indispensable part of making a defense of the faith that is within us.

CHAPTER SIX

Missiology in the Postmodern West

A Radical Reformation Perspective

NANCEY MURPHY

INTRODUCTION

The purpose of this volume is to reflect on the implications for Christian mission of the current epistemological crisis in the West. In chapters 1–3 this crisis was associated with the modern/postmodern divide. In this chapter, first I will make a proposal for distinguishing modern from postmodern thought. Second, I will describe some of the effects of modernity, so described, on Christian self-understanding. Third, I will employ some of the resources of Anglo-American postmodern philosophy to reflect on the nature of the missiological task. Fourth, I will present a modest proposal for a recontextualization of the Christian message suited to the particular needs of the contemporary Western world.

DISTINGUISHING MODERN AND POSTMODERN THOUGHT

Breaks between one historical era and another are never clean: there is continuity from one to another and wide variation in the way major intellectual shifts affect different aspects of culture, different subcultures within a society, and different geographical regions. Thus, the date of the dawn of modernity is contested. Scientists might choose 1632, the publication date of Galileo's *Dialogue concerning the Two Chief World Systems*. Philosophers tend to choose 1650, the date of the death of René Descartes. Modern theology, however, is taken to have begun only with the writings of Friedrich Schleiermacher (1768–1834). Without the benefit of hindsight, we should expect even more controversy regarding the *end* of modernity.

One indication that we *have* reached the end of the modern period is the fact that today's scholars have deeper insight into the characteristics of modern thought than their predecessors of even a generation ago.[1] This insight comes from the fact that presuppositions unquestioned a generation ago have now been called into question; thus they can be recognized as the presuppositions of the past.

I do not pretend to provide an exhaustive account of modernity, but I offer three philosophical positions as keys to distinguishing modern thought. (The emphasis on philosophy is not mere disciplinary chauvinism: philosophy is a second-order discipline that, when it does its work well, uncovers, studies, and perhaps reforms patterns of thought employed in other dimensions of culture.) The key philosophical positions are foundationalism in epistemology, referentialism in philosophy of language, and atomism-*cum*-reductionism in metaphysics.[2]

MODERN AND POSTMODERN EPISTEMOLOGY

I can be brief in describing the epistemological stance that is now widely designated as "foundationalism"[3] since this has been described in Part One. Foundationalist epistemology began with the requirement that all justification of beliefs be traced back to an *indubitable* starting point. In light of the development of weaker forms of foundationalism—the "chastened" foundationalisms of this century—it is important to say what foundationalism (now) amounts to. I claim that the major requirements are two: first, that there be some class of beliefs that are somehow immune from challenge, and second that all reasoning within the system proceed in one direction only—from a set of privileged beliefs to others, never the reverse.

Thus, the history of modern epistemology can be summed up as a series of answers to diverse questions, such as what category of beliefs (such as intuitions, sense data) will serve as the foundation, and what kind of logical construction will serve for building the rest of the system (e.g., deduction, induction, hypothetico-deductive reasoning). Modern epistemologists have ranged along a spectrum that spreads from the optimistic Descartes to

---

1. One of the most perceptive books here is Stephen Toulmin, *Cosmopolis: The Hidden Agenda of Modernity* (New York: Macmillan, 1990).

2. I owe much of this thesis to my husband, James W. McClendon, Jr. See our jointly authored "Distinguishing Modern and Postmodern Theologies," *Modern Theology* 5 (April 1989): 191–214. For a more detailed account see Nancey Murphy, *Anglo-American Postmodernity: Philosophical Perspectives on Science, Religion, and Ethics* (Boulder, CO: Westview Press, 1997).

3. Although Descartes's epistemology is now recognized to be characteristically foundationalist, the term "foundationalism" is relatively new. An indication of this is that there is no entry for foundationalism in the Collier-Macmillan *Encyclopedia of Philosophy*, published in 1967. For additional details on foundationalism, see Richard Rorty, *Philosophy and the Mirror of Nature* (Princeton, NJ: Princeton University Press, 1979), 157–63; Jeffrey Stout, *The Flight from Authority: Religion, Morality, and the Quest for Autonomy* (Notre Dame: University of Notre Dame Press, 1981), 3–5; and Ronald Thiemann, *Revelation and Theology: The Gospel as Narrated Promise* (Notre Dame: University of Notre Dame Press, 1984), 44–46.

the pessimistic (skeptical) Hume. Richard Bernstein rightly points out that most of the contemporary epistemological crisis is "Cartesian anxiety."[4] That is, it is due not to the influence of new, postmodern theories of knowledge, but merely to the growing recognition that there are no beliefs that serve the purpose of sustaining the unquestioned modern assumption that knowledge must have foundations.

A postmodern epistemological position is one that moves beyond these modern debates in a definitive manner, one that shifts the very terms of debate. W.V.O. Quine did so by offering a new image, that of a web or net, to replace the "building" metaphor lying behind foundationalism. As noted above, there has already been significant development of postmodern, "holist" theories in both epistemology and philosophy of science.

A major feature of these holist accounts is the recognition of the mutual conditioning of the various sorts of beliefs that foundationalists would distinguish. For example, in the philosophy of science it is now recognized that while factual statements justify theories, theories interpret, and thus partially constitute, facts. Neither sort is "privileged" in the old foundationalist way. Another significant feature is recognition that epistemology (theories of rationality, justification, and truth) is itself but a part of the web. Thus, epistemology provides no universal starting point for judging the validity of webs of belief.

Modern and Postmodern Theories of Language

The standard theory of language in the modern world has been referential and representative: language has been thought to obtain its *meaning* by referring to objects or states of affairs in the world; its primary *function* is to represent or mirror that reality. Since so much language fails to fit this model, however, a second theory of language has been developed, or, one might better say, a theory of second-class language. This "expressivist" theory states that nonreferential language may nonetheless be significant in that it expresses the attitudes, emotions, or intentions of the speaker. Thus, for example, we are presented with an emotivist theory of ethics, in which, to take one instance, the sentence "Murder is wrong" merely expresses the speaker's disapproval of murder.

The modern concept of truth as correspondence is the point at which modern referentialism relates to modern epistemology. According to the concept, a sentence is *true* if it accurately pictures the way things are. But this sentence-to-world relation (truth) requires a word-to-world relation (reference). We can accept the truth of sentences that do not picture empirical reality only if they are derivable in some justifiable manner from sentences that do bear such a relation to the world—that is, from an empiricist foundation.

---

4. Richard Bernstein, *Beyond Objectivism and Relativism: Science, Hermeneutics, and Praxis* (Philadelphia, PA: University of Pennsylvania Press, 1983).

Two mid-century philosophers brought about a revolution in theories of language. Ludwig Wittgenstein emphasized the *use* of language in its *social context:* he maintained that to utter a sentence is to make a move in a language game. There is no deeper "foundation" for the meaning of language than the social conventions that govern its use; nor need there be.

J.L. Austin developed a "speech-act" theory of language. If we regard language from the point of view of what we are doing when we use it, our attention shifts from the narrower (modern) question of meaning to the broader question of the conditions under which an utterance is successful; Austin called these conditions for the "happiness" or "felicity" of a speech act.

These conditions can be summarized as follows: first, there are conventions of a purely *linguistic* sort, such as grammar and word usage. Second, there are *social* conventions governing the necessary form for various speech acts, such as requests, promises, and objections in a court of law. Third, there is a *representative* or descriptive condition: the sentence must bear a relation to a state of affairs in the world. But appropriate reference is determined by the sort of speech act in question. For example, to request that someone close the door requires a different state of affairs than to thank the person for having closed it. Fourth, there is what I shall call the *expressivist* condition: the speaker must intend to perform the speech act involved, and must have whatever affect is appropriate, for example, sincerity when making a promise. Finally, there is the condition Austin calls uptake: the hearer must get the point of what is being said; he or she must understand that the speaker intended to perform this particular speech act by means of this sentence.

The multiplicity of these conditions well reflects the complexity, the multidimensionality, of the use of language. Any theory of language that proposes one of these dimensions as supplying *the* meaning of an utterance or text is clearly reductionist.

Modern and Postmodern Metaphysics

A third feature of modern thought is a view of reality in which complex wholes can be analyzed without remainder into their parts. This metaphysical assumption was promoted by the success of early modern physics and especially the gains that came from explaining chemical phenomena on the basis of physics. One expression of this thesis was the logical positivists' program for the unity of science—the reduction of all sciences ultimately to physics. A second is modern "generic individualism"—the view that the characteristics of societies are entirely determined by the characteristics of the individuals that make them up, conjoined with the view that individuals can all be treated alike for the purposes of ethics, political theory, and law. That is, individuals in a society are "interchangeable" in a way comparable to atoms in a molecule.

The postmodern successor to this position cannot be merely a shift in valuation from the individual to the collective, but rather the result of the recognition of a more complex relation between individual and society, part and whole. Here, a society is conceived more like a clock made up of a variety of complementary parts than a bag of marbles. In a sense, the parts are what they are only because of the function they play in the whole. So, the Enlightenment recognition of the importance of the individual need not be rejected, only the modern failure to recognize how part and whole mutually condition one another. In science, the successor position to reductionism is the recognition of "top-down" causation in the hierarchy of the sciences.[5]

MODERN AND POSTMODERN CULTURE

It is often said that we are living in a postmodern culture. My assessment is that what is called the "postmodern condition" is better understood as the full force of *modern* philosophical positions finally reaching the streets. That is, "the postmodern self" is merely a further atomization of the modern individual, a position already anticipated by David Hume in the eighteenth century.

I suggested above that much of the "postmodern" epistemological crisis is due exactly to the fact that skeptics have *not* relinquished the modern foundationalist doctrine in favor of a more realistic account of how knowledge actually works. The recent development of a variety of realisms is an attempt to salvage the modern representational-referential theory of language in the absence of adequate epistemological foundations.[6] It leads to the same sort of (unwarranted) skepticism as did early modern theories of perception based on "ideas" in the mind. In that earlier setting, one imagined one's sensations to be representations "in the mind" and then the problem as to how one could ever know that they accurately represented a real world outside the mind always arose.

Current preoccupation with realism substitutes linguistic representations for sensory ideas, bemoans the fact that we can never compare the-world-as-described-by-our-language-and-concepts with a world not so described, and thus creates a new form of skepticism. The solution is to abandon the "picture" image of language and recognize that language itself is *part of* reality, and a tool *by means of which* we know and adapt to nonlinguistic reality.

I believe, but cannot argue here, that much of what goes under the heading of "postmodernism" in Continental thought falls on the modern side of my set of distinctions. For example, deconstructionists argue for instability of textual meaning specifically because of the text's lack of an external referent, thus perpetuating the modern notion that (stable) meaning depends on reference.

5. See Nancey Murphy and George F.R. Ellis, *On the Moral Nature of the Universe: Theology, Cosmology, and Ethics* (Minneapolis: Fortress Press, 1996).
6. See Murphy, *Anglo-American Postmodernity*, chapter 2.

THE THEOLOGICAL COST OF MODERNITY

A variety of thinkers have noted the deleterious effects of modern presuppositions on understandings of Christianity. I have argued that the three philosophical presuppositions listed above are responsible for bifurcating Western Protestant theology into two strands, which can be identified loosely as liberal and conservative.[7] In brief, if theology must have indubitable (or at least universal) foundations, the only real options turn out to be either Scripture, preferably understood as inerrant, or some (universally available) human religious experience. Furthermore, if there are only two kinds of language, then religious language must be either representational, with its own kind of realities to represent, or it must be merely expressive. Finally, the atomist-reductionist worldview, coupled with a deterministic account of the laws of physics, make divine action problematic: how could God act in a world whose events are all determined by the laws of physics? Theologians have had the option of a view of divine action either as intervention or as immanent working in all the processes of nature and history.

Conservative theologians have generally been scriptural foundationalists, with a representational (propositional) view of religious language and an interventionist account of divine action. Liberals can be characterized by their preference for experiential foundations, expressivist accounts of religious language, and immanentist accounts of God's relation to the world. At this point, it should be clear that both of these basic strategies run into insuperable philosophical problems.

I endorse, therefore, Wilbert Shenk's critique of modern approaches to missiology. Shenk points out that the individualism of modernity has led to a view of evangelism that focuses almost exclusively on the individual and a view of Christian morality that concentrates on "personal" sins rather than structural evil.[8]

Lesslie Newbigin has provided a powerful critique of the way in which the modern rejection of tradition and the quest for certitude based in "objective" human reason have jointly led to the banishment of religion to the realm of the private.[9] His analysis is consistent with a critique of the expressivist account of religious language.

There is sad irony in this development. If Stephen Toulmin's account of the motives behind Descartes's quest for certitude is correct, it was the devastation wrought by the Thirty Years' War that led moderns to reject (reli-

---

7. See Nancey Murphy, *Beyond Liberalism and Fundamentalism: How Modern and Postmodern Philosophy Set the Theological Agenda* (Valley Forge, PA: Trinity Press International, 1996).

8. Wilbert R. Shenk, *Write the Vision: The Church Renewed* (Valley Forge, PA: Trinity Press International, 1995), chapter 3.

9. See, e.g., Lesslie Newbigin, *Truth to Tell: The Gospel as Public Truth* (London: SPCK, 1991); *Truth and Authority in Modernity* (Valley Forge, PA: Trinity Press International, 1996).

gious) tradition as a source of guidance in the public sphere.[10] So Christians' inability to settle their theological differences peacefully has led, ultimately, to the view that theology has no cognitive content and does not belong in the public sphere.

RATIONALITY AND MISSION TO THE WEST

Much of the contemporary epistemological crisis is a result of the following sort of reasoning: first, the justification of knowledge claims requires that they are derived from indubitable foundations; second, there are no indubitable foundations; therefore, third, there are no justified knowledge claims.

At this point, two responses are possible. One is to accept the final conclusion of the sequence, as many so-called postmoderns do.[11] The other option is to read the argument as a *reductio ad absurdum* and to reject the first Premise. This is what a number of Anglo-American philosophers have done, including Quine, Thomas Kuhn, Imre Lakatos, Richard Rorty, and Alasdair MacIntyre. But the defeat of modern forms of skepticism by means of the development of a holist epistemology may lead to a new epistemological problem, that of relativism. Epistemological relativism is reinforced in contemporary culture by a growing awareness of cultural pluralism, and also by its superficial resemblance to moral relativism. The latter, however, is also a product of modernity and of the assignment of morality to the private, expressivist domain.[12]

While many of these holist philosophers are content with a *limited* relativism,[13] there are also a few who provide strong normative accounts of rational adjudication among competing scientific research programs or large-scale traditions (in particular, Lakatos and MacIntyre). One response to the crisis, then, is simply to promote the views of these new-style rationalists. Lakatos's methodology can be applied to schools of theology;[14]

---

10. Toulmin, *Cosmopolis*.

11. See, e.g., Hugh H. Silverman (ed.), *Questioning Foundations: Truth/Subjectivity/Culture* (New York: Routledge, 1993): "The notion of 'foundations' hangs seriously in the balance" . . . "truth is the last lie." Truth itself must be "interrogated, questioned, placed in parentheses" (2–3).

12. See Alasdair MacIntyre, *After Virtue*, 2d ed. (Notre Dame: University of Notre Dame Press, 1984), for an account of the modern moves that have led to emotivism in ethics.

13. I stress "limited." In a seminar on contemporary relativism in the Anglo-American context we were unable to find any respectable philosopher who promotes a complete relativism. Although Paul K. Feyerabend is often associated with the motto "Anything goes," this is a quotation out of context and does not fairly represent his views. In contrast to those who see contemporary culture as unlimitedly pluralistic, he believes that it is becoming all too monolithic and that this uniformity is being rapidly exported to the Third World. Consequently, he argues for proliferation of competing viewpoints. See, e.g., *Farewell to Reason* (London: Verso, 1989).

14. See Nancey Murphy, *Theology in the Age of Scientific Reasoning* (Ithaca, NY: Cornell University Press, 1990).

MacIntyre's theory of tradition-constituted reason can be used to adjudicate among competing religious traditions.[15]

Such an approach, however, while valuable, is not a sufficient response to the missiological questions confronting us today. A central thesis of Bert Hoedemaker's *Secularization and Mission* is that the relation between Christianity and rationality itself has become problematic.[16] In the remainder of this section I hope to contribute to an understanding of this problematic relation. In the following section I hope to go some way toward its solution.

RELIGION, FAITH, AND RATIONALITY

Hoedemaker argues that secularization calls for a new reflection on what "mission" might mean, since secularization questions the very presuppositions underlying much traditional talk about religion, faith, and mission. Secularization involves the creation of spheres independent of religion, such as politics and economics. In these spheres of public life, a functional or instrumental sort of reason has come to dominate, geared toward the accomplishment of goals but not toward the evaluation of the goals themselves. The challenge, then, is to rethink the place of religion in culture, especially the privatization of religion that has acquiesced in the autonomy of these new, separate spheres.

Hoedemaker distinguishes between religion and faith. Religion, he says, is the human propensity for preoccupation with finitude, failure, suffering, the encounter of good and evil, the experiences of love and anxiety. Religion expresses itself in a variety of symbolic and ritual activities. By "faith" (he might better say, a faith *tradition*) Hoedemaker means the structuring of religious activities by way of a tradition, a community, and a story or revelation. A faith tends to assume social, cultural, and political significance, and thus to compete with rational systems. A faith is never merely externally related to rational systems, however, since the structuring of religious response into a faith system is itself an activity of reason. So faith is by its nature a bridge between religion and rationality.

Hoedemaker suspects that the Christian faith in the West has been in too close an alliance with rationality, especially with the functional rationality of the Enlightenment and post-Enlightenment eras. Secularization has brought about a disturbance of the relations between rationality, religion, and faith, and thus may present opportunities to readjust the balance. A missiology of Western culture, then, must involve creation of a new contextual faith. A major part of this recontextualizing must be in relation to reason, but with the recognition that reason itself is not merely external to faith;

---

15. See Nancey Murphy, *Anglo-American Postmodernity*, chapter 6; and "Overcoming Hume on his Own Terms" (forthcoming, in a volume to be edited by D.Z. Phillips).

16. Bert Hoedemaker, *Secularization and Rationality: A Theological Essay* (Valley Forge, PA: Trinity Press International, 1998).

rather, some form of reasonableness will be inherent in that development.

The relation between faith and reason is an interaction. The Gospel must challenge culture, and one point at which Western culture is in need of challenge is in its assumptions about rationality.

MacIntyrean Reflections on Religion and Rationality

Hoedemaker's concern in *Secularization and Mission* is with practical rationality, that is, with an account of what makes it rational to *act* in one way rather than another. A major concern of the present volume, however, is with "pure" reason, that is, with what makes it rational to *believe* one thing rather than another. These two sorts of rationality are intrinsically connected, in that we can ask what makes it rational to *believe* that one account of *practical* rationality is superior to another. Thus, I want to extend Hoedemaker's questions about the relations between practical rationality and mission to include those about pure reason and mission.

My resource here will be the recent writings of Alasdair MacIntyre. MacIntyre's primary concerns over the past two decades have been largely with practical reason, with ethics. His major ethical work, *After Virtue*, mounts a critique of Enlightenment theories of ethics, including a scathing indictment of the role of instrumental reason in the spheres of business and therapy. He concludes that the best hope to remedy both the instrumentalism and the moral relativism of contemporary culture is to rejuvenate the Aristotelian tradition of moral reasoning. Two later books turn to the task of defending this thesis and thus involve MacIntyre in proposing an epistemological account adequate to the task.[17]

It is possible here only to give a very brief account of MacIntyre's method for adjudicating among rival traditions. In addition, I shall extract from his writings some useful materials for extending Hoedemaker's work on rationality and mission.

MacIntyre's account of the nature and development of *traditions* is a valuable resource. One of his central insights is that all reasoning takes place within the context of some tradition. This recognition is an improvement over Quine's atemporal and universalist account of holist epistemology.

All traditions, according to MacIntyre, originate with an authority of some sort, usually a text or set of texts. They develop by means of successive attempts to interpret and apply the text in new contexts. Application is essential, for traditions are socially embodied in the life stories of the individuals and communities who share in them, and in institutions and social practices.

MacIntyre's first concern was with traditions of moral reasoning; for example, he traced the development of the virtue tradition from Homer

---

17. Alasdair MacIntyre, *Whose Justice? Which Rationality?* (Notre Dame: University of Notre Dame Press, 1988); *Three Rival Versions of Moral Enquiry: Encyclopaedia, Genealogy, and Tradition* (Notre Dame: University of Notre Dame Press, 1990).

through Aristotle and Thomas Aquinas to the Scottish Enlightenment. In considering the question of the rational adjudication among competing traditions, however, he came to recognize that traditions of moral reasoning are themselves embedded in what he calls "large-scale traditions," which tend to include epistemological theories, as well.

So the problem of rational adjudication among competing traditions is acute. Each tradition has its own set of authoritative texts; each is embodied in its own social world, and each will have its own (internal) account of standards of rationality, definitions of truth, and so forth. There is no tradition-neutral place from which one can judge. MacIntyre's insight is that a traditon can fail *on its own terms*, and can thus be judged less adequate than its immediate rivals. Traditions fall into epistemological crises and it is then an open question whether the tradition will contain resources that can be reformulated so as to overcome the crisis. One such crisis in Christian history was the clash between Augustinian Christianity and the Aristotelian world-view when the latter was introduced into medieval Europe. Thomas Aquinas showed that the Christian tradition did have adequate resources to meet the challenge, by incorporating into itself much of the science of the Aristotelian worldview, while reformulating its theology and epistemology.

In short, a tradition can be said to be rationally justified when it has been subjected to challenges from new experiences and rival traditions, and in each case has been able to overcome those challenges in a way faithful to its original texts. One tradition can be shown to be superior to its rival when the rival fails to pass such a test, and especially when the former provides intellectual resources for resolving not only its own but also the rival's epistemological crisis.

If we substitute MacIntyre's more general concept of a tradition for Hoedemaker's concept of faith, we can see that MacIntyre's account of the incorporation of theories of rationality, justification, and truth as integral parts of a large-scale tradition both reinforces and extends Hoedemaker's recognition that rationality is always already involved in faith: not just practical rationality, but concepts of pure reason as well.

Paul Feyerabend suggests that "Reason" in the West is, itself, a tradition. So our intellectual situation may be conceived as a complex one in which we have a variety of Christian subtraditions, each incorporating or tacitly employing some concept of rationality; a variety of rationalist subtraditions, such as Platonism, Aristotelianism, Enlightenment rationalism, and empiricism; and finally, certain large-scale traditions that are in competition with Christianity (such as other religions and scientific humanism), each of these with its own complex relations to the subtraditions of reason.

One of the most interesting features of MacIntyre's historical account, for present purposes, is his claim that Christian subtraditions have not only incorporated rationalist subtraditions, but have *reformulated* epistemology in line with their accounts of God and of human nature. For example, the Augustinian tradition began with a Platonic epistemology, but adapted it to its theology. Augustine transformed Plato's *ideas* into exemplars of created things in the mind of God. It is God present to the mind, as light is to the eye, that enables humans to apprehend truth. Augustine's conception of the fallen will had a tremendous impact on his epistemology. MacIntyre says:

> The intellect and the desires do not naturally move towards that good which is at once the foundation for knowledge and that from which lesser goods flow. The will which directs them is initially perverse and needs a kind of redirection which will enable it to trust obediently in a teacher who will guide the mind towards the discovery both of its own resources and what lies outside the mind, both in nature and in God. Hence, faith in authority has to precede rational understanding. And hence, the acquisition of that virtue which the will requires to be so guided, humility is the necessary first step in education or in self-education.[18]

In this account of theology *preceding* epistemology, we also find an example of morality preceding knowing, ethics preceding epistemology. Notice how thoroughly MacIntyre's account of tradition-constituted rationality overturns modern foundationalism. For the foundationalist, rationality was universal and timeless. It provided the standard by which any account of reality (theological or otherwise) and any account of morality was to be judged. Epistemology was thus logically prior to theology, ethics, and every other discipline. Here we see clear historical evidence that theology may be logically prior to both ethics and epistemology, and that moral formation may be temporally prior to the pursuit of knowledge.

REFRAMING THE QUESTIONS

So in place of Hoedemaker's threefold relation among religion, faith, and rationality, I propose that we think in terms of interacting traditions, both Christian and rationalist. Traditions of rationality interact with Christian subtraditions; a Christian tradition can both absorb and revise accounts of rationality. I also propose an alternative to Hoedemaker's "religion," which is too much influenced by the modern expressivist account of theology. The question, then, is what to call the third term of the relation. A "particularistically" Christian term is desirable, but not one that is biased in favor of any single contextualization of Christianity. I propose for this purpose a term from James McClendon's theology. To refer in a neutral manner to that which theories of salvation attempt to describe, he speaks simply of "the new in Christ."[19]

Thus, we can describe the very complex interactions as follows: contextual responses to *the new in Christ* result in the development of a variety of

---

18. MacIntyre, *Three Rival Versions*, 84.

19. James McClendon, Jr., *Doctrine: Systematic Theology*, Vol. 2 (Nashville: Abingdon, 1994), chapter 3.

Christian subtraditions, interacting in various ways with other *large-scale traditions*, absorbing into themselves various *epistemological traditions* and sometimes changing those traditions in so doing. The most familiar examples include the Hellenization of Christianity, which involved the absorption and transformation of Platonic epistemology, as already noted. There was also the contest between the Augustinian and Aristotelian traditions in the Middle Ages. These were two large-scale traditions, each with its own epistemology and account of ultimate reality, reconciled into a single tradition by Thomas Aquinas.

We may not be in position to provide such neat summaries of more recent history, but several tantalizing fragments of the interactions between Christianity and Reason have been charted. Jeffrey Stout provides an account of the crisis for theology that resulted from theologians' inability quickly to jettison medieval epistemology and adapt to the new "probable reasoning" of modernity.[20] Ronald Thiemann explores the effects of the incorporation of foundationalist epistemology into theology in the guise of theories of revelation.[21] The questions facing missiologists in the West, then, include the following:

1. What are the epistemological assumptions woven into our various Christian subtraditions at this moment of history? Hoedemaker, Newbigin, Thiemann, and others have begun to answer this question, and all have argued that these syntheses can no longer be seen as adequate.[22]
2. What are the most recent developments in the tradition of Reason? The first part of the present volume attempts to answer just that question and makes it clear that we need to consider two fairly independent subtraditions, conventionally designated the Anglo-American and the Continental. A clear distinction between postmodern developments and the last gasps of modern epistemology is also crucial.
3. Is Christian belief justifiable in light of one or more of these traditions of rationality? I believe that all reasonable strategies for employing modern epistemology in this task have been tried, and have run into insurmountable obstacles, sometimes distorting theology in the process.[23] Continental developments, of course, call the entire rationalist project into question. Yet, prospects for justification in light of the works of the more rationalistic of postmodern Anglo-American philosophers are promising. Note that pursuing the justification of Christian belief in light of current (Anglo-American) epistemological developments is what the "postepistemologists" such as Rorty mean to call into question—not only foundationalist accounts *in* epistemology, but also the assumption of the priority of epistemology to all other disciplines. As MacIntyre and Hoedemaker have each made clear in his

---

20. Stout, *The Flight from Authority.*
21. Ronald Thiemann, *Revelation and Theology.*
22. See also Murphy, *Beyond Liberalism and Fundamentalism,* chapter 1.
23. See ibid., chapter 3.

own way, the more interesting (and more pressing) questions are the following:

4. How is Christian thought itself to be reconceived, i.e., transformed in these new contexts?

5. What might the Christian tradition (or a Christian subtradition) have to offer for the development of new traditions of reason/antireason? To these last two questions I turn in the final section.

RADICAL REFORMATION THEOLOGY AND EPISTEMOLOGY

MacIntyre distinguishes three rival versions of moral enquiry, which he labels Encyclopaedia, Genealogy, and Tradition. The first is named for its classic text, *The Encyclopaedia Britannica* (ninth edition), which enshrined the Enlightenment view of objective standards of rationality and universal morals. This tradition, he claims, has been effectively criticized by the Genealogists, i.e., Friedrich Nietzsche and his followers. As a current competitor to the Nietzschean view that all moralities need to be unmasked to reveal the interests behind them, MacIntyre offers his renewed version of the Aristotelian-Thomist tradition. I believe this is a helpful starting point for mapping the current scene in the sphere of practical reason. It is also helpful for mapping the current epistemological scene, since each tradition of moral enquiry involves broader epistemological commitments. So here we have the answer MacIntyre would give to Hoedemaker's question: If it is time for Christianity to sever its ties to Enlightenment instrumental reason, then what comes next?

MacIntyre sees two options: Thomas or Nietzsche. I see three. MacIntyre's account is typically Catholic. I suggest that the Genealogical tradition is in the line of descent from Augustine to the mainline Reformers, in that Nietzsche's view of knowledge as the will to power is much like what an Augustinian would expect, apart from any concepts of grace, regeneration, and revelation. The fact that these two options can be associated with major theological positions suggests that we might find other possibilities by considering different *theological* positions. I shall attempt to develop a third option using resources from a third major Christian tradition, originating in the Radical Reformation of the sixteenth century.

The Catholic Option

In general, Catholic theologians have been more optimistic than Protestants regarding human capacities for knowledge. This optimism can be traced to the fact that Thomas developed an account of the hierarchical ordering of the capacities of the soul that was different from the account Protestants inherited from Augustine. For both Augustine and Thomas the soul was conceived as hierarchically ordered, and the proper "chain of command" was from higher faculties to lower. For Augustine, the will was the highest function of the soul, above the intellect. Thus, when the will falls it corrupts all lower faculties, including the intellect; in Calvin's terms, the fall entails total depravity.

Thomas took the intellect to be the highest of human faculties. Since it is above the will the fall does not affect it directly. Humans can still fall into error, when the will leads them to form judgments prematurely, but the capacities for knowledge are not intrinsically darkened or depraved. In MacIntyre's version of Thomistic epistemology, he concentrates on the intellect *embodied in social practices*. A *social practice* is an important concept for MacIntyre for a variety of reasons. He defines it as follows:

> By a "practice" I am going to mean any coherent and complex form of socially established cooperative human activity through which goods internal to that form of activity are realized in the course of trying to achieve those standards of excellence which are appropriate to, and partially definitive of, that form of activity, with the result that human powers to achieve excellence, and human conceptions of the ends and goods involved, are systematically extended."[24]

What is important for our purposes is the specification that social practices aim inherently at the realization of *goods* internal to those practices. Thus, MacIntyre's account of the socially embodied intellect is one in which the intellect itself aims intrinsically at a variety of goods. This is not to say that social practices, including those relating to the acquisition of knowledge, cannot be deformed or distorted (by corrupt institutions, or by the lack of appropriate virtues on the part of participants), but it is a more optimistic view of the nature of social practices than we find in the Genealogical tradition.

THE GENEALOGICAL OPTION

Nietzsche set out to show that the will-to-power conceals itself under the guise of the will-to-truth. If we redescribe Nietzsche's will-to-power in theological terms as wanting to be like God (cf. Gen. 3:5), his account is strikingly like what an Augustinian Christian would expect.

Michel Foucault, an important interpreter of Nietzsche, has developed a view of knowledge parallel to MacIntyre's in many respects; however, the similarities make the difference at one point all the more striking. Both are thoroughly historicist in their understandings of epistemology; both employ a genealogical method; both regard knowledge as originating from social practices. But whereas MacIntyre takes such practices to lead to truth, Foucault concentrates on practices of social control and aims to show how they distort human knowledge. For Foucault, there is an essential connection between knowledge and power, and it inevitably deludes us.

---

24. MacIntyre, *After Virtue*, 187.

A RADICAL REFORMATION ALTERNATIVE

James McClendon has set out to produce a systematic theology in light of the Radical Reformation heritage, a tradition begun in the sixteenth century and carried on in a number of contemporary Christian communities, including the Mennonites and Brethren, some Baptists, Methodists, Disciples of Christ, Pentecostals, and some intentional communities. In his first volume, *Ethics*, he makes use of MacIntyre's account of a social practice, but calls into question "the generally optimistic and progressive ring of MacIntyre's overall account of practices."[25] By invoking the biblical concept of *principalities and powers*, McClendon forges a concept of *powerful practices* that has neither the essential optimism of MacIntyre's account nor the essential pessimism of Foucault's account of the relations between power and knowledge.

The biblical concept of the powers has been lost to view in the course of Christian history, having been identified with the angels and demons of the medieval worldview. The biblical concept of the powers developed from the concepts of the alien gods of Old Testament understanding. In the Near East, power was inevitably associated with gods, and gods were linked with politics and society. "In the New Testament the powers retain their status subordinate to God, and also their political role: they are God's creatures (Col. 1:15–17), fallen and rebellious (Eph. 2:1ff; Gal. 4:1–11), and may be identical with empire and its lords (Rom. 13:1–4)."[26]

The mission of Jesus is understood as conflict with and conquest of these powers. In the epistles this conflict is typically represented in summary form, as in Colossians 2:15 (REB): "There he disarmed the cosmic powers and authorities and made a public spectacle of them, leading them as captives in his triumphal procession." In the Gospels, this conflict is portrayed in narrative form, and the opponents are no longer called the "principalities and powers," but are human overlords of state and temple, or demonic forces that sponsor illness and madness. McClendon observes "that the contra-power that Jesus (and through him, God's Spirit) mounts against these is nothing less than the whole course of his obedient life, with its successive moments of proclamation, healing, instruction, the gathering of a redemptive community, and costly submission to the way of the cross and its death and resurrection."[27]

Wherever Christ's victory is proclaimed, the corrupted reign of the powers is challenged, and yet they remain in being; in the time between the resurrection and the final coming of Christ, they remain in an ambiguous state. They delimit and define the social morality of Jesus' followers; to them the disciple must witness concerning the reversal of power documented in Christ's resurrection.

---

25. James McClendon, Jr., *Ethics: Systematic Theology*, vol. 1 (Nashville: Abingdon, 1986), 173.

26. Ibid., 174.

27. Ibid.

There is a hint in the New Testament that the final destiny of all these powers, civil, military, economic, traditional, cultural, social, *and religious* will not be their abolition but their full restoration (Eph. 1:10; 3:10). "So the task of Christians confronting a world of *powerful practices* (as we may now call them) requires almost infinite adjustments, distinction, and gradations."[28]

Just as Jesus recognized the religion of his own day as among the powers, Christians today must recognize the power of institutionalized religion. Yet, this need not deter them from the attempt to witness to the powers of the world by forming communities in which social structures and practices can more closely approximate God's will for the ordering of human life. Here is a powerful antidote to modern individualism: the church must be a new countersociety.

The Radical Reformers

For four centuries the Anabaptists or "rebaptizers" were associated almost exclusively with radical sects such as the Münsterites and thus dismissed from mainline church histories. Exactly how and when the movement started is still in dispute. One important event in the consolidation and definition of this form of Christian life, however, was a meeting of leaders of the Swiss Brethren at Schleitheim, on the Swiss-German border, in 1527.

The Schleitheim Confession presented Anabaptist distinctives: those points on which the Radicals differed from the other Protestants. These seven distinctives were: first, baptism was to be reserved for believers; second, unrepentant sinners were to be admonished and, if necessary, banned from the congregation; third, the breaking of bread was to be reserved for those who were baptized and at peace with one another; fourth, the church was to be separated from the world; fifth, shepherds (pastors) were to be chosen from among the congregation; sixth, "concerning the sword," Christians should not use any punishments other than the ban to enforce church discipline, and should not engage in combat or any other civic duties that involve violence; and seventh, Christians should not swear oaths of loyalty to the government.[29] A document concerning congregational order was apparently circulated with the seven articles. It urged frequent meetings for study and the Lord's Supper, admonishing of sinners, simple living (there should be no frivolity or gluttony), and the communal ownership of goods.[30]

A contemporary version of the Radical Reformation heritage may provide a suitable recontextualization of the new in Christ for our own day:

1. *The Separation of Church and State.* Although state-sponsored church bodies still exist in Europe, the separation of church and state and volun-

---

28. Ibid., 176.
29. John Howard Yoder (ed.), *The Legacy of Michael Sattler* (Scottdale, PA: Herald Press, 1973), 27–54.
30. Ibid., 44–45.

tary church membership are no longer considered radical ideas. However, John Howard Yoder, one of the most significant contemporary theologians of the Radical tradition, points out that more insidious elements of the wedding of church and empire still remain. Yoder calls the development of state churches "neo-Constantinianism."

The next shift came with the Enlightenment and with revolution, leading to the decoupling of church and state as *institutions*. Yoder calls this "neo-neo-Constantinianism," since Christians' *moral* identification with the state was little changed. Ironically, he notes that "once the separation of church and state is seen as theologically desirable, a society where this separation is achieved is not a pagan society but a nation structured according to the will of God."[31] Especially in the U.S., patriotism has remained highly religious.

Yoder sees the establishment of "people's democracies" in Eastern Europe as a further stage of development. In this arrangement, which could be called "neo-neo-neo-Constantinian," the government may actually oppose Christianity, while Christians, despite criticism in detail of their disestablished position, remain patriotic.

There is yet one more step: Christians can identify God's cause, and Christians' loyalty, with a regime that is future rather than present—with a revolution or liberation that will bring about a better power system. This would be called "neo-neo-neo-neo-Constantinianism." Theologians of this sort prefer models of partnership with power, even though the friendly sovereign is not even there yet. Yoder says:

> Each view along this progression is clear in rejecting the former one as having been wrong, and in blaming the blindness of earlier generations of churchmen for having accepted such identification with an unworthy political cause. This sense of rightness over against the others blinds each generation to the fact that the basic structural error, the identification of a civil authority as bearer of God's cause, has not been overcome but only transposed into a new key.[32]

Yoder believes that the later positions are more dangerous to Christian faithfulness than the earlier: at each level the church's capacity to be critical decreases; least of all can one be concretely critical of a projected future.

Yoder makes perceptive remarks about the relevance of a non- or anti-Constantinian understanding of power for missiology:

> On the one hand, "mission" by definition should mean a forsaking of the Constantinian setting for a pilgrim status in someone else's world. The "forsaking" in mission has been as complex and as burdened with unpurged vestiges as the "overcoming" in Western experience. Suffice

---

31. John Howard Yoder, *The Priestly Kingdom: Social Ethics as Gospel* (Notre Dame: University of Notre Dame Press, 1984), 142.

32. Ibid., 143.

it to suggest that "to deconstantinize" or "disestablish" might be a more concretely usable verb for the critical changes still needed than are the more current verbs "to contextualize" or "to indigenize," because the changes include: an element of repentance and judgment on the Western past; an awareness of the centrality of the power problem (whereas some discussion of "contextualizing" is often more narrowly semantic); a warning against a too easy conformity (to the indigenous scheme) to correct for the old ("foreign") one.

To conclude with a biblical vocabulary; if kenosis is the shape of God's own self-sending, then any strategy of Lordship, like that of the kings of this world, is not only a strategic mistake likely to backfire but a denial of gospel substance, a denial which has failed even where it succeeded."[33]

Yoder's comment that a church morally allied with the state loses its ability to criticize relates to McClendon's claim: Christians' participation in Jesus' conflict with the principalities and powers involves the formation of communities of disciples who engage in reformed social practices. As Yoder says, it is only in contrast to the peaceful practices of the church that the world can see itself *as world.*

It is important to mention here that direct descendants of the Anabaptists have been justly criticized for complete withdrawal from the surrounding social order. Yoder and a number of others emphasize that the point of being separate from "the world" was not the purity of the church or abandonment of society, but rather to maintain a position uncompromised by power structures in order to be a transformative force in society.

2. *Simple Life-style.* A second aspect of Radical Reformation Christianity relevant for the current situation in the West is simplicity of life. This emphasis began as a proscription of excessive consumption—"All gluttony shall be avoided among the brothers . . . for eating and drinking are not the kingdom of heaven"—so as to "permit no brother to be in need."[34] Apparently, as Mennonites and other descendants of the early Radicals reestablished themselves after persecution, and their simple living allowed them to amass wealth, the very meaning of "simplicity" changed to that of avoiding frills and new technology.

Were the church as a whole to recover the Radicals' original call to simple life-style this would be a timely message—one that Westerners desperately need to hear as the disparity between rich and poor grows wider throughout the world, and as Westerners consume resources and create pollution at an unsustainable rate.

3. *Nonviolence.* A third distinctive of the Radical Reformation whose time has come is the refusal of violence. Renunciation of "the sword" among the early Radicals was connected with their call for voluntary church

---

33. Ibid., 145.
34. "Congregational Order," in Yoder (ed.), *The Legacy of Michael Sattler,* 45.

membership and separation of church and state. Physical punishment was not to be used to compel religious conformity, since only a voluntary commitment mattered in God's eyes. Yet, if violence was not to be used in the service of this most important of causes, much less should a Christian use it for other purposes.

Radicals in the meantime have extended the prohibition against capital punishment and military service to include a positive call to engage in ministries of peacemaking. John Yoder sees peacemaking as central to the new in Christ, and in fact interprets the theological concepts of justification and reconciliation not (merely) as making things right between God and the individual sinner, but in the first instance as reconciliation among classes of people formerly at enmity: males and females, slaves and free, and especially ethnic groups.

Justification (being set right with God) is accomplished when Christians are set right with one another. In Paul's ministry the reconciling of Jews and Gentiles was primary. The "new creation" is a new "race" of humans where the Jewish law no longer forms a barrier between Jew and Gentile, and where gender and economic differences are reconciled as well. Yoder writes:

> But it is *par excellence* with reference to enmity between peoples, the extension of neighbor love to the enemy, and the renunciation of violence even in the most righteous cause, that this promise takes on flesh in the most original, the most authentic, and most frightening and scandalous, and therefore the most evangelical way. It is the Good News that my enemy and I are united, through no merit or work of our own, in a new humanity that forbids henceforth my ever taking his or her life in my hands."[35]

In an age when violence in our cities and ethnic conflicts abroad take center attention in the news, Yoder's account of the Good News should be welcome indeed.

4. *Revolutionary Subordination.* This is a closely related emphasis in Radical Reformation Christianity. An examination of this issue will put us in position to return to the central topic of this section of my chapter and of the book as a whole: a Christian response to the epistemological crisis in contemporary Western society.

In the movie *The Witness*, a typical American hero finds it necessary to hide among the Amish in rural Pennsylvania. In one scene, a buggy, full of Amish and the hero, are accosted by young town bullies. The Amish sit patiently while they are taunted and smeared with ice cream. When the hero jumped out and attacked the youths with his fists, the immediate reaction of the audience in the theater was to cheer.

---

35. John Howard Yoder, *The Politics of Jesus*, 2d. ed. (Grand Rapids, MI: Eerdmans, 1994), 226. For a systematic survey of Yoder's theology, cf. Nancey Murphy and George F.R. Ellis, *On the Moral Nature of the Universe: Theology, Cosmology and Ethics* (Minneapolis: Fortress Press, 1996), chapter 8.

This scene and the audience's reflex response suggest that in our culture we see only two options: either to meet an assertion of power with a counterassertion, or to wait passively to be run over by the aggressor. Jesus' command to turn the other cheek has, unfortunately, been used as a label for the second of these two options. Hence, it is no surprise that Christian ethicists have sought to restrict, as far as possible, instances where Jesus' injunction is thought to apply.

I believe that knowledge of the context of Jesus' teaching will make it clear that Jesus is not enjoining mere passive acceptance of abuse. Walter Wink points out that in first-century Mediterranean culture, a backhanded slap was a gesture used to dishonor an inferior person. Thus, husbands could slap their wives and children in this manner; slave-owners their slaves; landowners their peasants. There were severe penalties, however, for striking an equal in this humiliating manner. Another relevant factor is that the left hand was never used for anything except unclean purposes. Thus, a backhanded slap would necessarily be made using the right hand and would fall on the recipient's right cheek. Note that Jesus is recorded to have said explicitly: "If anyone slaps you on the right cheek, turn and offer him the other also" (Matt. 5:39b REB). If the recipient then turns the left cheek, the "superior" is forced to strike with the fist or slap with the palm—gestures reserved for one's equals.

So Jesus, whose followers were mostly from the inferior classes, was suggesting a way of asserting one's equality, of upsetting the social hierarchy, yet without violence to the attacker.[36] Jesus' teaching can be seen as offering a third option—a way of living without worldly power, whilst retaining one's dignity and confining oppression and violence.

All four of these Radical Reformation distinctives, in fact, can be seen as strategies for living in such a way as to curb the *will-to-power*. Nonviolence is the refusal to use physical force against another. Revolutionary subordination is a strategy for righting injustices without the use of any power other than that of the imagination. The separation of church and state (and yet more thorough deconstantinization) is the rejection of institutional longing for alliance with the power of the state. Finally, learning to live with less reduces the need for power to defend one's economic privilege.

Epistemology and the Will-to-Power

I have suggested in the preceding subsection that the Radicals' emphasis on living without worldly power is highly relevant for recontextualizing Christianity in the West today. I now want to argue that this same tradition, this same emphasis on doing without worldly power, answers major epistemological problems in a way that its rival traditions cannot.[37]

---

36. Walter Wink, *Engaging the Powers* (Minneapolis: Fortress Press, 1992), *passim*.

37. I emphasize the rejection of worldly power; the New Testament emphasizes the transformative power of love, truth, and suffering. So "worldly power" here means the forms of power sought by the Johannine "world," that is, the system opposed to God and God's Word.

I believe that MacIntyre's account of the epistemological scene is the best available.[38] Yet his account has two major weaknesses. First, it is overly optimistic in its evaluation of social practices and thus of the capacities of the (socially embodied) intellect. Second, he has not been able (in his own estimation) to provide conclusive reasons to the Genealogical tradition. I claim that his epistemological account can be repaired, first, by *acknowledging* the (measure of) truth in the Genealogists' account of the epistemic distortions caused by the will-to-power, and, second, by providing a more nuanced account of the powerful practices involved. On McClendon's view, one does not have to settle either for MacIntyre's blanket optimism or Foucault's assumption that practices inevitably distort the quest for understanding.

So a synthesis that grafts MacIntyre's epistemological work onto a Radical Reformation social analysis will provide the best understanding of the epistemological task. In addition, I would claim that an adequate response to the current epistemological crisis calls for the adoption of Radical Reformation *practices*. These practices are of two sorts: first, those of nonviolence, simple living, and revolutionary subordination as strategies for living without the assertion of power. Second, Radical Reformation churches have contributed to the development of what might be called "Christian epistemic practices"—communal practices aimed at the pursuit of truth. In general, such practices involve procedures and criteria for judging whether teaching, prophecy, and decisions are of the Spirit of Christ, or not.[39]

For the Radicals the principle of consistency with Scripture (particularly the New Testament) took such a prominent place among their criteria for decision making that discussion of these matters by contemporary historians often falls under the topic of "Anabaptist hermeneutics."[40] Judgment always took place in the context of the need for guidance in questions concerning a local congregation's practice. John Howard Yoder points out that, since the Holy Spirit was promised to the church in the context of a reconciling approach to wayward members (Matt. 18:19–20; John. 20:22–23), the mandate and enablement to discern the will of God were seen as provisions not primarily for scholars, but for the concrete congregation in its struggle with differing visions of what obedience meant in its own time and place. This is not to say that scholarship had no place in the community; only that it must be relevant to shaping the community's common life.

The Radical Reformers called on the congregation to make decisions in three types of cases: public disputations, synods, and the discipline of individuals. We see an example of the first in Balthasar Hubmaier's debate (1524) with the Catholic John Eck. The key provision in Hubmaier's proposed rules for the disputation was drawn from 1 Corinthians 14:29: "Two

---

38. See Murphy, *Anglo-American Postmodernity*, chapter 3.

39. For a more detailed account of these practices, see Murphy, *Theology in the Age of Scientific Reasoning*, chapter 5.

40. Cf., e.g., John Howard Yoder, "The Hermeneutics of the Anabaptists," *Mennonite Quarterly Review* 41 (October 1967): 291–307.

or three prophets should speak, and the others should weigh carefully what is said." The audience for the debate would be placed within the framework of a congregation gathered for worship. The congregation would listen as the two speakers expressed their convictions, and then decide who had spoken more nearly in accord with the Scriptures.[41]

Perhaps the most significant synod in the earliest years of the movement was the meeting at Schleitheim, mentioned above. Two hints about the procedure of the meeting stand out. One is that participants in all cases are referred to as brothers *and sisters*, suggesting that women were full participants. The second is that the expression "we have been united" is used frequently, the passive voice suggesting that unanimous agreement of the congregation was taken as a sign of the action of the Holy Spirit.

The Anabaptists practiced communal discipline according to the instructions in Matthew 18, even to excess in some communities. The practice of discussion between the community and the wayward individual, however, was often effective in creating unity in thought and life-style.

Whereas consistency with the Scriptures served as the *criterion* for decision making among the Radicals, the *practical test* of consistency was the agreement of the entire community—whether the issue be the conduct of an individual in the local community, the distinctives of the Radical movement as a whole, or a theological debate with outsiders. The *means* of reaching agreement was open discussion in the context of prayer. This is an instance of a social *practice* as defined by MacIntyre.

There is an important connection between discernment, as the Radicals understood it, and the power-limiting practices described above. Pilgram Marpeck (1495?–1556), a leader of the Radical movement in the south of Germany, wrote extensively and participated in a number of public disputations. Like the others, he was committed to the *sola scriptura* principle. But, without the aid of the Holy Spirit, he maintained, the scriptures could not be interpreted or explained. The most subtle temptation besetting the Christian is to ascribe to the Holy Spirit what is actually one's own human opinion. "Ah, my brethren, how diligently and carefully we have to take heed that we do not consider our own impulses the impulse of the Holy Spirit, our own course the course and walk of Christ."[42] We might say, how easy it is to be self-deceived about self-serving teachings, and how tempting it is to invoke the authority of the Holy Spirit to augment one's own power.

Consequently, Marpeck offered four signs by which to judge the impulses behind one's own or a fellow Christian's teaching:

> First is love for God and to grant to my neighbor that which God has granted and given me for His praise and the salvation of my soul. Second is a devaluation and giving up of life unto death to suffer for

---

41. The rules proposed in Balthasar Hubmaier's *Axiomata* (1524) are cited in Yoder, "The Hermeneutics of the Anabaptists."

42. "Two Letters by Pilgram Marpeck," *Mennonite Quarterly Review* 32 (July 1958): 198.

the sake of Christ and the Gospel and all patience. Third, to realize when God unlocks or opens a door that one may enter the same with the teaching of the Gospel. No one shall open a door which God has not opened, in order that the office of the Holy Spirit remain His own and free. For He it is who opens and no one closes, He closes and no one opens, in order that the pearls not be cast before swine. . . . Fourth, that one be free and sound in teaching and judgments and in truth, in order that none speak unless Christ work through his Holy Spirit. . . . These four parts are the true proof that the compulsion is of the Holy Spirit; also that it brings forth fruit at each season.[43]

The criterion of willingness to suffer and even to die is particularly interesting, for our purposes, in that it is a clear acknowledgement of the potential connection between theological teaching and self-interest. Consequently, teaching that is clearly in disregard of one's own survival has greater warrant to be accepted as authentic. The fourth criterion, the freedom of the teacher, arose from Marpeck's reaction to teaching distorted by the attempt to maintain church-state unity.

I suggest that what we see here are social practices aimed at faithfulness (practical reason) and truth (pure reason), which adequately take account of the distorting influences of the will-to-power and, in the happy case, counteract it in a variety of ways: by listening to the least of the brethren (and sisters), by requiring unity, by deliberately favoring teaching that flies in the face of the will to survive. And all of this is taken to be a means of allowing the Holy Spirit (rather than self-interested individuals) to have the last word. While these practices were developed for practical decisions within the church, they are not irrelevant to scholarly enquiry, as their adaptation to the theological disputation demonstrates.

CONCLUSION

I began with an account of the divide between modern and postmodern intellectual assumptions, and suggested that much of what is called the postmodern condition is merely the effect of widespread awareness of intellectual problems created by those very modern assumptions. Thus, one could expect many such issues to dissolve as truly postmodern positions take their place.

One issue that will not dissolve is relativism: given a holist epistemology, the question will always arise of what one is to do when faced with competing, equally coherent wholes. Alasdair MacIntyre is one of few philosophers who have provided guidance for rational adjudication among competing "large-scale traditions," each of which incorporates its own account of the nature of rationality.

I have endorsed the conclusions of Hoedemaker and others that the passing of Enlightenment views of rationality provides as much promise as it

---

43. Ibid., 199.

does threat to Western Christianity. I have especially endorsed his call to seek for a new balance or synthesis between the Christian tradition(s) and newer versions of the tradition of Reason.

My proposal involved the synthesis of insights and practices from the Radical Reformation tradition with the epistemological contributions of MacIntyre. I have argued that these insights and practices remedy the most important defects in MacIntyre's account of rationality. In particular, I have argued that the power-renouncing practices of the Radical Christians reflect both a recognition of the role of the will-to-power in knowledge and an anti-dote to its distorting effects.

Along the way, I suggested that a variety of emphases found throughout the history of this minority Christian tradition could now be brought to the fore to produce a version of Christian faith and practice especially suited to challenging the assumptions and social structures of contemporary Western society—its militarism, its violence, and its consumption—while at the same time challenging the church's long-standing willingness to profit from the West's power and wealth.

CHAPTER SEVEN

The Trials of Truth

Mission, Martyrdom, and the Epistemology of the Cross

KEVIN J. VANHOOZER

INTRODUCTION

What might Christian theology have to contribute by way of response to the epistemological predicament of postmodernity? This essay explores a number of parallels and contrasts between the narrative of the trial of Jesus and the contemporary trial of truth by the postmodern masters of suspicion. The "trials of truth" signals, in the first place, the severe troubles faced by the concept of truth in contemporary culture and contemporary thought. Second, the notion of the "trials of truth" leads to a renewed appreciation of the role of the person in staking a claim. It also focuses on "testifying" as a speech act, rather than on restricting the discussion either to basic propositions or to justificatory procedures.

My goal is to offer an expansionist account of epistemology by thinking through its relation with ethics. This leads to a reflection on recent "virtue epistemologies" that highlight the role of intellectual virtues in achieving justified belief and that make wisdom rather than mere knowledge the ultimate goal of cognitive endeavor. Rationality, I argue, is a matter of developing epistemic virtue and wisdom rather than merely acquiring knowledge. Finally, a contrast of the trials of Socrates and Jesus brings my discussion of the intellectual virtues into relation with the so-called "theological virtues," highlights the importance of the concept of testimony, and clarifies the peculiar intellectual virtues associated with the "epistemology of the Cross."[1]

---

1. I offer these reflections in part to commemorate the 150th anniversary of the publication of Kierkegaard's "On the Difference between a Genius and an Apostle" (1847),

CRUSADE, PILGRIMAGE, OR MISSIONARY JOURNEY?

Knowledge claims are today poised unsteadily between epistemology, missiology, and ideology. A truth claim is a statement on a mission; to be precise, a statement on a mission of truth, whose goal is to procure universal acknowledgement.[2] The problem is how to construe the nature of this mission: is it heroic or hopeless? imperialistic or impotent? Will the claimant return covered in glory or empty-handed?

THE PROJECT: THE EVANGELICAL TRUTH CLAIM

The theologian's primary task is faithfully and intelligibly to render the claim that "God was in Christ reconciling the world to himself." But there is an important preliminary task as well. Today it is not discrete packages of truth content that need to be defended so much as the concept of truth itself. How can truth claims fulfill their mission in a postmodern world? Three intimidating obstacles bar the way to success: (1) *The problem of perspective and partiality*. What people see is affected by where they are standing, when they are living, why they are looking, and who they are. (2) *The problem of power*. Both propositions and the processes of legitimating them as knowledge are commonly seen as implicated in the material conditions of social life. That is, language and ideas intersect with and are complicated by relations of domination.[3] (3) *The problem of pluralism*. For many today, the one clear, distinct, and incontrovertibly true idea is that the contemporary situation is marked by rival truth claims that compete and conflict with one another. To some, it follows that truth is exclusive, and thus that claims to truth are necessarily oppressive. To others, it follows that truth must be inclusive, embracing all claims in its fulness.

In response to these and other problems, it has become fashionable to abandon talk about truth and to limit one's claims to justification instead.[4] This approach consigns authority either to a material norm (e.g., founda-

---

an essay that has proven to be of seminal value in regard to the conception of the present work.

2. Cf. Alistair McFayden, who argues that if something is true, it is true for everybody, and will be seen to be true once all the distortions and limitations of partiality are stripped away. "Truth as Mission: The Christian Claim to Universal Truth in a Pluralist Public World," *Scottish Journal of Theology* 46 (1993): 437–56.

3. See John B. Thompson, *Studies in the Theory of Ideology* (Cambridge: Polity Press, 1984). Later in this essay I shall contrast the postmodern tendency to link ideology to power relations with the biblical ideology of vulnerability and suffering.

4. Hilary Putnam is a good example of this trend: *"truth is not the bottom line*: truth itself gets its life from our criteria of rational acceptability." *Reason, Truth and History* (Cambridge University Press, 1981), 130. Kierkegaard would doubtless reply that if truth is neither more nor less than rational acceptability, then it's "good night, Christianity" (see his "On the Difference between a Genius and an Apostle," in Alter Lowrie and Alexander Druanda (eds.), *The Present Age and Two Minor Ethico-religious Treatises* (Oxford: Oxford University Press, 1940), esp. 139.

tional beliefs), to a rational procedure (e.g., tradition-based fallibilism), or to a reliable belief-forming mechanism (e.g., reliabilism). There is, however, considerable dispute over what it is that makes one's believing *right*. Moreover, to restrict one's epistemological mission to showing that one is entitled to hold certain beliefs removes one of the most important reasons for believing something, namely, *because it is true*. The Christian theologian must today show how truth is accessible and why truth matters.[5]

The Theologian's Task: To Stake a Claim about God

What is truth? According to William Alston, a proposition (what a statement asserts) is true if the world is the way the proposition says it is; if, that is, the state of affairs asserted *obtains*.[6] Jesus, one might say, is God's truth claim: the divine self-revelation in history, the Word above all words that can be relied on—the Word (a person rather than a proposition) whose life, death, and resurrection, taken together, display how things (ultimately) are (or will be).[7] The truth of Jesus Christ has a propositional component, summed up by his names—"Savior," "Messiah," "God with us"—and by the New Testament confession that "there is no other name under heaven by which one may be saved" (Acts 4:12). Specifically, Christian theology makes a truth claim about Jesus' passion: "God was in Christ . . . reconciling all things to himself" (Col. 1:20). I call this the "evangelical truth claim" and I contrast it with merely empirical or existential claims, for it is primarily a claim about the reality and activity of God.[8]

This theological claim arises from a tradition that ultimately goes back to the authors of the New Testament (viz., the apostolic preaching). Yet, it is also a universal truth claim, because it is a claim about the one Creator God and, hence, about the nature of ultimate reality.[9] The evangelical truth claim

---

5. William Alston offers an apology for the concept of truth, even for the epistemological purposes of justification, in his *A Realist Conception of Truth* (Ithaca and London: Cornell University Press, 1996), chapter 8. Truth matters, he says, "because it is important for us to determine what states of affairs obtain where that has a bearing on our practical or theoretical concerns" (235). It should be obvious that theological statements meet this latter requirement. Alston also argues in the same chapter that "Doing without truth leaves us without any way of framing an adequate concept of epistemic justification" (255). It is an important part of virtue epistemology that epistemic virtues are motivated by a desire for truth.

6. Alston names his theory a "minimalist realist theory of truth" because, while he maintains that truth is a matter of the relation between propositions and facts, he does not undertake to specify the nature of the correspondence relation between the two. See his *A Realist Conception of Truth*, chapter 1.

7. Bultmann famously commented that the riddle of the New Testament is how the proclaimer became the proclaimed. My view is similar, but slanted toward epistemology rather than homiletics: how did the truth-teller come to be identified with the truth itself?

8. As we shall see, this reference to God—the transcendent—is for Kierkegaard what sets the apostle, and the witness, apart from the philosopher-genius.

9. McFayden and Pannenberg both defend the universality of Christian truth claims

is thus a claim about *the meaning of the whole*. In order to do justice to the nature of theological truth claims, therefore, it will be necessary to recover two notions that have been rather neglected in contemporary epistemology: understanding (a grasp of meaning) and wisdom (an understanding of the whole).

How can we rationally commend Christian truth? Are theological truth claims inherently oppressive, in which case staking a truth claim would be like waging holy war? Is the apologist a crusader, with the cross emblazoned in crimson upon his breast? There is a real danger of making truth the instrument of power and of ideology, of turning the cross into "the swastika on our breasts." Perhaps we should rather think of theology as a pilgrimage, in which case staking a truth claim would be what happens at the end of a quest for the epistemological Holy Grail. On this model, we will exchange tales with our fellow pilgrims, and it is possible that our journey will lead to Birmingham rather than Canterbury, or to Delhi rather than Jerusalem.

Philosophy has traditionally been conceived as such a quest, in which the philosopher-pilgrim seeks wisdom. Theology, in my opinion, is different. An incarnational theology that confesses the Word made flesh contends that wisdom has found a way to us.[10] An apprentice of wisdom, theology now carries a double burden: to seek understanding (rendering faith for ourselves) and to share the good news (commending faith to others). I shall therefore picture the theologian neither as pilgrim nor crusader, but as an itinerant evangelist on a never-ending missionary journey. The task of the theologian is to make evangelical truth publicly accessible. I shall argue, however, that more will be involved in staking a truth claim than proclaiming it.

What Is at Stake: A Way of Wisdom

How can we make the idea of truth intelligible in an age rife with suspicion and cynicism? Today it is no longer enough merely to justify propositional truth claims. For what is at stake is the very concept of truth, that is, the notion that truth is meaningful and that truth matters. What Kierkegaard said of individuals can be stretched to apply to whole communities: what is needed in an apathetic age is a truth for which we can live and die. But before we can articulate this "saving" truth we need first to secure the very idea of truth. Truth matters because "truth is that on which we necessarily or ultimately rely."[11] The truth claims that will here

---

by appealing to monotheism: the unity of the world, even if it is an eschatological unity, ultimately finds its unity in God. Universality is implicit in what I have called the evangelical truth claim: God through Christ reconciles *all things* to himself.

10. This is yet another way of articulating what Kierkegaard saw as the crucial difference between the apostle and the genius: the apostle proclaims a message that is not a product of his own devising.

11. I am here adapting Rowan Williams's definition of metaphysics as the discourse

be of interest are those that are implicit in our way of life. This is another reason for redirecting epistemology toward wisdom rather than toward knowledge only.[12]

This expansionist approach to epistemology is in accord with Kierkegaard's view that philosophy, especially in its Greek origins, is not so much a subject as a way.[13] What is at stake in a theological truth claim, I contend, is whether we can gave an explicit account of those Christian convictions about the meaning of the whole that our most important practices implicitly presuppose. Articulating the meaningfulness of the idea of truth involves showing how truth claims are implicit in the way we live, in our commonsense practices—in what might be called our "metaphysical competence" (viz., wisdom).

A theological truth claim will be a statement about the meaning of the whole and, as such, will *matter to everyone.* Such a claim must involve propositions (objectivity) and passion (subjectivity). A theological truth claim will ultimately be about the Word of God and the difference it makes to human being. What is finally at stake in the epistemological crisis of Christian mission is the wisdom and way of Christ. As we shall see, to stake a theological truth claim is to undertake a missionary journey that, ultimately, involves both propositions and passion, and participates in the trinitarian "missions" of Son and Spirit.

Theology as Passion for Truth

Theology is the discipline that cultivates Christian wisdom and makes disciples. But surely, one might object, Christian theology has no monopoly on passion or truth, or on wisdom for that matter. Jesus and Socrates alike aim at inculcating wisdom in their followers. In what comes next, therefore, we shall have to be sensitive to what, if any, difference there may be between philosophical and theological truth claims. An examination of the respective trials of Socrates and Jesus may prove to be of help in this regard. For the moment, let us define theology as the discipline that trains disciples how to render for themselves and commend to others (1) the utter reliability of the Word of God; (2) the meaning and truth of the claim that "God was in Christ reconciling all things to himself"; (3) the wisdom of the Cross.

---

about the underlying intelligible structure of our commitments, "what constitutes them as more than arbitrarily willed options." Cf. his "Between Politics and Metaphysics: Reflections in the Wake of Gillian Rose," *Modern Theology* 11 (1995): 6.

12. The Christian way may involve countercultural wisdom (e.g., the first being last and the last being first) but this is not the same as irrationality. It may well be, however, that the apostle will appear less like a genius and more like a fool (though of the Shakespearean variety).

13. So David J. Gouwens, *Kierkegaard as Religious Thinker* (Cambridge: Cambridge University Press, 1996), 28.

The Challenge: Trial by Nietzsche

Staking a theological truth claim requires a three-dimensional strategy. There is first a negative moment of exposing the beliefs of my conversation partners (call it "the moment of truth"), a moment that may involve naming the idols (e.g., ideology critique). This corresponds to the Socratic "examining." There follows a positive moment where one seeks understanding by establishing one's own reading of reality. With this second stage, one effectively stakes a claim about how things are. Finally, one gives an account of how the evangelical truth claim can be rationally established and, if need be, defended. It follows from the nature of the claim, however, that the person making it, as well as the proposition, must also be tried and tested. The present essay focuses on the third of these stages.[14]

In the first part of this volume the contemporary epistemological predicament has been set out. To that general sketch I now wish to add a few concrete conversation partners. This is better than debating with straw men; there is little virtue in staking truth claims in undisputed territory. I will therefore stake my claim on ground contested by Van Harvey, an historian and representative of modernity's passion for the truth (e.g., autonomy, criticism), and Nietzsche, representing postmodernity's hyperbolic hermeneutics, for whom there are no facts, only interpretations. Both Harvey and Nietzsche have tried traditional ways of staking the evangelical truth claim and found them wanting.

Van Harvey's *The Historian and the Believer* represents one of the most powerful modern challenges to the evangelical truth claim.[15] Harvey believes that rational thinkers should be committed to an ideal of judgment which is also a morality of knowledge. Rationality for Harvey is a matter of doing one's intellectual duty. He appeals to the metaphor of the law court and casts the historian in the role of a prosecuting attorney who cross-examines witnesses and tears their stories apart.

For his part, Nietzsche represents a hermeneutics of extreme suspicion, for whom all truth claims are really reflexes of the will-to-power. He contends that Christians inhabit a fictional world rooted in the hatred of everything natural and life-enhancing. The idea that one has to die in order to live is for him the denial of reality. Nietzsche represents an explicitly anti-

---

14. I have rather freely adapted a model drawn from ancient biblical hermeneutics: *explicatio* (unfolding the hidden theological presuppositions that undergird one's interpretation of the world), *meditatio* (establishing one's interpretation of reality by reflecting on parts in the light of the whole), and *applicatio* (applying the interpretation by demonstrating its practical implications). My method thus includes the three moments that John Frame calls offense (exposing belief/unbelief), proof (presenting a basis for belief), and defense (answering objections to belief) in his *Apologetics to the Glory of God: An Introduction* (Phillipsburg, NJ: Presbyterian & Reformed Publishing, 1994). It is also similar to the development of a chess game, with opening moves, consolidated middle position, and an end game.

15. Van Harvey, *The Historian and the Believer: The Morality of Historical Knowledge and Christian Belief* (Philadelphia: Westminster Press, 1966).

Christian interpretation of reality, and in particular a misreading of the cross of Christ. In attacking truth in general and Christian truth in particular, therefore, Nietzsche stakes an important countertheological claim.

My last dialogue partner is, appropriately enough, Socrates. We have already seen that Socrates stands for philosophy's independent attempt to cultivate the way of wisdom, to reach the truth about the whole by means of unaided reason. He too is engaged in mission (so too, for that matter, are Harvey and Nietzsche). Socrates represents both philosophy's passion for truth and its sustained examination of every claim to truth. Accordingly, Socrates symbolizes both rationality's constitutive principle and its intrinsic limitations.

EXPOSITORY EPISTEMOLOGY

As its name indicates, this methodological first step *exposes* belief (Latin *exponere*, "to put out"). It is a preeminently postmodern move, but postmoderns were hardly the first to make it.[16] Indeed, Socrates exemplifies this negative hermeneutic of suspicion, for he too, like Nietzsche and the postmoderns, is concerned to expose what is falsely called knowledge.

Expository epistemology aims to uncover one's ultimate beliefs or presuppositions. The theologian takes Bultmann's hermeneutical maxim—exegesis without presuppositions is impossible—and translates it into epistemology: behavior without belief is impossible. Rowan Williams has recently defined metaphysics as the attempt to clarify those basic insights into the nature of the real to which our practice commits us.[17] What is to be examined and exposed are those commitments about the way things are which are implied in our most familiar and important practices. If we ask why these practices are other than arbitrary, the discussion quickly becomes metaphysical. Expository epistemology must include a "hermeneutics of practices." In short, the transcendental question—what are the necessary conditions of this way of life?— exposes that on which one's belief, or suspicion, is ultimately grounded.

Socrates' expository method is grounded in his sense of mission: to show people who think they are wise that they are not. The goal of the typical Socratic dialogues is to demonstrate that Socrates' interlocutors do not actually know "the most important things" they think they know (e.g., what is holiness, goodness, knowledge, justice, etc.). Socrates puts his dialogue partners to the critical test and finds them wanting. This epistemological method is the subject of Kierkegaard's study, *The Concept of Irony, with Constant Reference to Socrates*.[18] Socrates feigns ignorance in order to show the wise

---

16. John W. Cooper rightly reminds us that twentieth-century Dutch Calvinists (e.g., Cornelius Van Til, Hermann Dooyeweerd) had earlier challenged the alleged neutrality and autonomy of human reason ("Reformed Apologetics and the Challenge of Post-Modern Relativism," *Calvin Theological Journal* 28 [1993]: 108–20).

17. Williams, "Beyond Politics and Metaphysics," 3–22.

18. Kierkegaard, *The Concept of Irony* (Princeton, NJ: Princeton University Press, 1989).

that they are not really wise about "the things that really matter." For Kierkegaard, the irony of this epistemology is more a quality of Socrates' person than of any single argument. It is Socrates' ignorance that challenges knowledge, offers no answers, and then claims to make wise. For Kierkegaard, Socrates' epistemological midwifery is "infinite negativity": Socrates prepares the way for the truth by deconstructing the false opinions of those who think themselves wise.

Nietzsche also uses irony to question assured beliefs.[19] Like Socrates, he wants to show his readers that they do not really know "the most important things." Whereas in verbal irony one does not say what one really means, in what I call *metaphysical irony* one does not really believe that one's concepts and theories actually correspond to the world. Humans are "all too human" either to know God or to know as gods.

Unlike Socrates, however, Nietzsche was persuaded of the fundamentally nonrational character of the world and of human life. In this he anticipated the postmodern preoccupation with the "all too human." What is left of epistemology in postmodernity is rationality among the ruins. Socrates and Nietzsche yield only an ironic wisdom concerning the limits of reason, a "wisdom" that ultimately undoes the picture of knowledge as justified true belief. Philosophical examination in the mode of irony instead becomes never-ending critique.[20]

Nietzsche and his contemporary followers believe that religion is an imaginative projection that sacrifices the truth that all is metaphorical projection and interpretation for a lie. He assumes the prophetic mantle against Christianity and presents himself as the defender of the truth: namely, that the world is not a good creation but a field of conflicting forces without any inherent structure of final purpose. Ironically enough, Nietzsche speaks as if he knows what the truth is (e.g., *not* Christianity). Absolute suspicion, like absolute skepticism, is impossible in practice. What we have in Nietzsche and his ilk is finally an apologist for *another* faith. Unlike much modern Christian apologetics, I am concerned in the first instance to expose not *unbelief*, but rather *alternative* control beliefs. The risk of offending, however, is perhaps just as great, for no one likes to be shown to be inconsistent or idolatrous (or metaphysical!). Yet this is the aim of this initial expository

---

19. Friedrich Schlegel's definition summed up the Romantic variation of irony popular in the late eighteenth and nineteenth centuries: "the recognition of the fact that the world in its essence is paradoxical and that an ambivalent attitude alone can grasp its contradictory totality" (cited in René Wellek, *A History of Modern Criticism (1750–1950): The Romantic Age* [New Haven: Yale University Press, 1955], 14).

20. In the light of Kierkegaard's analysis, we might venture to suggest that the deepest irony in Socrates, and perhaps in all philosophy, is that it seeks infinity within human being itself. As we shall see, Kierkegaard associates Socrates with the religion of immanence. Perhaps irony is the inevitable result of an approach that seeks transcendence through introspection. The question that Kierkegaard poses is whether the philosopher can ever get beyond immanence, that is, whether the philosopher can ever know more than his own mind.

work: to make explicit the fundamental commitments to which our most important practices implicitly bind us.

HERMENEUTICAL EPISTEMOLOGY: READING REALITY

Expository epistemology must be balanced by a positive moment (from *ponere*, "to put [forward]") that establishes one's own position.

WHY HERMENEUTICS?

"Positive" has another meaning as well. The core beliefs of Christianity are "positive" in the sense that they are grounded not on universal reason but on testimony to specific historical figures and events (e.g., revelation). The scandal of the cross is epistemological, at least in part, and follows from the positivity and particularity of the Gospel. Yet, it is precisely this positivity that, according to Kierkegaard, gives rise to the difference between the apostle and the genius. The nature of the theological truth claim is such that neither its source nor its norm can be located in the sphere of immanence, i.e., "within the limits of reason alone."

There are a number of reasons for discussing theological truth claims under the rubric of hermeneutics. First, hermeneutics is a viable alternative to the either-or of objectivism and relativism. Objectivism is the belief that there is some permanent framework to which we can appeal in determining the nature of rationality, knowledge, truth, and rightness. An objectivist might say that philosophy's job is to identify and defend the objective structures of reality and rationality alike. My counterthesis is that, while we may not have such a universal framework, we do have a number of relatively adequate frameworks for this enterprise.[21] As Ricoeur puts it, we must choose between absolute knowledge and hermeneutics. Our age is one that acknowledges the theory-ladenness of data, the "impurity" of reason. It is increasingly difficult to take seriously those who maintain that their thought is free of cultural, historical, and linguistic conditioning. Yet, we can continue to stake theological truth claims in the hermeneutical age of reason.

Second, hermeneutics is perhaps the discipline that best corresponds to the nature of a theological truth claim, not only because the latter concerns biblical testimony, but because it deals with the *meaning of the whole*. Hermeneutics thus allows us to recover a neglected theme in epistemology, namely, understanding.[22] This involves leaving behind "the Cartesian per-

---

21. I am thinking here not only of diverse disciplinary perspectives, but also of the diverse literary forms of biblical discourse, each of which constitutes a way of experiencing and seeing the world. See my "Language, Literary Hermeneutics, and Biblical Theology: What's Theological about a Theological Dictionary?" in Willem A. VanGemeren (ed.), *The New International Dictionary of Old Testament Theology and Exegesis* (Grand Rapids: Zondervan, 1997), vol. 1, chapter 1.

22. Linda Trinkaus Zagzebski observes that contemporary epistemology neglects both understanding and wisdom. When understanding is mentioned, she says, it is usually

spective," in which the focus is on the single beliefs of a single person and the goal is to attain propositional knowledge.[23] On the other hand, understanding, according to Linda Zagzebski, "is not a state directed toward a single propositional object at all. . . . One understands p as part of . . . one's understanding of the whole pattern of a whole chunk of reality."[24]

To see knowledge as a form of interpretation, then, is to *expand* and *enrich* the traditional notion of epistemology. It allows us, moreover, to reclaim the imagination—the capacity to see things together in terms of whole patterns. This self-conscious appropriation of the imagination is crucial, for the most intimidating obstacle to the Christian apologist is not this or that argument, but rather the monolithic secular culture or framework that has taken thought captive to a flattened-out naturalism that pretends to be comprehensive. In sum, a hermeneutical model of reasoning allows both for a negative and for a positive moment in one's theology (e.g., exposing and proposing), as well as for critical testing, as we shall see in due course.[25]

Text and Interpretation as Epistemological Concepts

The world has rightly been called the Book of Nature. For those who subscribe to naturalism, the world does not mean anything, it just is; for others, however, including Christians, the world cries out for interpretation. Nietzsche portrays with insight human beings as "*homo hermeneuticus*, an organism that invariably and necessarily interprets," though he mistakenly denies that interpretation can be a form of knowledge.[26] Knowledge in the hermeneutical age of reason may be a context-dependent affair, relative to paradigms and frameworks, though in a critically realist account it is nonetheless knowledge for that.

According to Martin Buber, however, it is Christianity that gives the world hermeneutics, that is, the confidence that there is a correct interpre-

---

identified with a minimal grasp of the sense of an isolated proposition. My definition of theological truth claims as claims about the meaning of the whole enable me to amend both of these oversights. In this section, the focus is on understanding, but in the penultimate section, the "epistemology of the cross," I shall return to the theme of wisdom. See Zagzebski, *Virtues of the Mind: An Inquiry into the Nature of Virtue and the Ethical Foundations of Knowledge* (Cambridge: Cambridge University Press, 1996), 43–51.

23. For an account and critique of "the Cartesian perspective," see Jonathan Kvanvig, *The Intellectual Virtues and the Life of the Mind* (Lanham, MD: Rowman & Littlefield, 1992), 181–82.

24. Zagzebski, *Virtues of the Mind*, 49. It is important to add that the "whole" that understanding grasps is not simply a matter of theory or of propositions, but includes different kinds of facts and contexts. Hermeneutics is also holistic in the sense that it looks at the speech act as a whole, and not only at its propositional content.

25. I am here correlating expository theology with the hermeneutics of suspicion, and positive theology with the hermeneutics of belief.

26. Karen L. Carr, *The Banalization of Nihilism: Twentieth-Century Responses to Meaninglessness* (Albany: SUNY Press, 1992), 28.

tation of the Word, and of the world: *God's* interpretation. The Word of God is, for Christians, the basic text that provides the lenses through which one seeks to understand God, the world, and oneself. The revelation of God in Christ, together with the witness of Scripture, generates a distinctively Christian worldview. This basic text provides concepts for the descriptive task of understanding the "most important things" and imperatives for the prescriptive task of living them out.

A worldview is a comprehensive interpretation of individual, social, and cosmic reality, of the "meaning" (the origin, nature, and destiny) of life. Let me propose yet another definition of theology as *the reflective and active rendering of the Christian interpretation of reality*.[27] The Christian interpretation of reality is a function of its interpretation of Scripture, of those books set aside as authoritative testimony to the Gospel. We may call it a philosophy of "canonical sense." It is the sum total of the biblical books, the various parts in their interrelatedness, that communicates the wisdom of the Christian way, which is the wisdom of Christ and the wisdom of the cross. Faith in the God of Israel and of Jesus Christ commits Christians to a supreme interpretive norm: the Scriptures.

Yet, all attempts to secure this canonical norm philosophically are bound to fail. So, while one may have an absolute commitment to Christ, one need not be committed to a single conceptual scheme: objective truth need not entail objectivism. A hermeneutical theology neither aspires after certainty nor rests content with faith, but makes a case for or against various proposed interpretations of that to which our most important Christian practices, generated by Scripture, ultimately commit us.

The only kind of fideism to which I might subscribe, therefore, would be a *hermeneutical fideism*. This is not a statement that "I believe in order to avoid thinking," nor "I believe in order to lord it over others," nor "I believe in order to immunize myself from criticism," but rather "I believe *in order to understand*."[28] What we, as theologians who stake truth claims, are exposing and proposing is ultimately the rationale for our beliefs and actions. Hermeneutical theology is about the justification of the ways of wisdom that are generated by and embodied in our canonical texts and community practices.

---

27. Note that this entails a new definition of truth as well: truth is God's interpretation of reality. Cf. Kant's tacit understanding of the noumenal as the object of God's knowledge (*Critique of Pure Reason*, B 72).

28. I shall return to fideism toward the end of the essay and ask whether the *Shorter Oxford* definition is correct: "A mode of thought in which knowledge is based on a fundamental act of faith." Kierkegaard's distinction of the apostle from the genius obliges us to ask whether it is rational to believe what the apostle tells us. Can fideism—the position that religious truth is based on faith rather than evidence or a process of reasoning—nevertheless be rational?

TRAINING IN IMAGINATION: CULTIVATING CHRISTIAN PHRONESIS

"Christianity is praxis, a character task." (Kierkegaard)[29]

It may help to understand the implications of the above saying if we sum up the argument to this point. I have argued that formulating and defending the Christian worldview is like interpreting a text. We expose our presuppositions and we propose an interpretation, a way of describing, knowing full well that there are other interpretations that arise from other perspectives. How, then, do we cope with the conflict of interpretations?

Nietzsche thought that, because religion was an imaginative projection, it was necessarily false. Ironically, the self-proclaimed champion of creativity turns out to have a low view of the imagination. Imaginative projections are fictive constructions and do not correspond to the way things are. His criterion for preferring one interpretation rather than another had to do with its "life-value" (does it enhance life?), not its truth value. In contrast, I argue for a perspectival realism: the imagination, formed and guided by the canon, may be an organ of truth. *It may be that some of our perspectives— the biblical "wordviews" to be exact—allow us to imagine reality rightly.* The worldview one holds, however, is a matter of one's moral and spiritual dispositions as well as one's cultural and linguistic position. A world view, that is, is not merely an intellectual tool, but the product of an intellectual outlook which, I shall argue, is ultimately a matter of ethics, even spirituality.

Right interpretation depends not only on having the right procedures, but on having the right habits of perception as well as a desire to understand the whole.[30] We often need to be trained in order to perceive things correctly. Theology both announces past fact (indicative) and draws our attention to what should follow from it (imperative). The intelligibility of the claim, however, is a matter of both theory and practice. To stake a theological truth claim ultimately demands practical reasoning, something akin to Aristotle's *phronesis*. It is a matter of grasping the significance of the biblical story and of the contemporary situation, so that we know what a particular situation requires of us as persons staking the evangelical truth claim.

Thus, staking theological truth claims is a product neither of instrumental nor of speculative reason, but of practical reason: a type of reasoning about moral action and a type of reasoning for which one may be held morally responsible.[31] Indeed, according to some recent virtue epistemolo-

---

29. Cited in Gouwens, *Kierkegaard as Religious Thinker*, 209.

30. A hermeneutical model oriented to understanding and right interpretation can easily assimilate commonly cited epistemological criteria: personal disclosure value, empirical fit, logical coherence, to name but a few. Rationality in hermeneutics, as in science, is a matter of submitting one's interpretation to critical tests in a free and open conversation. It is this willingness to submit one's interpretation to critical tests that prevents hermeneutical theology from becoming an irrational fideism.

31. Paul Helm suggests that *believing* too can be a species of practical reason: "The practice of believing may be considered a means of gaining a chosen end, the possession of the truth." See *Belief Policies* (Cambridge: Cambridge University Press, 1994), 143.

gists, rationality just is a form of being moral—of ethics applied to the intellect—a point to which I shall return below.[32]

The above leads me to my major thesis in this section: *theology in a post-modern context must reorient itself to wisdom rather than to knowledge.* Wisdom, I believe, is the means of integrating what modernity and post-modernity alike have torn asunder: metaphysics and morals, theory and practice, fact and value. Wisdom is a matter of knowing certain things but also of making one's knowledge fruitful. It is a matter of being able appropriately to apply truth to the matter at hand. Wisdom provides an effective means for integrating seeing and doing, judging and acting. The wise person knows what to do in a given situation; the wise person understands. Wisdom thus provides a way of integrating universals and particulars. Truth and metaphysics return to postmodernity on this view not as correlates of *episteme* or theoretical reasoning, but rather as correlates of *phronesis*.

Scripture, inasmuch as it trains the imagination and generates interpretive frameworks for describing experience, is the central means for cultivating Christian *phronesis*. The task of the Christian theologian is to demonstrate the rational superiority of the Christian way and Christian wisdom in whatever situation one finds oneself. One who would stake a theological truth claim, then, must show that its descriptions and prescriptions make wise unto creation. What the theologian ultimately proves, I submit, *is not so much the existence but the wisdom of God.*[33]

Can Christian truth claims be verified? Not, perhaps, according to *episteme* or *techne*. There is no proof or process that can conclusively verify a theological truth claim. If reason were ultimately the judge of revelation, says Kierkegaard, then "God and the Apostle have to wait at the gate, or in the porter's lodge, till the learned upstairs have settled the matter."[34] There may nevertheless be a kind of verification in the domain of practical reason or *phronesis*. We verify or corroborate biblical wisdom in situations where, in the light of a Christian vision of the whole, we are able to act well.

Disputes with non-Christians about how to live well usually turn on competing descriptions of the situation in which we find ourselves. The theologian offers biblical perspectives on the world. Those who wish to stake theological truth claims must show that folly follows the bad descriptions of an atrophied imagination: e.g., descriptions of sexual intercourse as a merely physical encounter and bodily movements, or of justice as the will of

---

I further explore the ethical dimensions of epistemology below.

32. See, e.g., Linda Zagzebski, "The place of Phronesis in the Methodology of Theology," in Stephen T. Davis (ed.), *Philosophy and Theological Discourse* (New York: St. Martin's Press, 1997), 204–23; James A. Montmarquet, *Epistemic Virtue and Doxastic Responsibility* (Lanham, MD: Rowman & Littlefield, 1993).

33. Belief in the existence of God may be a necessary component of the evangelical truth claim, but it is hardly sufficient: "even the demons believe and tremble" (Jas. 2:19). Assent to propositions, in other words, is not yet wisdom. I discuss below the question of whether one can be held culpable for unbelief in God.

34. Kierkegaard, "On the Difference between a Genius and an Apostle," 148.

the majority. If theology is the discourse that articulates the underlying intelligible structure of our commitment to the Christian way, truth, and life, the "proof" of its nonarbitrariness is in "following the argument where it leads." We begin to understand and to commend theological claims only as we begin to take up our Procrustean beds and walk. In short, acquiring wisdom is the payoff of Christian interpretations.

One cannot force the truth on others. This is the crusader model of staking a claim, and it does not work. Theological knowledge is ultimately gained through obedient action (John 7:17). Again, right imagination is needed for right action; *phronesis* is a matter of seeing well and doing well. We can only fit into a situation appropriately if we are able to envision it aright. The imagination, the faculty of perceiving the whole, is an integral ingredient in wisdom. The wise person relates to God, the world, and others in a way that is fitting, and hence in a manner that leads to human flourishing (and to the glory of God): "In all that he (she) does, he (she) prospers" (Ps. 1:3).

Theories, worldviews, and the like can be tested and tried to see if they are progressing or degenerating: "You shall know them by their fruits." Pannenberg comments: "All interpretation, whether private or official, is measured against the truth of the subject matter, which is not decided by any one expositor but in the process of the expository debate."[35] True enough. And yet, when it comes to examining a theological truth claim (the Christian way), the ultimate test is not debate but a trial of life and death. Christian wisdom is fruit-conducive.[36]

AN EPISTEMOLOGY OF THE CROSS: THE WITNESS TO WISDOM

To this point, I have argued that theology's task is to read reality rightly, with the goal of showing how human beings may fit in or relate to it for their own good and for the glory of God. But can we really dignify this hermeneutical approach with the epithet "epistemology"? Is it possible rationally to justify the evangelical truth claim? The obstacles to doing so appear formidable. Who, after all, is in a position to know whether "God was in Christ reconciling all things to himself"? And, in a pluralistic world, why should we attend to the Christian testimony about the meaning of the whole (assuming there is one) any more than any other?

I began this essay by asking what Christian theology could contribute to the project of staking truth claims, given the contemporary epistemological predicament. Surely I am not suggesting that theology, which is a specific academic discipline with a peculiar remit and a very distinct subject matter, has something to say to epistemology in general about how to sort out

---

35. Wolfhart Pannenberg, *Systematic Theology*, vol. 1 (Grand Rapids: Eerdmans, 1991), 15.

36. Note the intimate connection between ethics and epistemology. As we shall see below, an intellectual virtue is epistemically privileged because it is truth-conducive. Conversely, wisdom is ethically privileged because it is fruit-conducive.

knowledge from opinion or to justify belief? Athens and Jerusalem we know, but the epistemologist is apt to be as incredulous as Nathanael and ask, "Can anything good come out of Nazareth?" (John 1:46). The simple answer is, "Yes, Jesus Christ."

Jesus associates his own person and work with the concept of truth in the clearest possible way: "My task is to bear witness to the truth" (John. 18:37). A consideration of the narrative of Jesus, and especially of his trials, yields an enriched account of what is involved in making, and staking, truth claims.[37] In the Christian tradition, testimony is a way of knowing, and the Greek term for one who testifies—*martyr*—catches both the aspect of "giving witness" to and "giving one's life" for the truth. Martyrdom, I shall contend, is ultimately what is required in staking a theological truth claim, for it is the whole speech act of testifying, and not only the proposition, that ultimately communicates truth claims about the way of wisdom. The martyr's witness responds both to the postmodern critique of traditional modes of justification and to the postmodern indifference toward the concept of truth.

I shall be particularly interested, therefore, in noting the ways in which martyrdom contributes to a virtue-based epistemology. I shall contrast the respective trials of Socrates and Jesus in order to consider the objection that a martyrological approach is neither unique to theology nor truth-conducive, since passionate commitment alone is an insufficient criterion of rationality ("The fanatic you shall always have with you"). Before I can show how theology qualifies epistemology, however, it is necessary to introduce the notion of an intellectual virtue.

Virtue Epistemology and the Desire for Truth

Virtue epistemology may be said to begin with the insight that we are responsible for what we believe. Since believing is something we do, it is subject to evaluation; it can be right or wrong, done poorly or done well. A virtue is an acquired excellence and involves "a characteristic motivation to produce a desired end and reliable success in bringing about that end."[38] It was Aristotle who first distinguished the intellectual from the moral virtues.[39] The intellectual virtues differ from their moral counterparts in two important respects: (1) they

---

37. My wager in what follows is that just as a study of biblical interpretation yields insights for general hermeneutics, so an examination of what is involved in making a theological truth claim yields dividends for epistemology in general. Theology's contribution to the discussion is best seen, I contend, if one espouses virtue epistemology, though this is hardly the only reason to subscribe to such an approach. Nevertheless, virtue epistemology appears to be especially well suited to staking the evangelical truth claim, provided that epistemology is informed by the properly theological virtues as well (see below). To anticipate: if, as Montmarquet says, "the epistemic virtues turn out to be qualities that a truth-desiring person would *want* to have" (*Epistemic Virtue and Doxastic Responsibility*, viii), might not the epistemic virtues be more completely displayed by qualities of a person with a *passion* for the truth?

38. Zagzebski, *Virtues of the Mind*, 137.

39. Cf. his *Nicomachean Ethics*, book 6. It is important to note, however, that virtue

arise from the general motivation for truth, and (2) they cultivate habits that reliably attain the aims of this motive.

Virtue epistemology aims to elucidate the normative element in believing: i.e., what makes believing *right*. The basic idea, roughly, is that truth is acquired through acts of intellectual virtue.[40] An intellectual virtue—such as open-mindedness, conscientiousness, and impartiality—is one that is conducive to knowledge and truth, that is, to "cognitive contact with reality."[41] It begins with the desire to attain truth. According to Zagzebski, "The motive for truth is a component of epistemic goodness."[42] It is important not to confuse an intellectual virtue with an intellectual skill: the latter is a capacity, the former an excellence. Moreover, a virtue is a character trait: a deep and enduring acquired excellence that is learned primarily by imitating virtuous persons.[43] Epistemic virtues, then, are traits of character "generally conducive to the discovery of truth, irrespective of subject matter."[44]

The concept of an intellectual virtue thus focuses on persons rather than processes and contends that virtue is the most useful criterion for determining the rightness of an act (ethics) or of a belief (epistemology).[45] A belief is justified, in other words, when it is held by a person with epistemic virtue: "An 'epistemically responsible' person, then, will be *trying* (his or her best) to arrive at the truth and to avoid error."[46] It follows, then, that justification—that extra something that makes a belief *right*—is a secondary trait that emerges from the primary, inner traits of persons of intellectual virtue.[47]

epistemologists dispute Aristotle's claim that intellectual virtues differ from their moral counterparts in kind. Both Zagzebski and Montmarquet, for instance, argue that rationality is a way of being moral, and that morality and rationality alike should be governed by *phronesis*. See Zagzebski, *Virtues of the Mind*, 137–58, and Montmarquet, *Epistemic Virtue*, chapter 2.

40. Montmarquet offers the following definition: "S is justified in believing p insofar as S is epistemically virtuous in believing p" (*Epistemic Virtue*, 99).

41. Zagzebski, *Virtues of the Mind*, 168. Note here the definition of "knowledge" as "a state of cognitive contact with reality arising out of acts of intellectual virtues" (270). Note also that virtue is a "success" term that refers to a competence to achieve a result (e.g., the competence to arrive at true beliefs).

42. Zagzebski, "The Place of Phronesis," 209.

43. Zagzebski doubts that the virtues can be learned through following rules or procedures. It is better to be apprenticed to those who have the virtue, or what is second best, to read narratives about such persons (181).

44. Montmarquet, *Epistemic Virtue*, 19.

45. Cf. Ernest Sosa, "The Raft and the Pyramid: Coherence versus Foundations in the Theory of Knowledge," in *Studies in Epistemology*, Midwest Studies in Philosophy 5 (Notre Dame: University of Notre Dame Press, 1980) and "Knowledge and Intellectual Virtue," *Monist* 68 (1985): 226–45, for earlier statements of the proposal that epistemologists focus on intellectual virtue (the property of a person) rather than on properties of belief (e.g., foundationalism) or of rational procedures (e.g., coherentism).

46. Montmarquet, *Epistemic Virtue*, 21.

47. How do we know which personal traits are truth-conducive? Why, for instance, are lucky guesses not epistemic virtues? Zagzebski believes it is because guessing is not a reliable procedure for producing true beliefs. Moreover, "An awareness of the unreliability of guessing is something within my sphere of responsibility." (The Place of

For my purposes, virtue epistemology highlights one especially notewor-
thy idea, namely, that epistemology is an affair of the heart. Everything
begins with a desire for truth. As we shall see, however, this desire by itself
does not suffice for rationality. Nevertheless, it has been said that genius is
nine-tenths passion. Certainly a passion for the truth is a requisite when it
comes to the knowledge of God, for this is an affair which engages the
whole person: "You shall love the Lord your God with all your heart, and
with all your soul, and with all your mind" (Matt 22:37). Insofar as there
is an incipient epistemology implicit in Scripture, it is one that deals not only
with the head but with the core of one's personal being: "For a man believes
with his heart and so is justified" (Rom. 10:10). Virtue epistemology thus
has the merit of admitting long-neglected factors back into the conversation
about knowledge, truth, and rationality.

THE EPISTEMOLOGY OF THE CROSS AND THE EPISTEMOLOGY OF GLORY

It is but a short step from the notion of epistemic virtue to that of epistemic
vice or noetic sin. One besetting epistemic vice is intellectual pride: the tendency to think too highly of one's arguments or conclusions. Theologians in
particular should beware what we might call, after Luther, an "epistemology of glory": the belief that human beings, through their native powers of
ratiocination and intellectual works, can achieve knowledge of God (and
thus of the evangelical truth claim).[48] Kierkegaard's careful distinction
between a genius and an apostle could likewise be taken as an attack on an
epistemology of glory and on the idea that one can "by reason find out
God."[49] The glory of the genius shines only in the realm of immanence, and
that only for a time; the genius is simply the first to discover what humanity
will eventually learn anyway as it develops.

An epistemology of glory is a strategy for self-transcendence whereby a
knower surmounts his or her own subjectivity by means of some process
(justification) that purges beliefs of the wrong kind of supports. For instance,
modern philosophy tended in its heyday to equate Reason with a God's-eye

---

Phronesis," 209). Which processes are reliable? This is determined by "the nature of the
believer and the 'fit' between the believer and the knowable world" (210). Montmarquet
concurs: the epistemic virtues are qualities that a truth-desiring person, given the conditions that obtain in the world, would want to emulate (*Epistemic Virtue*, 30).

48. An "epistemology of the cross" is implicit in Luther's "theology of the cross." In
his *Heidelberg Disputation* (1518) he contrasts Scholasticism's natural theology with his
own attempt to know God through God's self-revelation in the life, work, and especially
death of Christ. Luther's contrast of the two epistemologies is his way of pointing up the
differences between philosophy and theology as ways of knowing God. My own adaptation of Luther's phrase, developed below, puts the accent in a slightly different place,
namely, on the importance for epistemology of the theological virtues (including humility) and of discipleship.

49. The notion of epistemic virtue provides another way of drawing this distinction.
The genius is one gifted with intellectual skills; being an apostle—one who believes on
reliable authority and responsibly gives testimony—is not so much a matter of intellectual skills as intellectual (and moral) virtue.

point of view. The more muted postmodern epistemology of glory is content with the severely limited transcendence of intersubjectivity, that is, communities can achieve what the individual cannot ("it takes a village . . ."). But is community consensus sufficient insurance against the possibility that our beliefs are anything more than mass opinion? It is widely believed that either the quality of the evidence or the process of testing it justifies belief. But who, and what, guarantees the evidence and the justificatory procedures?

Paul Helm suggests that belief policies are not themselves determined by evidence (or by procedures of justification), but are rather a matter of choice, and are thus subject to the possibility of weakness of will and self-deception. An example of a weak will, says Helm, is "when a person does not believe when there is good reason to believe."[50] Hence, it is not enough to want to avoid error; one has to love the truth more than one's own ideas. Pascal notes that everyone has an aversion for the truth in different degrees "because it is inseparable from self-love."[51]

One displays a distinct lack of virtue, for example, by ignoring the evidence. Moreover, according to Montmarquet, such ignorance results not in bliss but in blameworthiness. Virtue epistemology provides a fascinating lens through which to read familiar passages such as Romans 1:18–23. The apostle Paul speaks of those who "by their wickedness suppress the truth" (v. 18). Though what can be known of God is plain, leaving unbelievers without excuse, the crucial evidence was neglected, apparently for moral as much as for intellectual reasons. False beliefs arise not only from error, but from "leaving undone the things we ought to have done." It would appear that Luther's *simul iustus et peccator* has important epistemological implications, applying to philosophers and theologians alike.

Justifying belief is not an impersonal intellectual procedure but is rather a person-relative process. Different people work with contrasting styles of assessment; for instance, willing believers have a lower threshold of justification. Helm views the adoption of a belief policy as an action for which individuals are responsible.[52] After considering the skepticism of Sextus Empiricus, Helm formulates the following belief policy: *believe only what keeps you from disquiet or anxiety.*[53] Now it is an open question whether belief in God fosters peace or disquiet. To many, like Nietzsche, the notion of a creator-redeemer God is distinctly unsettling (cf. Sartre's belief that the choice was between "either God or human freedom").

The volitional component in belief policies may explain why the most intransigent resistance to Christian truth claims is located not on the plane of intellectual argument so much as on the ethical level. Unbelievers resist,

---

50. Helm, *Belief Policies*, 148. Helm does not explicitly relate his account to virtue-based epistemology (though see 4), but the connection is easily made. Self-deception, for instance, is ethically qualified ignorance; it is an intellectual vice. It would be interesting to rethink Helm's account of belief policies in terms of Zagzebski's account of the intellectual virtues. Unfortunately, neither author seems aware of the other.

51. Cited in Zagzebski, *Virtues of the Mind*, 147.

52. Helm, *Belief Policies*, 164.

53. Ibid., 159–60.

sometimes culpably, theological truth claims. To be fair, however, we should acknowledge that perhaps the biggest single reason for resisting the evangelical truth-claim is Christians themselves, because of the way in which they stake the claim. The most frequent objection to the Christian faith, at least in the popular if not the philosophical arena, is an account of what some Christians or the church have done. Actions refute claims more quickly than words.

If justification is to some extent a matter of adopting a certain belief policy, and if individuals and groups allow interests other than an interest in truth to determine their choices, then the theologian should be wary of adopting an epistemology of vainglory that pretends to represent reason alone. The epistemology of the cross is far more deconstructive of human ideologies and belief policies than anything postmodernity has yet produced. That God reveals himself on Christ's cross as one who suffers and dies is an implicit correction, if not outright rejection, of the attempt to think God on the basis of reason alone: "Has not God made foolish the wisdom of the world?" (1 Cor. 1:20).[54]

This is why the confessions of Reformed churches recognize the inherent corrigibility of theological formulations. The confessions themselves have only relative and provisional authority; they are under the Word of God, and thus subject to correction from it. There is thus a built-in iconoclasm, an intrinsic guard against the tendency to let a community's language and concepts dictate what can be known of God. An epistemology of the cross incorporates ideology-critique into its very fabric.

EPISTEMOLOGY AND MARTYROLOGY:
THE RATIONALITY OF TESTIMONY

Staking the evangelical truth claim, I submit, is a matter of demonstrating wisdom rather than knowledge, and so demands that one justify not only particular propositions but a certain kind of practice, both in order to make wisdom intelligible and in order to "try" it. In short, staking a theological truth claim requires the (virtuous) practice of "taking up one's cross." This is the probationary moment of practical reason, the moment when the theological truth claim is tried and tested. What happens to virtue epistemology when it encounters the peculiarly theological virtues—faith, hope, and love—associated with Christian discipleship and martyrdom?

In this section I reclaim the category "martyr," in its dual sense of witnessing and suffering, for the sake of an enriched concept of knowledge that does not favor either epistemology or ethics, but rather seeks to preserve both propositions *and* persons, both procedures *and* practices. *Witnessing is the way to put others in the position of coming to know (i.e., to believe and to understand) evangelical truth.*

---

54. At the very least, the cross represents a significant correction to the concept of perfection with regard to God as the "most perfect being."

In a postmodern setting it is no longer enough to justify truth claims propositionally. An epistemology of the cross will not be merely evidentialist. It is not enough to state a proposition; one must stake a claim, and ultimately oneself, and this for two reasons. First, the truth of the claim is not a matter of propositional content only. What is at stake is the very notion of truth as a way of life, and thus the notion that truth matters (individually and socially). What is needed in an apathetic age and situation of ironic indifference is a truth for which one can live and die (Kierkegaard). In the second place, the martyr displays several character traits related to the epistemic virtues. If justification arises from acts of intellectual virtue, it may be that martyrdom could serve as a normative component of justified true belief. Indeed, martyrdom may well be an instance of epistemic responsibility taken to the limit. A belief is justified, in other words, when it is held by a person with epistemic virtue, who knows of what he speaks and is willing to suffer on its behalf.

The Trial of Jesus and the Trials of Life

Jesus' theological truth claim—"I am the way, and the truth, and the life; no one comes to the Father, but by me" (John 14:6)—seems to have led directly to his trial.[55] Jesus' passion for the truth ultimately resulted in his passion and death. As Moltmann observes: "At the center of Christian faith is *the passion of the passionate Christ*."[56] Jesus staked his claim, then went to the stake for it. Both stakings were integral to his mission, which was in part the epistemological one of making known the truth about God and about salvation.

How does one "try" Jesus' claim to be "the way, the truth, and the life"? "To try" admits of an interesting double meaning, which I shall explore below. Here I want only to point out that what is on trial is Jesus' whole life. The trial narratives make this explicit. The various trials of Jesus recounted in the Gospels oblige us to take the role of judge or jury and thus to make judgments about the whole of his life. In so doing, the story tests the reader for practical wisdom.

---

55. I cannot here deal adequately with the historical reconstructions of the accusation against Jesus: was it blasphemy (a religious charge), sedition (a political charge), or perhaps the claim to be and do all the Temple was and did, in which case it would be both religious and political (see Bruce Chilton, *The Temple of Jesus* [University Park, PA: Pennsylvania State University Press, 1992])? There is a similar ambivalence over the charge against Socrates as to its religious or political motivation (see Brickhouse and Smith, *Plato's Socrates* (Oxford: Oxford University Press, 1994), chapters 5 and 6. What we can say with some certainty is that the charges against Jesus and Socrates were attempts to defeat their respective missions.

56. Jürgen Moltmann, *The Way of Jesus Christ: Christology in Messianic Dimensions* (Minneapolis: Fortress, 1993), 151.

*The Judiciary: The Economy of Works
(Law) and the Sphere of Immanence (Religion A)*

The trial of truth involves certain judicial procedures, procedures for making right legal judgments. To make such judgments is to speak in the name of the law. But which law? What kind of authority gives these judicial procedures legitimacy? In modernity, philosophers like Kant happily spoke of reason in juridical terms; not so in postmodernity. According to the postmodern critique, reason is not blind but biased. Hence the difficulty of having to make judgments in the absence of an impartial judge. Some philosophers, such as Habermas, appeal to the regulative notion of an impartial communicative process. The account of Jesus' trial, however, is far from picturing the ideal speech situation. On the contrary, it illustrates how religious and political interests and perspectives affect the participants' judgments despite the presence of evidence and the existence of judicial procedures. The trial of truth by the judiciary is something of a travesty. Doing one's intellectual duty, I shall argue, involves more than following procedures.[57]

Jesus was, in fact, tried more than once before different "publics," and was thus subjected to more than one judicial procedure.[58] Before Caiaphas and the Sanhedrin, Jesus was judged according to the Law and the prophets (though, in fact, it was tradition rather than Scripture that ultimately carried most weight). Before Pilate, Jesus was judged according to a different, explicitly political, standard, though the procedure still aimed at rendering justice. Jesus' third trial, before Herod, seems to have been conducted according to more eccentric standards. Herod, aware of the plurality of pretenders claiming to be Christ, "was hoping to see some sign done by him" (Luke 23:8).

The fourth "trial," before the crowd, was conducted according to the slimmest of judicial procedures. It was trial by mass opinion, and the mob duly displayed its lack of practical wisdom by choosing Barabbas over Jesus. Interestingly, the evangelists highlight the presence of mockery during *all* of Jesus' trials. Jesus was correctly hailed as "King of the Jews" but for entirely the wrong reasons. The soldiers' ironic identity description of Jesus does not therefore count as justified true belief. In the final analysis, it is difficult to say whether any of these judicial procedures satisfied their epistemic duties by rendering a true judgment.

---

57. Zagzebski notes that the traditional view of epistemology "identifies justification with both the component of knowledge in addition to true belief and the idea of doing one's epistemic duty" (*Virtues of the Mind*, 31). She is quick to point out that deontological theories do not exhaust the nature of morality. Virtue theory (and consequentialism) represent other approaches to morality that have their epistemological analogues as well.

58. Again, I do not have time to go into the historical dimension of Jesus' trial (e.g., the question of whether the Sanhedrin had the authority to try Jesus, as they did, at night).

In the context of epistemology, the "judiciary" refers primarily to those procedures by which beliefs are deemed right. Rationality here appears to be a matter of due process or of doing one's epistemic duty. Zagzebski points out that almost all contemporary epistemic theories take an "act-based" moral theory as their model.[59] It is precisely this focus on justifying individual beliefs, however, that has led to the neglect of understanding and wisdom in much contemporary epistemology. I share this concern but see an additional one as well. To what extent are the judicial procedures of reason confined to the sphere of immanence, to what Kierkegaard calls Religion A? How successfully can traditional epistemology cope with Jesus' fifth trial, the one he endured before the world, on the cross? Significantly, Karl Barth discusses the resurrection of Jesus under the heading "the verdict of the Father."[60] Given the intrinsic limits of human reason (Kant), can reason alone do justice to the evangelical truth claim?[61]

The Fiduciary: The Economy of Witness (Testimony) and the Sphere of Faith (Christianity)

Is the epistemology of the cross, then, fideistic? Yes, in the sense that faith yields knowledge of God; no, in the sense that one may not justifiably believe irrationally or against the evidence. In my view, fideism is a matter of belief policy where one decides that accepting certain forms of evidence—apostolic testimony, to be exact—is a rational, intellectually virtuous knowledge-producing act. The epistemology of the cross I am here trying to sketch is fideistic in the sense that, with regard to the evangelical truth claim, it displays a certain epistemic humility as to the unaided powers of human reason and makes a *reasoned* case for the necessity of trust.[62] From another angle, an epistemology of the cross does not renounce the role of evidence but *expands* it to include testimony. Trusting testimony, however, is more than a matter of epistemic duty; it is, as we shall see, a matter of epistemic virtue. In an epistemology of the cross, to anticipate the later discussion, faith is not only the first theological virtue but a prime epistemic virtue as well.

---

59. Zagzebski, *Virtues of the Mind*, 1–15.

60. A number of commentators have observed that, in the Fourth Gospel, it is the world that is ultimately on trial. As in the Hebrew Scriptures, God in Christ is prosecuting a kind of cosmic lawsuit, and the way people respond to his Word provokes a judgment on themselves ("He who does not believe is condemned already, because he has not believed in the name . . ." John 3:18).

61. The reader must keep in mind that I am considering the evangelical truth claim. I agree with Paul Helm that "it is extremely difficult to maintain most forms of fideism consistently as belief-policies across the whole body of a person's beliefs" (Helm, *Belief Policies*, 192). I am not, therefore, suggesting that rational procedures are unhelpful in most domains, but only inquiring into their role in judging "the most important things."

62. Helm speaks of a "second-order" or rational fideist "who provides reasons and arguments for fideism" (Helm, *Belief Policies*, 210).

Testimony (the first sense of "martyrdom") occupies a central place in the narratives of Jesus' trial. Indeed, the Fourth Gospel as a whole is an extended testimony to God's truth claim that aims to persuade its readers to make the judgment for themselves that Jesus is the Christ, the Son of God (John 20:31). The Fourth Gospel parades a host of witnesses on Jesus' behalf. John the Baptist "bears testimony" to Jesus as the Saviour of the world (John 1:7–8; 3:26). The so-called "testimonies" of the Hebrew Scriptures are adduced as additional evidence of Jesus' true identity. Moreover, the works that Jesus does also constitute testimony of his origin (John 5:36). In the same way, Jesus' miracles are "signs" (*semeia*) that confirm his identity and mission. Lastly, the Spirit of truth is an "Advocate" who bears witness to Christ (John 15:26), and even God the Father is said to bear witness to Jesus (John 5:37). Of course, there were many at Jesus' trials who bore false witness as well. Nevertheless, the centrality of testimony, together with the possibility of false witness, requires a more careful analysis of what I am calling the *fiduciary*.

Contrary to Plato and Locke, testimony yields not mere opinion, but evidence, even a way of knowing. C. A. J. Coady's book, *Testimony: A Philosophical Study* argues that testimony as a mode of knowledge fell out of favour in modernity, due in large part to the dominant individualistic ideology: "It may be no accident that the rise of an individualist ideology coincided with the emergence of the theory of knowledge as a central philosophical concern but, accident or not, the coincidence was likely to cast into shadow the importance of our intellectual reliance upon one another."[63] Coady's thesis is as simple as it is bold: "our trust in the word of others is fundamental to the very idea of serious cognitive activity."[64] It may also be fundamental to our ability to make cognitive contact with reality.[65]

David Hume maintains that one can always reduce testimony to some other, more basic form of evidence (e.g., observation). His critical attitude toward testimony is shared by a good number of modern philosophers who agree that we need sufficient reason before believing in testimony.[66] Neither Hume nor Harvey allows testimony itself to count as a sufficient ground for believing what we have been told. Indeed, they reckon one who believes something on the basis of testimony alone to be epistemically irresponsible. The main difficulty seems to be their assumption that testimony does not constitute "sufficient evidence" for belief. This is problematic on two counts. First, what is the warrant for that assumption? And second, is there an obvious answer to the question of what sufficient evidence amounts to?

Testifying—giving testimony—is a speech act. We are invited to accept *p* because A says that *p*, and because A is in a position to say so; in other

---

63. C. A. J. Coady, *Testimony: A Philosophical Study* (Oxford: Clarendon, 1992), 13.
64. Ibid., vii.
65. Recall Zagzebski's definition of knowledge as "a state of cognitive contact with reality arising out of acts of intellectual virtue" (*Virtues of the Mind*, 270).
66. See W. K. Clifford, "The Ethics of Belief," *Lectures and Essays* (London: Macmillan, 1886), and Nicholas Wolterstorff, *John Locke and the Ethics of Belief* (Cambridge: Cambridge University Press, 1996).

words, A's stating *p* is offered as grounds for accepting *p*. The legal act of testifying only "adapts and solemnizes an everyday phenomenon."[67] Thomas Reid classifies testimony, along with other speech acts such as promising, as "social operations of the mind," and complains that philosophy has overlooked their significance.[68] Testimony, like language itself, is essentially social. Coady, similarly, argues that trusting the word of others is implicit in our actual cognitive procedures.[69] In believing testimony, then, we are *believing in* the speaker. This need not lead to blind faith: "We may have 'no reason to doubt' another's communication even where there is no question of our being gullible; we may simply recognize that the standard warning signs of deceit, confusion, or mistake are not present."[70] Significantly, no such warning signs seem to be present in the apostolic testimony to the event of Jesus Christ.

H. H. Price's "Principle A"—"Believe what you are told by others unless or until you have reason for doubting it"—is a kind of restatement of Thomas Reid's "principle of credulity."[71] Trusting the word of others is socially expedient and socially indispensable. Trust is an intellectual virtue because relying on what other people say is often truth-conducive. The knowledge we gain from others is not inferential but properly basic; in many cases, there are no other grounds for a belief. There are additional reasons, however, why trust is important in discussions concerning the evangelical truth claim. As we have already suggested, there are good reasons to acknowledge that knowledge about God may be beyond the reach of unaided human reason. Significantly, Zagzebski lists "reliance on truthworthy authority" on her list of intellectual virtues.[72] A person with a passion for truth should count divine revelation as a reliable authority, though of course identifying divine revelation with Scripture requires *phronesis*. Trust is the virtue of "knowing when to rely on others" and is the "reverse side of autonomy."[73] Montmarquet unifies the virtues under two headings: honesty (a regard for the truth as such) and charity (a regard for others, not least as potential sources of truth). It remains to be seen whether faith is not the intellectual virtue that involves a proper regard for God. In any case, we

---

67. Coady, *Testimony*, 26.

68. Thomas Reid, *Essays on the Intellectual Powers of Man* (Cambridge, MA: MIT. Press, 1968), essay 1, chapter 8.

69. We may relate this to George Steiner's suggestion that belief in God underwrites language (*Real Presences* [Chicago: University of Chicago Press, 1989]).

70. Coady, *Testimony*, 47.

71. H. H. Price, *Belief* (London: George Allen and Unwin, 1969), chapter 5. Reid acknowledged that our propensity to believe others will be qualified by experience. On the basis of my experience, for instance, I am more likely to believe what I am told in *TIME* than in the *National Enquirer*.

72. Zagzebski, *Virtues of the Mind*, 98.

73. Ibid., 160. Credulity should not be confused with gullibility. In the first place, we are only rational in trusting others who are reliable in showing us the way or in giving us the truth. Most to be trusted, therefore, are those who are demonstrably knowledgeable or wise. Second, credulity, as an intellectual virtue, should not stand alone but must always be tempered by the other intellectual virtues.

have established that belief in apostolic testimony may well be the rational response of a person of epistemic virtue.

Hume reduces testimony to first-person observation. In other contexts, however, he appeals to natural laws, which are but inferences from the observations of a large number of people. He has here to rely on a notion of the common experience of humanity rather than his own individual experience. This is highly problematic, for the notion of "common human experience"—the criterion with which Hume evaluates reports of miracles— ultimately relies on testimony, on what others have reported to be common in their experience. *Hume's distrust of reports of the miraculous is therefore a performative contradiction.* The only escape would be to check the experience of others against our own individual experience. But this is to be mired in the worst kind of solipsistic relativism. Our reliance on testimony "goes beyond anything that could be justified by personal observation."[74] Coady thus concludes that testimony is an irreducible form of knowledge.

Justification in a fiduciary scheme has to do not with "founding" the evidence given by a witness, but with trusting it. Testimony makes the past and present perception of others available to those who did not, or could not, perceive for themselves. Propositional truth—a report about what happened in history—is thus one element in testimony. As Coady observes, reporting "is probably the dominant form of assertion."[75] Yet, my argument is that the witness's whole speech act, taken as part of a broader way of life, is part of the package that certifies the validity of the claim being made. At least with regard to claims about ways of wisdom such as the evangelical truth claim, the life of the witness and the testimony itself are inseparably intertwined.

To stake a theological truth claim, therefore, is to make a self-involving speech act that requires the speaker to take a stance toward his or her own words, toward others, the world, and perhaps God. One who testifies must redeem Habermas's validity conditions for communicative acts in general as well as an additional validity claim, namely, that this is a truth for which one is prepared to live and die. As we have said before, in the current epistemological climate of postmodernity, justifying propositions is not enough. What needs to be validated is not only the proposition but the entire speech act of testifying. The present expansionist account of epistemology requires us to consider not only procedures but practices, the performance not only of epistemic duties but, more importantly, of epistemic virtues.

Testimony and "Incredible" Reports

Hume and others like him would like to establish a criterion by which to rule certain types of testifying out of court, without having to consider the particular circumstances of the speech act. Harvey agrees with Collingwood:

---

74. Coady, *Testimony*, 93.
75. Ibid., 154.

"In so far as an historian accepts the testimony of an authority and treats it as historical truth, he obviously forfeits the name of historian."[76] Testimony must be tested because there is false testimony, as the penultimate prohibition of the Ten Commandments reminds us: "Thou shalt not bear false witness" (Exod. 20:16).

No witness, of course, hands down a complete, photograph-like description of an event. Rather, one selects and interprets what one reports. Here most moderns and postmoderns are in agreement. An element of judgment is necessarily present. These judgments, as F. H. Bradley pointed out, presuppose other judgments and beliefs that have been influenced by one's culture and worldview. The task of the critical historian is to cross-examine the witness with the aim of removing obsolete world view accretions and of recovering the literal core: namely, what a person today would have observed had he or she been there. In this fashion, says Harvey, "The historian *confers* authority upon a witness."[77]

F. H. Bradley argues that all testimonies to the "non-analogous" should be rejected.[78] Unless the witness's experience is like our experience, it does not count as evidence. Critical history involves rethinking the judgments of others according to the criterion of present knowledge and experience.[79] This is, to say the least, a rather legalistic "morality of historical knowledge," one that partakes of the judiciary and privileges the desire to avoid error to the exclusion of the fiduciary and the desire to gain truth.

Is it necessarily a defect of testimony that a past witness "saw" things differently than we might have seen them? Is this not simply to acknowledge that *testimony itself is an interpretation?* And might it not be that the witness's judgments and interpretive framework are as indispensable for our appreciation of a claim as a mere report of a raw perception? It seems unlikely, for instance, that we could ever assess the claim "Jesus is the Christ" without some appreciation of the Hebrew Scriptures. One could never directly observe Jesus as the Christ. That claim—and perhaps the evangelical truth claim as well—is more of a judgment than an empirical observation. By treating common human experience or universal natural laws as our critical criteria, then, we are choosing to attend to testimony with a blind eye and a deaf ear.

In testimony, there is both "mere observation" and "worldview." *Both* have to be tested, and we have to be clear about which we find objectionable, and why. Coady states: "Unless we register quite a lot we cannot act,

---

76. R. G. Collingwood, *The Idea of History* (Oxford: Oxford University Press, 1946), 256.

77. Harvey, *The Historian and the Believer*, 42.

78. F. H. Bradley, "The Presuppositions of Critical History," in *Collected Essays* (Oxford: Oxford University Press, 1935). Harvey cites Bradley's essay with obvious approval.

79. Bradley states: "The view I have put forward is this, that every man's present standpoint ought to determine his belief in respect to *all* past events" (Bradley, "Presuppositions," 2).

select, and interpret at all. The real story is quite complex and multi-layered: neither the picture of wholly passive registration nor that of furiously active invention is adequate."[80]

Witnessing involves fact (reporting events) and interpretation (describing their meaning). What, after all, is more marvellous: that a dead man came back to life, or that God is described as one who forgives sinners? Testimony need not be exhaustive in order to yield knowledge. A critical realism of testimony recognizes the value of multiple perspectives or voices and insists that, through serious interpretation, the reader can make cognitive contact with that to which the witnesses testify.

The Theologian as Witness

"Is the cross an argument?" (Nietzsche, The Antichrist §53)

The witness is one who first acquires a belief, then attempts to pass it on. While testimony may or may not be the source of the witness's belief (i.e., the mechanism by which the belief is acquired), it is certainly the result. The reliable or authoritative witness becomes a conduit of rationality. One important aspect of the vocation of the theologian is to witness to the truth: not just to the evangelical truth claim, but to the notion of truth itself.[81] Moreover, bearing witness to truth involves a way of life. The witness, especially the martyr, displays the meaning of the evangelical truth claim by readiness to stake not only the claim, but his or her life. This involves moral and intellectual courage. *Bearing witness is ultimately a matter not of epistemic duty but of epistemic virtue.*[82]

In Kierkegaard's view, the problem with Christianity is that it has too many teachers and not enough witnesses. For the teacher, Christianity is essentially doctrine. This only takes us as far as *episteme* and *theoria* (theoretical knowledge), not as far as *phronesis*—the way, the truth, and the life. It is important to note that for Kierkegaard, the witness does not speak a private, but a public language. Though Kierkegaard never abandons his emphasis on inwardness (e.g., one's subjective passion for the truth), he does develop the implications of inwardness *outwards*. One's life must conform to one's message. A politics must follow from a passion. The witness unites in his or her person the private/passionate and the public/political realms, for the sake of the wider community. In this way, private responsibility and public accountability alike are satisfied. A witness with personal integrity stakes himself or herself in a public manner. Accordingly, the "wit-

---

80. Coady, *Testimony*, 268.

81. This is particularly so given Jesus' claim to be the truth (John 14:6). Can persons as well as propositions be truth-bearers? Perhaps so, if the truth concerned is a matter of that upon which a "way and life" ultimately relies.

82. I am not sure what Zagzebski, to whom my account of epistemic virtue is largely indebted, would make of this claim. She does recognize that courage is an intellectual virtue, but there is no discussion of testimony, and no index entry for "credulity," in her work.

ness" is the fullest expression of "the individual," yet not in such a way that leads to privatization.

Witnessing is a practice that displays not only the witness's sincerity with regard to the truth claim but often its very *matter*: "the self, language and world coexist in relations of mutual implication."[83] Questions about meaning and truth—about God as well as about everything else—will be related to the way we actually live. One's active witness, therefore, can disclose to others not only the meaning of the evangelical truth claim, but the intelligible structure of the world as interpreted by Christians as well. Doing the truth is one way of showing what the truth is, what the world is really like. Living the Christian way helps form sensibilities that allow others to perceive better the summons which a situation represents.

Aristotle says that moral education begins with a child's learning to be appropriately ashamed at what is shameful. We might similarly say that Christian education begins when a disciple learns why one need *not* be ashamed of the gospel. My thesis is that Christian discipleship is conducive to forming certain epistemic virtues, especially the theological virtues of credulity and humility, and that these virtues are in turn conducive to appreciating the truth that "God was in Christ reconciling the world to himself."

Martyrdom as Communicative Action

"The martyrs have harmed the truth." (Nietzsche, The Antichrist)

Christian witnesses are not only speakers, but sufferers too. This was a constant theme in Kierkegaard's works. Neither orthodoxy nor "Christendom" is enough; Christian truth demands passion or inwardness. Yet, subjectivity is not the whole story for Kierkegaard either. In his later writings, discipleship becomes more and more important. "Dying from the world" means not withdrawing from the world, but following Christ without being dominated by worldly matters. Being a Christian is recognizable "by the opposition one suffers."[84] Discipleship inevitably leads to suffering. Kierkegaard speaks of "suffering for the truth" or "suffering for the doctrine." The truth *has* to suffer; Christ's persecution was not accidental. The cross of Christ symbolizes what is involved in having a passion for the truth. It is not that the disciple seeks suffering, but rather that the world inevitably persecutes the truth. Why should this be so? Because the truth is not ultimately of this world. It is eschatological, not immanent, and cannot be contained within a worldly framework.

Both the form and the content of the evangelical truth claim work against the notion of "Christendom" and its imperialistic overtone of imposing truth on others. Those who stake theological truth claims, then, should not

---

83. James Fodor, *Christian Hermeneutics: Paul Ricoeur and the Refiguring of Theology* (Oxford: Clarendon, 1995), 11.

84. Cited in Gouwens, *Kierkegaard as Religious Thinker*, 214.

oppress but rather suffer oppression. To associate the theological truth claims with expressions of the will-to-power is effectively to contradict Christian witness. The power associated with Christian truth has little to do with force (except the force of testimony and perhaps that of the better argument) and nothing to do with violence. The power of the cross is the weakness and wisdom of God (1 Cor. 1: 23–24). From the perspective of an epistemology of the cross, truth—even rationality—is vulnerable.

Christ's passion becomes for Kierkegaard the pattern for Christian witness. When Kierkegaard declares that "truth is subjectivity," he is speaking the language not of postmodernity but rather of the gospel. Subjectivity, for Kierkegaard, is an intellectual virtue that calls people to relate to the truth as if their lives depended on it (which they do). To say truth is subjectivity is just another way of talking about "passion": about passion as an epistemic virtue (i.e., a burning desire for the truth) and about the passion of Christ (i.e., a definitive suffering for the truth). Christ's passion is a model for how we should stake truth claims today (e.g., as a suffering witness): "Christ is the truth [but] to *be* the truth is the only true explanation of what truth is."[85] The witness to the truth is one whose life displays the rightness of the believing, and thus the rightness of the belief. Only personal witness—an integration of speech, belief, and life—can ultimately legitimate the wisdom of the Christian way. George Malantschuk's comment is apt: "Kierkegaard's subjectivity is a blend of truth and what is individual, whereas Nietzsche's subjectivity is a blend of what is arbitrary and what is individual. For Kierkegaard, it is truth which determines and transforms the individual; for Nietzsche, it is the individual who determines what truth shall be."[86]

Martyrdom can be a powerful form of truth-disclosing action. Christian martyrs bear witness to the love of God and the Lordship of Jesus Christ—twin convictions that undergird the Christian way of life. As a practice that is peculiarly transparent to the ultimate commitments which found it, martyrdom displays the shape of Christian metaphysics as well as that of Christian morals. Coady aptly observes that we are oriented to reality by others as much as by our own intellectual powers. The Christian martyr not only declares but displays what it means to say "Jesus is Lord" or "God is love." Indeed, one might go further and say that without martyrs we simply would no longer have the meaning of these propositions. Martyrdom appears to be a form of what Kierkegaard calls "indirect communication," and is thus an appropriate response to the epistemological predicament of postmodernity.

The evangelical truth claim, precisely because it is as concerned with the way to live as with correct ideas, is staked best not through direct communication (i.e., by theoretical knowledge) but indirectly, through the expansive category of the speech act "testifying." Of course, if we ask

---

85. Ibid., 218.
86. George Malantschuk, "Kierkegaard and Nietzsche," in *A Kierkegaard Critique*, H. Johnson and N. Thulstrup (eds.) (New York: Harper and Brothers, 1962), 124.

whether the commitments implied by one's testimony are arbitrary, we begin to do metaphysics. But this is precisely my point: martyrdom is a form of "indirect metaphysics."[87] Faithful Christian witness thus involves naming God *and* a particular way of being-toward death. Speaking the truth in love is tied up with bearing witness, that is, with learning how to be a Christian martyr.

CROSS-EXAMINATION: PASSION AND TRUTH

> *"A man's virtues are called good depending on their probable conse-quences not for him but for us and society. . . . When you have a virtue . . . you are its victim." (Nietzsche, The Gay Science)*

The witness/martyr, I have argued, has a passion for truth. Is this fact of any epistemological significance? We have seen that virtue epistemology con-ceives justification as something that emerges from the inner traits of per-sons rather than something that attaches to impersonal processes. Did not the Greeks develop an interest in philosophy and epistemology precisely in order to get beyond subjectivity and to counter the irrational force of the passions? In giving pride of place to passion, am I not playing into the hands of the postmodern relativists? On the contrary, I view passion as the epis-temic virtue that is perfectly suited to staking the evangelical truth claim in an age marked by irony and indifference towards the truth. Passion, I shall argue, is an epistemic (and ethical) virtue that, just because it is truth-con-ducive, leads also to martyrdom.

Here I Stand

> *"Stand firm in your faith. . . ." (1 Corinthians 16:13)*

Luther's terse formula—"Here I stand"—allegedly spoken in the context of his own trial, displays two important intellectual virtues: humility and con-viction. *Here* I stand. This is a confession of humility, an admission of the contextual conditioning of one's thought.[88] Humility, as an intellectual virtue, recognizes that in some areas I must think others more epistemically privileged than myself. It predisposes one to trust the testimony of those who are reliable authorities. It also means that I must stand prepared to be corrected by better arguments (or, in Luther's case, by the Word of God). Humility is perhaps the prime feature of an epistemology of the cross.[89]

---

87. It would be a misunderstanding of my proposal to see it as reducing truth to truth-fulness, or correspondence to sincerity. Speech acts have various kinds of validity con-ditions, and sincerity is only one of them. I shall consider below the objection that my proposal is unable to distinguish the martyr to truth from the foolish fanatic.

88. The Incarnation, especially the *kenosis* of Christ, shows that even God's truth claim was contextualized in "the form of a servant . . . in the likeness of men" (Phil. 2:5–11).

89. Interestingly, Aristotle (whom Luther calls the "philosopher" behind the theology

Epistemic humility leads to an abandonment of the epistemology of glory, of the project of finding out God through theoretical argumentation or of thinking that one can, through reason, attain a context-free God's-eye perspective. Intellectual humility means that I, and my whole community, must acknowledge the provisionality of our claims ("Here *we* stand, in the West, at the end of the twentieth century"). To stress humility is thus to emphasize the corrigibility of interpretive traditions. Yet humility remains an intellectual virtue; those who have it stand a better chance of apprehending the truth—of knowing God—rather than their own ideological projections.

"Here *I stand*." Luther can also be read as displaying a second epistemic virtue: intellectual courage, the courage of one's convictions. Sometimes, one has literally to stand in order to stake a claim (i.e, to stand and be counted). Luther's standing was a sign of his conviction and commitment to the truth. One stands for truth because truth is for everyone. Luther the private individual had a passion for public truth. The evangelical truth claim, of all possible truth claims, is eminently public: it is good news for the whole world. In standing for Christian wisdom, then, one proclaims its ability to transform any situation or society where people are willing to take it seriously and follow its way.

Endurance as a Criterion of Truth (James 1:12)

"What does not destroy me, makes me stronger." (Nietzsche)

These two virtues, each an aspect of passion, are, I submit, the virtues of the martyr who bears witness to and suffers for something that he or she has received from another. But why should passion, which in this context refers to suffering, be truth conducive? And what distinguishes Jesus' passion from that of Socrates, the Christian martyr from others who are willing to die for the truth, particularly the fanatic? This is an important query. My thesis is that *humility and conviction are epistemic virtues, and so truth-conducive, because together they lead one to believe that which can be relied on ultimately.*

The belief policy of the Christian martyr is not "believe whatever you're told no matter how seemingly ridiculous," but rather "believe what you are told about God by those who have it on good authority and whose testimony—which includes their lives (and deaths)—are reliable indicators of practical wisdom." If I may again appeal to Luther: properly to state Christian truth involves *oratio* (prayer), *meditatio* (interpretation), and *tentatio* (the experience of testing through affliction). In brief: the connection between humility, conviction, and rationality is to be found in the critical test of *endurance.*

---

of glory) appears to have thought humility a vice (see Zagzebski, *Virtues of the Mind*, 88). Zagzebski, however, is not so negative: "But if humility is the virtue whereby a person is disposed to make an accurate appraisal of her own competence, intellectual humility could reasonably be interpreted as a mean between the tendency to grandiosity and the tendency to a diminished sense of her own ability" (220).

To stake the evangelical truth claim means to be able and willing to render Christ in one's daily living—or better, to *surrender* everything for the sake of this claim. In particular, theologians, in imitation of Christ, must humble themselves and not retreat to commitment nor hide behind ecclesial authority.[90] No special privileges or prerogatives should be allowed to insulate theological truth claims from the crucible of testing. To pour oneself out for the sake of the evangelical truth claim means making the way of Christ intelligible, both theoretically and practically. It means living a life that embodies the Word in the power of the Spirit in such a way that it is able to meet and pass the critical tests of human reflection and human existence.

Displaying humility and conviction is analogous to fallibilist theories of rationality according to which justification involves a process of critical testing. *Epistemic humility means being tolerant, not in the sense of embracing plurality and difference, as would a postmodern relativist, but rather in the sense of enduring it.* This is, in part, what it means to suffer for the truth. The epistemically virtuous person endures critical testing of beliefs. The virtuous believer/witness tries to pass the greatest test of all: the test of time.[91] Ultimately, to stake a Christian theological truth claim is to embark on an endurance test for which we have only the firstfruits of verification.

The witness implicit in this standing is that the truth is strong enough to absorb everything the world has to throw at it. Endurance does not mean duration, for truth is not merely a matter of *surviving* critical testing. On the contrary, to "endure" means "to harden"; it is not merely a matter of staying the same over time, but of becoming stronger. The truth is that which endures and that which edifies. The steadfast faith is the faith that stands fast (Col. 2:5; Jas. 1:3). Knowledge, then, is neither a pyramid nor a raft, but a tree whose roots extend ever deeper and whose branches bear ever more fruit.

As did Jesus in his trials, so his disciples too often have to stand and take it. As we have seen, this is precisely the way the virtues are learned: through doing what a person with *phronesis* would do in similar circumstances, by imitating a master. Christian discipleship is, at least in part, an apprenticeship in the intellectual as well as the properly moral virtues.

Jesus and Socrates

> *"If this undertaking is of men, it will fail; but if it is of God, you will not be able to stop these men." (Acts 5:38–39)*

Surely I have proved too much. Every faith has its martyrs; yet, unless we side with postmodern relativists, not all faiths can be true. To what extent,

---

90. This seems to be the application to epistemology of Jesus' renunciation of divine glory or "equality with God" (Phil. 2:6).

91. There is a sense in which endurance is formally analogous to Alistair MacIntyre's suggestion that traditions are best tested over time. To highlight humility is to make "willingness to submit one's beliefs (or oneself) to critical testing" an epistemic virtue that is conducive to truth.

then, does an epistemology of the cross really help in discerning true knowledge from knowledge falsely so-called? In particular, why should one not follow a genius, like Socrates, rather than an apostle, like Paul?[92]

Socrates, we may recall, was on an epistemological mission too; one, furthermore, that was commissioned by a god (though philosophers do not like to be reminded of it). Indeed, at his trial Socrates claimed to be "god's gift to Athens."[93] His task was to make people wise. Like Jesus, Socrates was brought to trial because of his single-minded passion for his mission. Again like Jesus, he claimed that he had never done anything wrong and had never acted against the gods.[94] Moreover, Socrates, again like Jesus, chose to die for his mission; even Kierkegaard admired Socrates' passion.

How, then, does Jesus' martyrdom differ from that of Socrates, from others who have died for a righteous cause, or, indeed, from that of a fanatic? Let us begin with Socrates. For what belief did Socrates die? In the first place, he died to maintain his personal integrity. He had the courage of his convictions. Kierkegaard, however, rightly observes that Socrates did not die for the truth—that is, for some positive message—but rather for a principle, for the sake of making a formal protest. In other words, he dies for a negative reason; and the wisdom he left his students was largely negative too (i.e., dialectic, critical thinking). On the one hand, he has lived a life free of the evil of thinking that he was wise when he was not; on the other hand, he has not achieved a positive truth. He dies for a question, not for an answer. Socrates, in the end, is only half a martyr; he dies, but his is the death of a genius, not of a witness, and certainly not of an apostle.[95]

Socrates dies, moreover, in the vague belief that he will not be worse off in death than he is in life. Brickhouse and Smith observe: "although he never claims to be wise in this all-important matter, Socrates believed there is good reason to thinking everyone will be better off dead."[96] While he may well have been right about eternal life, he could surely not be said to have knowledge of it. As Kierkegaard observes, the difference between transcendence and immanence is that, when Jesus and Socrates both say, "There is eternal life," only Jesus has the authority to do so; only Jesus *knows*, for only he has it on reliable authority.[97] Lastly, Socrates dies in his old age with a joke on his lips. In the final analysis, Socrates' parting wisdom about life and

---

92. "Apostle" here means "one sent on a mission." Though Jesus sent others, he too was sent, by the Father (cf. John 15–17).

93. Plato, *Apology* 30d7–e1.

94. Ibid., 37b2–5.

95. Significantly, though his *daimonion* tells him what *not* to do, Socrates does not really receive any other positive revelation than the original delphic oracle that pronounced him the wisest of men!

96. Thomas C. Brickhouse and Nicholas D. Smith, *Plato's Socrates* (Oxford: Oxford University Press, 1994), 202.

97. Christ was not a genius who communicated his own ideas. As Kierkegaard points out, the statement "There is eternal life" is not particularly profound. That is not the point. What counts is that the one who said it is sent from God ("On the Difference between a Genius and an Apostle," 156–57).

death lacks authority. In short, his testimony is not apostolic, but a proud protest limited to the sphere of immanence, to what unaided human reason can know. On closer inspection, then, there is reason to question whether Socrates' death displays the epistemic virtues associated with passion (e.g., credulity, humility, conviction). Socrates does not give his followers a sufficient reason to follow his example. It is thus questionable whether he is an example of one who lives, and dies, well.

In contrast to Socrates, Jesus died in anguish, in his prime, at the hands of others. In submitting to an unjust penalty, in being willing to die for a message (e.g., concerning the kingdom of God) he had received on authority, Jesus put those who observed his life and death in a position to see, and to *feel*, the force of his claim. Jesus' martyrdom (the cross) was therefore not only truth, but transcendence-conducive. The way Jesus lived and the way he died communicated to and convinced others of the truth of his claims. The centurion at the foot of the cross, when he saw how Jesus died, confessed, "Surely this was the Son of God" (Mark 15:39).[98]

An Objection: The Epistemic Fanatic

To stake a claim is to act as a witness to some state of affairs. My thesis is that the way one witnesses is an important part of assessing the content of what is said. But could it not be argued that fanatics have the same kind of passion as that evidenced by Jesus? If the intellectual virtues arise out of a love of the truth, must we not say that the fanatic is a person of epistemic virtue?

The first thing to determine is whether the fanatic really desires the truth rather than the truth of his own ideas. To be passionate only about one's own ideas is to lack the epistemic virtues of humility and open-mindedness. This kind of love for the truth partakes more of eros than agape. Let us assume for the sake of discussion, however, that the epistemic fanatic really desires truth. The first thing to be said is that the mere desire for truth is not enough to qualify one as epistemically virtuous. Sincerity alone is insufficient, for sincerity alone is not necessarily truth-conducive. One can be sincerely wrong. Second, the epistemic fanatic is often not a martyr. Take, for example, the members of the Heaven's Gate sect. No one persecuted them; they were not martyrs. Their suffering was self-inflicted. In choosing death, the only thing they witnessed to was their own confusion.

Third, and most important, the fanatic's passion for the truth is untempered by the other intellectual virtues. This is a most important point.

---

98. Jesus' sufferings were for others—for the whole world: "Jesus suffers them in solidarity with others, and vicariously for many, and proleptically for the whole suffering creation" (Moltmann, *The Way of Jesus Christ*, 152). Of course, not everyone can see the truth in Jesus' death, for many lacked the right imagination, not to mention the requisite epistemic (and spiritual) virtues. Knowers require not only training but sanctification in order to acquire the virtues that put them into cognitive contact with divine reality.

Though passion for the truth can be a virtue, when unchecked by the other epistemic virtues it ceases to be truth-conducive. The fanatic is, epistemologically speaking, a tragic hero whose downfall is due to an excess of one intellectual virtue.[99] As Montmarquet points out, the desire to attain truth must be regulated by the other epistemic virtues.[100] Fanaticism, therefore, is best described as a *deregulated* passion for the truth. The epistemic fanatic, to put it another way, is one who fails to integrate and to unify the intellectual virtues in his or her person. In short, the fanatic lacks *phronesis*, practical wisdom, the supreme regulative virtue. It is the task of *phronesis* to balance the virtues and to judge, say, when to persevere with a belief and when to give it up. A person of epistemic virtue must believe what a person with *phronesis* would in similar circumstances.[101] Fanaticism, to the extent that it is a matter of unregulated passion and therefore of what can ultimately only be foolishness, is a downright epistemic vice.

Epistemic and Theological Virtue

In Jesus' passion we see the wisdom of God personified: the divine *phronesis* made flesh. Jesus, then, displays epistemic virtues in his martyrdom that Socrates and fanatics alike do not. In particular, Jesus personifies the antidote to fanaticism, namely, humility: his teaching witnesses to what he has received, and his life is a pouring out on behalf of this same message. Epistemic humility, I suggest, is the intellectual virtue needed if we are to make cognitive contact with transcendent reality by trusting apostolic testimony. As I have argued, such trust is eminently rational, since credulity is an intellectual virtue. The witness acquires beliefs through credulity but commends them to others through humility, that is, by submitting them to critical tests. Christians testify not only to a set of propositions but to a way, and this way must be subjected to Socratic examination, perhaps even to persecution.[102] Only by such trials can this way be deemed wise and reliable rather than foolish and misleading.

Jesus' ability to endure critical testing stems not only from those character traits typically mentioned by virtue epistemologists, but from the properly theological virtues as well: faith, hope, and love. *Faith:* Jesus accepted

---

99. The analogy with moral tragedy may be helpful. Othello's love for his wife, taken to the extreme, becomes jealousy (a vice).

100. Montmarquet, *Epistemic Virtue*, 25.

101. There are prima facie problems with the criteria for recognizing *phronesis*. Zagzebski appears to think that good intellectual practice is, if not self-evident, at least widely acknowledged. More work probably needs to be done in this area. Zagzebski's comment is relevant, however: "It is often a difficult matter to decide what theological propositions to believe, but this is no objection to the appeal to practical wisdom unless it is a condition of adequacy of a methodology of theology that makes the difficult business of deciding what to believe easy" ("The Place of Phronesis," 221).

102. Moltmann comments: "The ancient church knew her martyrs, and knew also how to interpret the martyrdom of the witnesses theologically" (*The Way of Jesus Christ*, 197). See also 2 Cor. 4:10; Col. 1:24; and Phil. 3:10.

and held on to beliefs acquired through trusting the Word of God. *Hope:* Jesus' implicit trust in his Father and in the divine promise of new life allowed him to complete his mission. In turn, Jesus' resurrection inspires contemporary witnesses to hope that the evangelical truth claim will ultimately be vindicated by God himself. *Love:* it was Jesus' love for others, even for those who opposed him, that not only inspired his passion, but enabled him to endure it. As Paul has written, "Love bears all things . . . endures all things" (1 Cor 13:7).

An epistemology of the cross is humble, yet at the same time hopeful. Testifying, like promising, is a speech act in which speakers commit themselves to an eventual fit of words and world. Now, even an enriched epistemology will not be able to prove the evangelical truth claim. Yet, we need not go so far as to suggest that the cross fails to get us beyond the level of immanence.[103] On the contrary, the Fourth Gospel suggests that the cross itself is the moment of Christ's glorification (his being "lifted up"). In the final analysis, we must say that the cross is an *indirect* communication of divine transcendence. Jesus' resurrection is both testimony and promise: testimony to the fact that God was in Christ reconciling all things to himself, and a promise that all things shall indeed be reconciled. The cross is ultimately an apocalyptic witness to the meaning of the whole of world history. Martyrs, says Moltmann, "anticipate in their own bodies the sufferings of the end time . . . they witness to the creation which is new."[104] To testify to the resurrection is thus to participate, in anticipatory fashion, in the promise of the Kingdom of God. The Christian martyr, unlike Socrates, thus testifies in concrete terms to hope. This too is a matter of *phronesis:* knowing how, in every situation, to live in such a way that testifies not only to the wisdom of Christ, but to hope in his resurrection.

Barth spoke of resurrection as the "verdict" of the Father. Perhaps there is a lesson here for the contemporary minister of the Word as well. We can stake claims with humility and conviction, and show their reasonableness and wisdom by enduring trials and critical testing, but it is ultimately up to God to validate them. God raised Jesus from the dead; the apostles were only "witnesses of this fact" (Acts 2:32). The trial of truth may admit of no worldly resolution. The church today continues to witness to resurrection, not by eyewitness but by existential testimony that attests the promise and its power.

Those who stake theological truth claims, then, need not wield the sword; truth will be victorious, but its victory is not gained by overpowering its opponents. As Oliver O'Donovan says: "The church does not philosophize about a future world; it demonstrates the working of the coming Kingdom within this one. . . . This may lead to mutual service, or to martyrdom."[105]

---

103. As Thiselton apparently suggests in *Interpreting God and the Postmodern Self* (Edinburgh: T. & T. Clark, 1995), 147.

104. Moltmann, *The Way of Jesus Christ*, 204.

105. Oliver O'Donovan, *The Desire of the Nations: Rediscovering the Roots of Political Theology* (Cambridge: Cambridge University Press, 1996), 217 (order slightly changed).

Witnessing, I submit, is the epistemologically correct way of staking a theological truth claim. For postmodernity, in some respects, has not advanced beyond Socrates. Both present philosophies of immanence that fail to do justice to the absolute significance of the historical particular. Martyrdom, I suggest, is the most appropriate form of a claim that concerns the extraordinary in the ordinary; the eternal quickening of human history.

CONCLUSION:
THE THEOLOGIAN AS INTERPRETER-MARTYR

The vocation of the Christian theologian is to be an interpreter-martyr: a truth-teller, a truth-doer, a truth-sufferer. Truth requires evangelical passion, not postmodern passivity; personal appropriation, not calculation. The theologian is to embody in his or her own person the core of Christian culture, in order to provide a focus for Christian wisdom.

Making Christian truth claims ultimately is not a crusade, nor a pilgrimage, nor even a missionary journey, but rather a *martyrological* act. Genuine theology is not only about the art of reasoning well (rationality), but about living well (wisdom) and dying well (martyrdom). Martyrdom is a form of indirect epistemology that arises from acts of intellectual virtue (e.g., humility, conviction) motivated by the passion for truth.

Questions about the truth of our theology are thus tied up with questions about the effectiveness of our discipleship and martyrdom. There is a tie between defending the truth and living faithfully. The challenge of Christian mission today, the challenge of staking a theological truth claim, is nothing less than displaying in one's life the way of Jesus Christ: not Heidegger's (nor Socrates') "being-toward-death" but a distinctively Christian *being-toward-resurrection*. This is not a matter of epistemological foundationalism so much as it is a demonstration of the integrity and uniqueness of Christian wisdom. Such a demonstration can be made, of course, only by those who are willing to be martyrs. Staking a theological truth claim is a costly affair. To refer truly to God *is* to bear faithful witness to the way of Christian wisdom, a witness that embodies the Christian metaphysic.

Epistemology in the service of Christian mission means not only doing one's epistemic duty, but rather displaying intellectual virtue and pursuing epistemic excellence. Making a truth claim is both a relational and a propositional affair, involving persons and procedures. What theology gives back to epistemology is an expanded set of intellectual virtues (faith, hope, love, and humility) and the model of the martyr/witness who is prepared to endure anything for the sake of the truth. To stake a theological truth claim humbly yet hopefully is, finally, to *be* a truth to one's neighbor.[106]

---

106. I am grateful to my Edinburgh University doctoral students and Fergus Kerr, who comprise the "Whither Theology?" discussion group, for their comments and suggestions on an earlier draft of this paper.

CHAPTER EIGHT

Christian Mission and the Epistemological Crisis of the West

J. ANDREW KIRK

INTRODUCTION

There is a sense in which the epistemological crisis of any culture is the "mother of all its crises." Epistemology explores the very foundation of its modes of perceiving, thinking, communicating, and knowing. When there is a breakdown of the culture's consensus regarding the nature of reality, the possibility and criteria of truth, and the scope and function of reason, almost every other aspect of its existence—art forms, educational policies, attitudes toward health and healing, the working of its institutions, the position of its traditional religious undergirding, its patterns of family life, and many more—will be profoundly affected. Christian mission in the West, if it is to be self-reflective, has to explore with deep and sensitive understanding the issues that are involved in this crisis and ponder long and hard on its own specific response.

CHRISTIAN MISSION

Missiology as an intellectual discipline is concerned to reflect critically on the content and practice of the church's life and work as this is perceived theoretically and carried out in action. How does the church envisage its calling? Why does it implement it in particular ways? What are the reasons for its apparent successes and failures? Can one aim to discover the best practice in a wide variety of circumstances? It assumes that there is a given imperative which urges it on to undertake specific tasks and refrain from others, and a particular social, political, and cultural context in which to work out its mission.

In recent years there has been a vigorous debate across the whole spectrum of Christian churches worldwide concerning the extent to which mission is an unchanging task entrusted to Christian communities and the extent to which its implementation is freshly discovered (or rediscovered) in each new generation, acknowledging an always tentative, contingent, and fallible grasp of its nature. Whatever the balance of conviction and certainty any person or group may possess or lack, there can be no talk of mission without the assumption that there is a definite calling to which the response should be obedience and fulfillment.

Some people are convinced that the church needs to invent its mission imaginatively in response to the rapidly changing kaleidoscope of events that characterizes contemporary Western culture. The church, it is claimed, must learn to shed the accumulated baggage inherited from the past as simply the fallible attempts of former generations of Christians to make sense of their calling in vastly different circumstances. In the hands of such people, this stance may involve the virtual abandonment of any distinctive Christian content in their attempt to witness to their faith. Among contemporary theologians such a position is perhaps most clearly discerned in the case of Don Cupitt, though in varying degrees among several others as well.

Although the classical formulations of faith and traditional methods of mission may cause acute embarrassment to such people, they do not (cannot) start to think Christian mission as it were ex nihilo. Both their "mission" involvement and their reflection upon it will inevitably entail the acceptance of certain presuppositions which they take as substantive starting points. These, of course, may be just as much baggage from the past as the traditions which they believe to be no longer tenable.[1] Discarding any element from the past or present, if the process is to be self-reflective and not a matter merely of intuition or whim, necessitates a mechanism of justification based on more adequate grounding.

The question then becomes one of criteria. Here, I believe, there is no possibility of sheer invention, for, if it is true that all human beings are to a degree children of their age, they will use ideas, language, thought forms, and practices already available to them within their horizon of experience. There may be a certain amount of creativity discernible in new combinations of thought taken from different sources. It is extremely rare, however, that anyone in the field of Christian mission discovers genuinely unthought and untried concepts and practices. Those whose musings are declared by the media to be radical, in the sense of being shocking to conventional wisdom, are usually combining ideas taken from other traditions and applying them to their understanding of Christian faith, not abandoning tradition altogether.

This argument is designed to show that in practice, when considering Christian mission everyone is obliged to work with traditions that they have chosen to believe are more or less compelling. The vitality of their vision lies

---

1. In the case of Don Cupitt, for example, see the discerning analysis of his own particular indebtedness to the past in S. N. Williams, *Revelation and Reconciliation: A Window on Modernity* (Cambridge: Cambridge University Press, 1995), 113–42.

in the strength of their grounds for justifying it. For this reason it is much truer to actual procedure to talk about reinventing or rethinking Christian mission within changing contexts than to give the impression that one is capable of reinventing the wheel. It is true to experience that our reflection always happens on the basis of given traditions which we find sufficiently convincing because of their intellectual consistency, their ability to offer an explanation for the fundamental questions of existence, including those of other explanations, or their ability to achieve a fully satisfied life.

This essay is built on the conviction that there is no other way in practice in which we can proceed rationally. To the objection that explanations of life or the achievement of personal meaning offer futile and unprofitable expectations, I would reply that such a counterconviction can only mean anything on the basis of counterpresuppositions which, in turn, need justifying.

To envisage missiology as a discipline that seeks adequate criteria to discern between good and bad mission theory and practice means taking one's stance within a particular tradition that provides such criteria. Critical reflection means, in the first place, using the standards or norms of the tradition itself to judge the adequacy of the mission undertaken. Of course, it will also involve opening itself to criticism that comes from outside its own tradition, in order to reevaluate not only its current practice, but the adequacy of its justifying foundation.

In the light of the discussion so far, I would like to attempt a brief summary of what I take to be the foundation of Christian mission within the tradition inherited and accepted by the vast majority of churches and what I take to be certain aberrations which have been criticized from outside the tradition and found subsequently to be inconsistent with the norms of the tradition itself. Christian self-identity is built on the foundation of Jesus Christ, both as an historical person who lived in a particular way and communicated a particular message, and on the interpretation of his significance given by the original disciples (called apostles).[2] In other words, certain hypotheses concerning the nature and mission of Jesus Christ form the basis for Christian mission prior to the engagement of Christians with society and

---

2. The issues surrounding the interaction of faith and history in the shaping of the New Testament are immense; they have been explored from almost every conceivable angle by critical scholarship over a period of two hundred years. My own general view about this vast amount of work is that reliable historical method requires a rigorous distinction being made between a critical sifting of evidence and speculation. Skepticism with regard to the historical reliability of the New Testament has almost always arisen as a result of the overindulgence of speculative theories. The most recent survey of the evidence has been accumulated by Tom Wright in the first two volumes of his projected five-volume study with the overall title, *Christian Origins and the Question of God*: these are *The New Testament and the People of God* and *Jesus and the Victory of God* (London: SPCK, 1994 and 1996). He shows that historical investigation, shorn both of methodological naiveté and inappropriate rationalist assumptions, comes face to face with an uncompromisingly real person impossible to portray as a mere figment of faith.

culture. These hypotheses spring out of a particular interpretation of God's intentions in dealing with the Hebrew people.

The church has gone wrong, according to its own criteria of judgement, whenever it has sought secular power for itself as a means to achieve its missionary ends, whenever it has used coercion or unworthy incentives to force people into accepting its teaching, or whenever it has depended on a socially privileged position to spread the gospel. In the first instance, it has sought to represent the goal and interests of the whole of society, rather than being salt or leaven within society; in the second instance, it has used weapons, forbidden to it in its founding message, to bring about conversion or conformity; in the third instance, it has used ends to justify unacceptable means.

When speaking about Christian mission in the light of the epistemological crisis of the West, it is vitally important to know how to distinguish between the ends of mission and the means used to achieve them. In Christian thinking ends determine means and means either proclaim or distort the ends. What is justifiable to do is strictly controlled by the message itself. The import of these affirmations will become clearer as we seek to engage missiologically with the West's epistemological crisis. To this we now turn.

THE EPISTEMOLOGICAL CRISIS OF THE WEST

Many of the arguments advanced so far are based on lines of reasoning profoundly disputed by certain current epistemological conclusions. Thus, for example, the notion that one may still argue from the basis of foundational beliefs which do not need any further justification seems to have been refuted two and a half centuries ago by Hume's arguments in *A Treatise of Human Nature*. The desire to achieve some kind of indubitable foundation for all true knowledge is question-begging and therefore inevitably leads to a radical skepticism that anything can be known, outside the inclinations of the mind to believe something. Building on this criticism, Wittgenstein says that the justification for our beliefs cannot go beyond the acknowledgment that this is what we do. In other words, there is no way of adequately distinguishing between opinion ("this is what I happen to believe") and justified true belief ("this is what all self-critically thinking persons ought to believe").

The position advocated here, that Christian missiology begins with propositions that are, in principle, distinguishable from contingent cultural formulations of them, is radically disputed on a number of grounds that have almost become accepted as in themselves not depending on any further justified belief. There is the argument from relativism. All claims to knowledge and truth are relative to the times and circumstances in which they are formulated. There are no neutral criteria which can be universally applied to judge between standards of evaluation of these claims. The Christian claim that the New Testament message about Jesus Christ is universally valid and applicable is to be explained by the contingent necessities of historical context, cultural dominance, or psychological need, for it flies in the face of the multiple interpretations of reality for which, it is alleged, there is no adjudicating yardstick.

Closely connected to the relativism inherent in the acceptance of multi-cultural pluralism is the notion that truth claims invariably reflect the "will-to-power." Most powerfully stated in Foucault's work on the genealogies of certain institutions, this interpretation of human history makes much of the influence of official ideologies which are manufactured to justify a particu-lar status quo and then backed by the most powerful institutional authorities of the day. Of course, this argument works both ways, for the only way of identifying "false" consciousness—the mechanism by which ideologies work—is by assuming a normative, critical vantage point.[3] Otherwise, there is no defensibly good reason for objecting to the ideological manipulation of power. Truth claims then operate in society by excluding difference and, through enforcing consensus and uniformity, abolish the precious commod-ity of individual freedom. They are little more than adjuncts to the messy business of securing and maintaining the power of some over others.

Another way of approaching the question of truth is to deny the possi-bility of any access to objective reality. It is common today to find fault with the notion of reality as a picture or mirror of something that exists inde-pendently of the observing person and thinking mind. It may be argued that reality only exists as it appears and therefore that the real-in-itself cannot be distinguished from a reproduction or simulation of the real. Our apprehen-sion of what we take to be real is always situated in language systems, which are simply instruments that have evolved for thought and communication to be possible. Language is a sign system that, because it does not corre-spond to any univocal facts beyond the power of language to evoke them as such, is open to the endless play of invention. In other words, we create our own realities as we so desire.

There is a further logical step from this way of seeing reality to a prag-matic notion of truth. Truth is created in order to enable us to cope with our experience of life. What is true is what is good for us to believe if we are to function optimally in a given context. Clearly this may vary from situation to situation, and cannot therefore be prejudged.

FROM MODERNITY TO POSTMODERNITY

The epistemological crisis of the West is often summed up in the much-quoted but not very precise assertion that Western culture is in the process of transition from the age of modernity to the age of postmodernity. Epistemo-logically, modernity is characterized as that period of history in which the human person is conceived as a self-sufficient autonomous subject requiring no external support for his or her knowledge, either in God or in nature.[4]

---

3. See D. Hawkes, *Ideology* (New York: Routledge, 1996), 1–12.
4. See Richard Kearney, *Modern Movements in European Philosophy* (Manchester: Manchester University Press, 1994), 288.

Critical, enlightened human reason was adequate to comprehend all that was necessary for the ordering of human life on the foundation of scientifically demonstrable universal laws. From now on it would be possible for human society to base its knowledge on evidence accessible to all and intrinsically open to verification or falsification. Such a situation would lead, sooner rather than later, to humanity abandoning its commitment to unfounded beliefs whose conflicting nature could never be resolved, as they were based on unprovable presuppositions. History then became intrinsically open to the possibility of a unified human race in which everyone would accept the self-evident truths of reason and gladly agree to harness them to overcome ignorance, superstition, and intolerance, which so degraded the inherent dignity of human nature.

Postmodernity is the name given to the period of history in which the supreme value of critical reason as a foundation for the emancipation and progressive development of human life is no longer believed. It marks a dramatic act of unbelief or, as Lyotard stated it, "incredulity towards meta-narratives," in this case the self-legitimation of science as the bearer of internal and external emancipation.[5]

The critical element of doubt surrounds the ability to create an unshakable relationship between the observing, classifying, and understanding subject and the world of objects immediately accessible to intelligent assessment. In other words, the fundamental distinction between the real world of nature and the fictitious worlds of imagination has been broken. The situation then becomes one of "hyperreality" (Baudrillard), in which the distinction between objects and their representations becomes dissolved; one is left only with *simulacra*.[6]

What has led to the rejection of the exaggerated claims of modern rational thought is the suspicion, based on social and cultural analysis, that scientific method in all realms of investigation was being used to enhance the control of an elite minority of professionals over ordinary citizens (George Bernard Shaw defined a profession as a conspiracy against ordinary people). Excess dependence on rationality has led to an almost uncontrolled desire to use knowledge to dominate and manipulate. Because of its universalizing claim to be the measure of all things, there is no transcendent bar of accountability: reason is judge, jury, prosecutor, and counsel for the defense in its own cause.

Postmodernity is iconoclastic. Frederic Jameson has identified four critical models of understanding which have been pervasive in modern times, but that are now challenged to their core: the distinction between essence and appearance (e.g., in concepts of ideology and false consciousness); the gap between the latent and the manifest (e.g., in the Freudian understand-

---

5. See David West, *An Introduction to Continental Philosophy* (Cambridge: Polity Press, 1996), 189ff; Hans Bertens, *The Idea of the Postmodern: A History* (London: Routledge, 1995), 111–37.

6. See D. Lyon, *Postmodernity* (Buckingham, England: Open University Press, 1994), 16.

ing of repression); the choice between authenticity and inauthenticity (in the existentialist account of alienation); and the differentiation between signifier and signified (in theories of language).[7] The net result is an all-pervading sense of uncertainty and instability, a constant challenging of the once accepted, unshakable foundations of apparently well-tested knowledge of the real world.

THE CHALLENGES TO CHRISTIAN MISSION

Just when the churches of the West were coming to terms with the culture of modernity (in particular, with the strengths and weaknesses of a scientific worldview), a very different approach to the experience of life is presenting itself.[8] On the evidence of history so far, it may take a long time for the churches fully to appreciate the nature of the current challenges and, in particular, to be able to handle criteria sufficiently rigorous to give some confidence that it knows how to distinguish between genuine insights and false trails.

The sustained attack on foundationalism, particularly in its form of a metanarrative that claims to be able to give a comprehensive, intelligent, and consistent account of the great questions of human life, is serious for a faith that takes for its starting point a story. Because of the evocative power of storytelling and the intrinsic attraction of stories which encompass the full range of human life (epic, heroicism, tragedy, comedy, confrontation, reconciliation) told sometimes in straight narrative, sometimes in poetic form or through proverbs, metaphors, and symbols, Christians in the late twentieth century have increasingly emphasized the communicative power of the Bible as story and invited listeners to find meaning for their story in the light of *the* story.

Implicit in the method, however, is the claim that in the story of Jesus as told by his earliest followers is set forth the answer to the most perplexing conundrums of human life, wherever lived and by whomever. This story is the measure of all others. This life is the measure of the meaning of liberation and freedom.[9] All other stories, however profound and noble they may be, are ultimately defective in their ability to explain the greatness of human achievement and remedy the colossal effects of human failure.

As we have already seen, such claims appear no longer to be sustainable, even if they are shorn of all vestiges of triumphalism. For one thing, to use the terminology of one story is to be guilty, in the words of Roland Barthes, of an "authoritarian discourse,"[10] that is to say, a language of power intended to create submission. For another thing, one must not imagine that

---

7. See Kearney, *Modern Movements*, 166.

8. See, e.g., among many other works, M. Rae, H. Regan, and J. Stenhouse, *Science and Theology: Questions at the Interface* (Edinburgh: T. & T. Clark, 1994).

9. See my *Loosing the Chains: Religion as Opium and Liberation* (London: Hodder and Stoughton, 1992), 194–201.

10. Kearney, *Modern Movements*, 329.

the story encodes a fixed, clearly defined discourse with a fundamentally uni-vocal meaning. If one follows a poststructuralist stance then the text allows a libertine excess of multiple signification, an infinitely playful performance of signification. The importance of this point of view is that the claim to an authoritative interpretation of the text is subverted, undermining "all hier-archical systems of language which institutionalize one form of discourse by repressing all non-conformist alternatives."[11]

The consequence of this proposition is that no controlling meaning can be given to the text which would exclude any others.[12] People of other faiths and none may quite legitimately read into and out of the text whatever they please. The Christian claims are quite simply one possible perspective among equals. If this is an acceptable approach to the basic Christian text, then clearly claims to truth based on the singularity of its message and the origin of its thought have nowhere to go; they vanish ephemeral-like into the shadow world of every person's opinion.

Earlier we stated that Christian mission is based on a conscious response to an imperative understood to emanate unambiguously from God. However the imperative is thought to be mediated, mission by its nature is consequent upon the existence of an obligation acknowledged and acted on.[13] The language of imperative and obligation assumes some kind of unconditional responsibility laid upon one to act in a certain way. Such notions do not fit a culture in which the relativity of truth and values is taken as being beyond the need for demonstration. It is not surprising that the concept of Christian mission causes acute embarrassment to those who have imbibed the intoxicating pluralism of human self-expression.[14]

Pragmatic notions of truth are unlikely to sustain a sense of mission either. If the criterion of truth is its ability to illuminate an individual's expe-rience and orient him or her toward a goal in life which he or she finds per-sonally meaningful, then persuasion to believe and act on a particular message as the only one having the inherent power to make sense of life for everyone, however gently accomplished, will be sternly resisted on the grounds that what is "true" for one person may well not be "true" for another. What is important is that my sense of the divine and of right and wrong are made more coherent and serviceable. It is this attitude toward truth which underlies the notion that a Christian's greatest responsibility to

---

11. Ibid., 329–30.

12. See Nicholas Wolterstorff's presentation and critique of Derrida's theory of signi-fication, *Divine Discourse: Philosophical Reflections on the Claim That God Speaks* (Cambridge: Cambridge University Press, 1995), 157–69.

13. Paradoxically, this is true also for those who see their "mission" to be the debunk-ing of all claims to possess a mission.

14. Thus G. M. Thomas observes: "Freedom must consist (according to the moderns) in would-be monks being able to become monks and would-be tarts becoming tarts if they so wish. . . . Choices will have to be made in an unencumbered fashion from a vir-tually infinite menu of potentialities." See his "A Clarity Interfered With," in T. Burns (ed.), *After History: Francis Fukuyama and His Critics* (Lanham: Rowman and Littlefield, 1994), 89–90.

people of another faith is to help them, when invited, to deepen their commitment to their own traditions of symbolization as a means of integrating more consistently their own experience of life. Any other approach is rejected as overweening presumption.

WAYS OF RESPONDING TO THE CHALLENGES

Christians can and have reacted in a number of different ways to the mission challenges posed by the diversity of changes taking place throughout Western society. By adapting somewhat the typology suggested by Richard Niebuhr in his classic 1951 book *Christ and Culture*, we can identify the following four categories: escapism/privatization; absorption/cultural consensus; opposition/minority status; transformation/minority status.

Christians may decide that the issues (some of which we have identified here) are too complex and, in their opinion, too esoteric to bother about. In some ways it would appear to be easier not to have either to adapt to the changing scene by devising new ways of formulating the message or of communicating it, or to challenge the assumptions lying behind the changes. The task of the church remains, as it always has, the faithful exposition of an unchanging message to individuals. Irrespective of the cultural changes, the fundamental needs of human beings remain unchanged. The church's main responsibility is to offer God's forgiveness and strength in the call for a new style of living following the way of Christ. Human beings, universally, need a sense of worth, a community to live in that they can trust, a hope for the future, care when living through times of distress. All these are offered in the unchanging gospel.

At the opposite end of the spectrum, some Christians are convinced that the familiar categories of thought by which the church has expressed itself are no longer serviceable. The changes taking place in culture are irreversible. The message which the church has traditionally proclaimed is not so much unbelievable as incomprehensible. The imperative is to attempt to proclaim and live Jesus Christ from within the thought forms of a postmodern age. The cultural consensus is accepted: "God's death" is affirmed as a positive value, because most images of God (mainly male, white, heterosexual, middle-aged, and hierarchical) are repressive and, therefore, too dangerous to resurrect. The major contribution a Christian may be able to make within the cultural confusion left by the "shaking of the foundations" is to rediscover the identity of the self stripped of the false assurances of the past.[15]

There is a growing body of opinion that conceives the church's mission in terms of faithful opposition: not in the wholly negative sense of finding

---

15. Alain Touraine sees the greatest danger of the moment to be "a complete dissociation between system and actors, between the technical or economic world and the world of subjectivity." He believes this is a problem equally, though for different reasons, for those who defend the gains of modernity and those who believe the postmodern challenge is more hopeful. See his *Critique of Modernity* (Oxford: Oxford University Press, 1995), 5–6.

fault with every aspect of contemporary culture, but in the discerning attitude of providing a set of values, an intellectual perspective, and a community which offers a permanent alternative to current fashions.[16] The major hermeneutical key of such a position is the suspicion of idolatry on the part of institutions and intellectual trends. The abandonment of the God of the prophetic initiative (explicit in all death-of-God pronouncements) is not a liberating act, but the submission to the greater slavery of intellectual and moral anarchy and arbitrariness. Above all, the church must rigorously guard against all temptation to align itself with secular power, however sympathetic some programs and strategies may seem to be towards those values Christians would wish to defend.

The final category we have identified is that which, whilst also wishing to eschew the exercise of power *qua* church, believes that the main assumptions of contemporary Western culture, whether in its modern or postmodern appearance, need not only to be challenged but to be replaced. Whereas this position requires the church as an institution to keep itself clear of involvement in the running of the institutions of society, it encourages Christians individually or collectively to work within institutions for new attitudes toward human life which reflect the way of Christ. In other words, the goal of Christian mission is to seek a culture and society which, in every way, mirrors more closely the new resurrected order inaugurated by Jesus Christ.[17]

As with all categorization, there is a danger of caricaturing the different mission stances taken or of not allowing sufficiently subtle shades of differentiation. The four positions must be understood as general tendencies and as ones which are not necessarily mutually exclusive. I will continue by giving an account of what I consider is the best way of grasping the opportunities for missiology presented by the present epistemological crisis. I will use the heuristic device utilized so successfully by liberation theology, following the methodological lead given by Paulo Freire in his pioneering work in popular education—*see, judge, act*.

SEE, JUDGE, ACT

The first step for missiological reflection is carefully to examine through a systematic analysis the real nature of the crisis. This is not a task that Christians need necessarily initiate or carry through on their own. In many ways the work has already been done, either implicitly or explicitly, by many people engaged in the epistemological debate who may own a variety of different faith perspectives. In my estimation, the crisis can best be summed up in the word "inconsistency." Within the different thought processes exam-

---

16. The position has been associated in recent years particularly with Stanley Hauerwas; see his *After Christendom* (Nashville: Abingdon Press, 1991).

17. This position has been clearly set out in a number of significant books by Lesslie Newbigin; see, e.g., his *Truth to Tell: The Gospel as Public Truth* (Grand Rapids: Eerdmans, 1991).

ined in the first part of this volume which have provided such a multiplicity of epistemological options, one may notice in varying degrees a lack of consistency. This is true within the intellectual tradition itself; it often becomes even more evident when thought is applied to moral reasoning and ethical action.

Inconsistency manifests itself as a fundamental contradiction between two or more axioms or statements or between an intellectual stance and practical living. It means that if one is to be accepted as valid, the other has to be denied. It is based on the premise that two, or more, propositions cannot disagree and both be right. It may be discerned in a line of reasoning, when conclusions are reached that are incompatible with the premises of the argument. It is also obvious when moral positions are taken that seem to bear no resemblance to the logic of the person's theoretical stance. Its most celebrated formulation is in the so-called "law of noncontradiction" that asserts that when two (or more) statements contradict each other they cannot both be correct (though they could, of course, both be false).[18]

One might well ask why consistency in thinking and living is deemed to be such an important principle that it is erected into the key for understanding the contemporary crisis. After all, those who deny the universal applicability of the law of noncontradiction are not lacking. This has been particularly true in philosophical thought associated with Eastern religions. The response has to be twofold. First, in practice, there is literally no other way that thinking can proceed. In order to deny the law of noncontradiction, one has to invoke it. Second, to think coherently and to be able to make one's actions harmonize with one's thinking is to enhance the dignity of human life. Inconsistency degrades and debilitates the meaning of human existence.[19]

It is vitally important in a missiological perspective that one does not exempt the mission agent from the critique of inconsistency. An accusation directed elsewhere and refused for oneself is generally given the name of hypocrisy. Unfortunately, there is too much evidence of that within the thinking and practice of the church. Therefore, the analysis of the crisis must encompass the intellectual tradition and life of the Christian community.

---

18. There have been attempts to refute the law of noncontradiction in its form as "the law of the excluded middle" by asserting the ambiguity of referents in some sentences that appear to be contradictory. Once the meaningfulness in context of the proposition is established and the scope of the language is identified, however, the logic of the law holds. See Mark Sainsbury, "Philosophical Logic," in A.C. Grayling (ed.), *Philosophy: A Guide through the Subject* (Oxford: Oxford University Press, 1995), 81–84.

19. There are legitimate objections to what appears to be the rigid application of an invariable law. These encompass those situations where the only way of doing justice to a full range of complex evidence seems to be the formulation of explanations which appear to invoke contradictory statements. The two most celebrated, from very different disciplines, might be the formulation of the movement of light and the Christian understanding of God as Trinity. Whether or not these are exceptions to the general rule is debatable, and the discussion is beyond the scope of this essay; the important principle is that the law is valid because it demonstrably covers the vast majority of cases.

Let us now turn to the issues we noted when looking at the epistemological predicament of the West. The rejection of foundationalism may seem to be self-evident, because access to universally recognized and indubitable knowledge is simply not possible. The apparent alternatives do not seem to leave one with any resting-place at all, however. Thought is caught between the rock of skepticism and the hard place of relativism, neither of which can be consistently maintained.[20]

In practice all people, whatever their theory may say to the contrary, act on the basis of fundamental beliefs.[21] These are beliefs universally held by humankind and reflected in the common structure of all languages. Their negation is not merely false but absurd; they are necessary for engaging in the practical affairs of life.[22] It can be shown from careful observation of normal life that everyone acts on the basis of acquired knowledge, however fragmentary, which they do not justify by recourse to a deeper knowledge. Of course, such knowledge may be accepted as a working hypothesis and, therefore, be corrigible; but, at the point of action, it is decisive.

The questions of pluralism and truth may be dealt with in the context of moral reasoning. Again, in practice, no one seriously believes that moral action can be encompassed either as a matter of personal taste or of the enforced decision of state or family. Universally, human beings consistently make moral judgements that assume an absolute code of practice, at least in

---

20. For the impossibility of maintaining a relativistic approach to ethical values, see my argument in *Loosing the Chains*, 53–66, 165–76. With regard to skepticism, the commonsense argument of Thomas Reid (a contemporary of Hume) that life can only be lived on the basis that complete skepticism is unwarranted seems to be a sufficient rebuttal. We can only act on the assumption that effects have causes and that a real internal and external world exists. So, Stephen Nathanson, *The Ideal of Rationality: A Defense within Reason* (Chicago: Open Court Press, 1994), 208–12; and Robert Audi, *Epistemology: A Contemporary Introduction to the Theory of Knowledge* (New York: Routledge, 1998), 308–13.

My "foundationalism" is methodological: actions spring from faith, in the sense explored by Juan Luis Segundo, *Faith and Ideologies* (Maryknoll: Orbis Books, 1984), *passim*; when actions clash, the faith needs justifying; justification assumes a foundational authorization; when justifications clash, the authorizations are used as the ultimate judging criteria. My contention is that this is the way in which argumentation actually takes place, when there is a serious clash of interpretations about practice. I am not happy with the term "chastened foundationalism." Although I recognize in it the call to epistemic modesty, there is nothing to be ashamed of in adopting a carefully defined form of foundationalism. I would prefer to call it "modified" or "moderate presuppositional" foundationalism. I wish to explore this highly disputed territory at a later date in a substantial book on the subject of truth.

21. This is the case though many deny it to be. Their reasoning is careful and sophisticated and yet, in my opinion, ultimately inconsistent. When I appeal to foundations, I am not seeking to defend classic foundationalism, if by that is understood the possibility of acquiring for any belief or interpretation of life the three main "epistemic immunities"—immunity from error, from refutation, and from doubt.

22. See J. Dancy and E. Sosa, *A Companion to Epistemology* (Oxford: Blackwell, 1993), 72.

some instances. This is the only way one can make sense of the paradoxical intolerance that the most liberally inclined people show toward certain attitudes and actions. Though, according to a person's moral tradition, they may vary from case to case, there are moral limitations which everyone accepts. Perhaps the most universally accepted would be the wanton exploitation of and cruelty toward vulnerable people (like children, the mentally and physically disabled, and the old) and deliberate deceit. Even where a moral tradition allows an excess of moral liberty (as in libertarianism), it upholds the duty of all to respect the freedom of others.

The notion that truth can be identified with personal or group dispositions (what is true "for me" or "for us") is absurd. It empties truth of any meaning whatsoever, by allowing to it a purely private definition. Moreover, it makes a complete nonsense of the reality of error. If truth is identified with what seems right in my internal world, then what seems right is right. As long as I believe it, I cannot be in error. If, on the contrary, one acknowledges the possibility of error, then it follows that some criterion (external to myself) must be employed to distinguish what is false from what is true. Here, we do not have to argue from any particular definition of truth, only to demonstrate that in practice, invariably, people argue and act on the basis of believing that it exists as a reality external to individual desires and interests.

The belief that truth can be understood in pragmatic terms is question-begging. If the meaning of truth is to be defined by its utility in producing a good or useful outcome, the argument has not been advanced at all, unless we know what is the good and why. The good cannot be specified by appeal to the consequences it produces without further begging the question. Manifestly, the appeal to functionality is not an adequate explanation of ethical right, for wrong action can also work, according to the criteria adopted. There is no possibility here of short-circuiting the appeal to intrinsic values. Pragmatism is altogether too subjective to provide adequate guidance to right and wrong action, for as a guiding principle it is too easily confused with opportunism. Nevertheless, the consequences of actions do provide an important consideration in judging between alternative choices, but only when tested against norms right or wrong in themselves.

If it is widely conceded that the reductionist rationalism of modernity is inherently incapable of satisfying the deepest intellectual and moral questions posed by human existence, the postmodern denouement probably fares even worse. The problem of modernity does not lie with the limitations of reason or with the use to which it has been put (instrumental reason), but with the assumptions on which it has been used. It is a self-defeating exercise to attempt to begin with the empirical particulars of the natural world in the hope of being able to build theories that can make sense of the whole of experience. Explanations that begin and end with observable and verifiable causal sequences are doomed to conclude that human life is machinelike. The sensations of personal worth, moral values, and ultimate purpose in existing have to be incomprehensible. Rationalism is bereft of the instruments necessary to fathom out this part of human experience. In a very real sense, the modern predicament, by posing a dilemma which it does not have the instruments to solve, makes human beings inferior to animals, for the latter do not possess these sensations and therefore do not experience a need to explain them.

The dilemma began when the culture in general accepted (following the arguments of Hume and Kant) that intellectual probity necessitated the assumption that the uniformity of natural causes required a closed-order universe. As a result, just as nature gradually swallowed up grace in the theology of the medieval period, so nature took the place of the revelatory and reordering activity of God within the world. The dilemma is acute. No longer is there a sufficient reason for believing with certainty that anything exists, or that there is an adequate correlation between the observer (subject) and the thing observed (the object), or that a meaningful distinction can be made between reality and fantasy. As Kant observed, reason supplies the human mind with regulative ideals, not constitutive ideas. In ethics reason guides our choice of principles on which to act, but does not supply those principles. In decision making reason may help determine the means we appropriate to achieve desired ends, but the ends themselves are not discovered as necessary truths by rational intuition, as Descartes and Spinoza believed. Once revelation is considered impossible or irrelevant, the universe becomes silent except for the prolonged echo of merely human chatter reproducing itself.

In theological terms, the epistemological crisis is due to an idolatrous faith in the power of reason to bring the whole world of nature and of experience under its regulative principle. Reason itself is not at fault. The postmodern tendency, therefore, to delight in the irrational and the absurd kills the patient rather than curing the disease. The turn to carefree playfulness as a riposte to the drudgery of bureaucracy and the boredom and superficiality of endless consumerism marks a regress to childhood, not a development to a fully responsible adulthood. As a matter of fact, its attention to variety, choice, and the importance of minority interests is a perfect foil for the consumer culture. What may be said about the drive to consume may be said with identical language (substituting experience for goods and services) of the postmodern condition:

> In general terms, modern Euro-American societies are characterized by the strongly rooted belief that to have is to be . . . this is related to the privileging of a relationship between individuals and things in terms of possession. . . . Indeed, most people describe possessions as aspects of the self, and their loss is experienced as personal violation and a lessening of the self. It is in this context that possessions have come to serve as key symbols for personal qualities, attachments and interests.[23]

---

23. Celia Lury, *Consumer Culture* (Cambridge: Polity Press, 1996), 7.

The unpalatable truth is that postmodernity, if consistent to its own ideals, is pure escapism. Its deconstruction is reaction (and reactionary), for it has no grounds for reconstruction. Here again, it mirrors the results of the technological reason it so passionately despises: "It has been argued that consumption . . . is also driven by hedonism, escapism, fantasy and the desire for novelty or 'identity-value.'"[24]

The second step for missiological reflection is to invite contemporary Western culture to consider the thesis that the destructive consequences of the inherent contradictions in its mode of thinking and between its thinking and action can be turned into new life by accepting the gospel as the one perspective that gives sufficient grounds for the integration of thought and of theory and practice. This will be an arduous task, which, even if it is achieved in part, may not result in the invitation being accepted. Perhaps the hardest task for missiology is to procure a hearing: in the words of the title of this book, "to stake a claim" that is taken seriously.

As far as epistemology is concerned, this task of integration awaits another opportunity. It will be one of the assignments still outstanding at the end of this present project. If the argument of this chapter has any weight, it cannot be done in isolation from the work of the other subgroups, particularly those working on the self-identity of the church in history and on the meaning of the church today. Integration involves thinking, being, and doing. The subject of the missiological task must himself or herself seek, on the basis of the gospel, as consistent a unity among the three as is possible to achieve in an imperfect world. Otherwise, he or she will contribute no more to the promised banquet than the meager scraps with which the non-Christian world seeks to assuage its hunger.

---

24. Ibid., 46.

CHAPTER NINE

Mystical Knowledge,
New Age, and Missiology

LARS JOHANSSON

A magazine once arranged a dialogue between me and a well-known Swedish film director who regularly conducts seminars with a New Age orientation. As the discussion developed, he suddenly presented several rather controversial views which he claimed to be biblical. When I reached for a Bible and pointed to some passages in the New Testament which challenged his position he said, "Oh, but these verses are later additions." When I asked him how he knew, he replied, "I just feel it!"

References to direct intuitive knowing are increasingly common among the many seekers of spiritual truth who relate more or less closely to what has been called the New Age. Opposing the church as a dogmatic institution and Christianity as a dogmatic religion, they view themselves as being in touch with their feelings and intuition. They challenge Christians to make the same connections by embarking on a journey within to receive intuitive knowledge.

Also reacting against modern rationality, they affirm that ultimate truth is revealed in mystical experiences in altered states of consciousness, beyond words and concepts. Rejecting dependence on external authorities such as creeds, dogmas, written revelations, and given traditions, they say that such things merely block the way to the inner realm. Truth comes from within, experience is primary and dogma secondary. "Dogmas are merely frozen experiences," as one proponent proclaimed in a public dialogue in which I took part. The New Age criterion of truth seems to be subjectivist, pragmatist, and individualist: "Truth is what feels right and works for me." While on the surface level the New Age celebrates a postmodern plurality of ways and truths, at a deeper level it assumes an ultimate unity in the universe beyond fragmentation. Knowledge of it is gained through the journey within, taking us beyond the exoteric, outer forms of the different traditions to the esoteric, underlying core of common Truth behind all religions. Experience of a mystical nature is held to provide the prime key to this common Truth.

Primacy of the experiential with regard to religious truth, a dualism between experience itself and its interpretation in dogma, and an accompanying vague belief in some sort of universal religion have become elements of a powerful metanarrative within the New Age. It is a spirituality that is now establishing itself as the new folk religion of the West,[1] challenging the church to move back to the countercultural quarters she came from.[2] The opinions stated above are not restricted to the New Age alone. They are most often expressed in a self-evident way as soon as religion is debated in the public arena.

Realities like these need to be taken into account as we try to trace the epistemological predicament of the West. As the church today seeks to relate to the massive number of people who seek a new spiritual direction for their lives outside the church, it will find that epistemological awareness is indispensable. In this paper I will try to show that the New Age appeal to experiential knowledge is deeply rooted in our culture and in certain epistemological assumptions that have been taken over from the formative forces behind the New Age. I will point to the contextual nature of mystical knowledge, refering to a recent discussion on mysticism, and then move on to an analysis of some concrete cases in the area of alternative spirituality. I am quite convinced that the current claims to higher mystical knowledge among the spiritual seekers present the church with one of the greatest challenges in its mission in the West. In the final section I will try briefly to point to some missiological implications of this challenge.

CULTURE AND EXPERIENCE

The move toward subjectivity is an important aspect of recent cultural change, since modernization includes not only rationalization but also its opposite. The modern drama entails an increase of epistemological uncertainty both in the field of philosophy and in everyday life. When traditional patterns of social behaviour as well as belief systems and external authorities are being changed or eroded, modern individuals are left alone to find answers to the perennial question, "What can I know?"[3] When answers are

---

1. Olav Hammer, *På spaning efter helheten: New Age en ny folktro?* (Stockholm: Wahlström & Widstrand, 1997), 22.

2. Lars Johansson, "New Age: A Synthesis of the Premodern, Modern and Postmodern," in Philip Sampson, Vinay Samuel, and Chris Sugden (eds.), *Faith and Modernity* (Oxford: Regnum Books, 1994), 234. A definition of the New Age and a description of its significance is left out in the paper but can be found in Johansson, "New Age," 209, and Paul Heelas, *The New Age Movement: The Celebration of the Self and the Sacralization of Modernity* (Oxford: Blackwell, 1996), 106. The latter provides at present the most extensive and up-to-date description of its significance.

3. See Johansson, "New Age," 218, for an overview of different aspects of the split between society and the individual.

not provided objectively by society, the individual is compelled to turn inward, toward his or her own subjectivity, to dredge up from there whatever certainties he or she can manage.[4] Tradition no longer thinks in my place, as the German sociologist Thomas Ziehe says. Subjectivization is thus integral to modernization and can be defined as a structural process where people are forced to turn inward to find meaningful answers.[5] This process also fosters subjectivism which is a preoccupation with the undiscovered complexities of one's individual subjectivity, creating, among many corollaries, a therapeutization of culture and spirituality. The turning toward subjectivity is not only an ongoing everyday drama but can be seen also in Western philosophy since Descartes.

In the vacuum created by the loss of the traditional, the socialization of consciousness has increasingly been taken over by the market and the media. The latter, in particular, plays an important role in shaping the ways we know the world and ourselves in the postmodern context. Postman has argued that television contributes to subjectivization since it represents a considerable cultural move away from words and reason to images and experience/feeling. In the present postmodern context of media-created hyperreality, Jameson describes how experience is reduced to a series of pure and unrelated presents which become powerful and overwhelmingly vivid and material. He further implies that these immediate and intense experiences contribute to a loss of a sense of narrative and a disconnectedness with tradition and history.[6] "The immediacy of events, the sensationalism of the spectacle . . . becomes the stuff of which consciousness is forged," according to Jameson.[7] The world of media also contributes to the postmodern focus on the surface, a willingness to accept things as they are, on the surface, instead of seeking a deeper meaning.[8] The immediate and impressionist truth claims one often hears among New Agers are partly, I suspect, a reflection of our present cultural climate. Truth is what feels true for me, in the here and now.

Another background to our present climate of subjectivism could be described as a protest against the patterns of a highly demanding public sphere which is abstract, impersonal, rational, and utilitarian. This reaction bestows higher value on the concrete and personal, on experience, feeling,

---

4. Peter Berger, *The Heretical Imperative: Contemporary Possibilities of Religious Affirmation* (New York: Anchor Press/Doubleday, 1979), 21.

5. Johansson, "New Age," 219, and James Davison Hunter, *American Evangelicalism, Conservative Religion and the Quandary of Modernity* (New Brunswick, NJ: Rutgers University Press, 1983), 92.

6. Mike Featherstone, *Consumer Culture & Postmodernism* (London: Sage Publications, 1994), 58.

7. David Harvey, *The Condition of Postmodernity* (Oxford: Blackwell, 1989), 54.

8. Steinar Kvale, "Themes of Postmodernity," in Walter Truett Anderson (ed.), *The Truth about the Truth: Deconfusing and Reconstructing the Postmodern World* (New York: Jeremy P. Tarcher/Putnam Books, 1995), 24.

and the subjective.[9] Private life becomes a kind of compensation for public life, a place where subjectivity functions as an antidote.

The loss of a traditionally stable order and the subsequent turn within (subjectivization), the colonialization of consciousness by the media, and reactions against an impersonal public sphere have created a cultural seedbed for current expressivism, New Age being one of many examples.

NEW AGE AND *PHILOSOPHIA PERENNIS*

Tracing yet another source of subjectivity (and attitude toward dogma) within alternative spirituality we find an important clue in the formative forces behind the New Age. The spiritual hunger of the counterculture and the subsequent growth of New Age in the late 1960s and early 1970s was particularly nurtured by three developments in the U.S.: the 1965 change of immigration laws led to an influx of teachers from the Eastern religions; the 1960s saw an establishment of a number of theosophically inspired groups coming from England;[10] a blend between the American counterculture of the 1950s and humanistic psychology (Maslow, Rogers) led to the development of the Human Potential Movement and a new branch of psychology called Transpersonal psychology.[11]

The countercultural decade of the 1960s and the New Age sought inspiration in an idealized projection of the East.[12] The gurus from India came from a culture inspired by the reformed/neovedanta Hinduism of such figures as Ramakrishna (1836–86) and Vivekananda (1863–1903). According to their teaching, dogmas, images, and rituals are just outer manifestations. The common core of all religion is an experience of the divine reality; every religion is like a river that flows to the same ocean. Theosophical teaching was of the same sort. The Theosophical Society, founded by Helena P. Blavatsky and Henry Olcott in 1875, claimed to revive a secret wisdom that was common to all religions of the world. This common core of truth was discovered by experience and intuition. It was a kind of higher gnosis, presented as an esoteric, inner knowledge, quite different from the outer, exoteric teachings of respective religions. The famous dictum of the theosophical movement still is: "There is no religion higher than truth."

---

9. Peter Berger, Brigitte Berger, and Hansfried Kellner, *The Homeless Mind: Modernization and Consciousness* (Harmondsworth: Penguin, 1974), 180.

10. J. Gordon Melton, "Whither the New Age?" in Timothy Miller (ed.), *America's Alternative Religions* (Albany: SUNY Press, 1995), 349, and Catherine L. Albanese, "The Magical Staff: Quantum Healing in the New Age," in James R. Lewis and J. Gordon Melton (eds.), *Perspectives on the New Age* (Albany: SUNY Press, 1992), 73.

11. J. Gordon Melton, "New Thought and the New Age," in Lewis and Melton (eds.), *Perspectives on the New Age*, 18, and Kay Alexander, "Roots of The New Age," in *Perspectives on the New Age*, 36, 47.

12. Andrea Grace Diem and James R. Lewis, "The Influence of Hinduism on the New Age Movement," in Lewis and Melton (eds.), *Perspectives on the New Age*, 57.

Already by the end of the nineteenth century, Hindu philosophers such as Vivekananda met with the theosophical movement and they mutually influenced each other. It was, in fact, the Theosophical Society who successfully introduced Vivekananda to the West. Theosophical circles in England during the 1930s educated the British intelligentsia in Orientalism. Such leading figures in the Californian counterculture of the 1950s as Alan Watts and Aldous Huxley came out of this camp. They, as well as people like Kerouac and Ginsberg, had a deep affinity with both Eastern religions and Western esoteric teaching in its theosophical form.[13] As the countercultural experiments in personal growth of the 1950s met with theories on human growth within humanistic psychology, the Human Potential Movement was born.[14] After some time it came to recognize the transpersonal aspects of the "peak experiences" that Maslow tried to describe. The result was Transpersonal psychology, which sought to trace and record different kinds of mystical experiences and states.[15]

The eclectical spirituality of the New Age drew its inspiration from these three closely related developments which all had a similar mystical orientation. And already in 1945 Huxley published his book *The Perennial Philosophy* as a testimony of his spiritual heritage, presenting a perspective on mystical knowledge which would come to be fundamental to the New Age.[16]

The idea of a Philosophia Perennis, a concept coined by Leibniz (1646–1716), can, in the West at least, be dated to Marsilio Ficino in the Renaissance.[17] Zaehner defines the *philosophia perennis* as

> that philosophy which maintains that the ultimate truths about God and the universe cannot be directly expressed in words, that these truths are necessarily everywhere and always the same, and that, therefore, the revealed religions which so obviously differ on so many points from one another, can only be relatively true, each revelation being accommodated to the needs of the time and place in which it was made and adapted to the degree of the spirituality of its

---

13. Carl A. Raschke, *The Interruption of Eternity: Modern Gnosticism and the Origins of the New Religious Consciousness* (Chicago: Nelson Hall, 1980), 207, and James Webb, "The Occult Establishment," in Robert Basil (ed.), *Not Necessarily the New Age: Critical Essays* (Buffalo/New York: Prometheus Books, 1988), 59.

14. The encounter and exchange between Abraham Maslow and the founder of Esalen, Michael Murphy, was an especially important factor as this first and most important personal growth center started. Aldous Huxley, who besides his Eastern and Occult affinities was a pioneer in psychedelia, was also consulted as the new center developed. Alexander, "Roots of the New Age," 36.

15. Alexander, "Roots of the New Age," 44.

16. See Heelas, *The New Age Movement*, 26, and J. Gordon Melton, "A History of The New Age Movement," in Basil (ed.), *Not Necessarily the New Age*, 46.

17. Antoine Faivre, "Introduction 1," in Antoine Faivre and Jacob Neddleman (eds.), *Modern Esoteric Spirituality* (London: SCM Press, 1993), xiii, and Håkan Arlebrand, *Det Okända: Om ockultism och andlighet i en ny tidsålder* (Örebro: Libris, 1995), 31.

recipients. . . . All are facets of the same truth. . . . The truth itself is that experienced by the mystics whose unity of thought and language is said to speak for itself.[18]

Perennialism and mysticism have become popular for several reasons. First, mysticism seems to be a fascinating alternative to religion. It has come to be viewed as a storehouse of all that is best and still admirable in religion but one that is free from such no longer acceptable elements as dogma, authority, discipline, and respect for traditions.[19] Second, perennialism corresponds to an ecumenical desire to find something common in the spiritual life of all the world's people in a shrinking and increasingly globalized world.[20] It also represents the hope of finding some universal spiritual resource that could restore meaning to contemporary life in the face of the cultural crisis of modern society. In face of the present threats to human life, some writers are advocating the need for a holistic postmodernism in contrast to the fragmentation of deconstructive postmodernism. This includes a revival of the premodern, assuming perennialism[21] and a core teaching in the wisdom traditions.[22]

Third, perennialism and the primacy of the mystical have also been widely accepted since they have been part of the reigning orthodoxy among several influential scholars of mysticism such as William James, Walter Stace, Evelyn Underhill, Rudolf Otto, and R. C. Zaehner.

The perennialism and mysticism of the New Age is not only an inherited piece of goods, it also seems to be in tune with the needs of our time as well as with our intellectual heritage. It reflects a hitherto relatively strong interpretative tradition in the West.

MYSTICISM AND CONTEXTUALITY

Moving on to a deeper discussion of mysticism, it is first of all notable, as we have shown in the introductory chapters of this book, that an increased awareness of the contextual nature of knowledge is one of the more significant trends in recent epistemology. Our knowledge and even our language depend on practices which are a part of tradition and community. Does this new awareness apply to the area of mysticism and perennialism?

Since the 1980s several studies have appeared which have questioned the reigning orthodoxy of mystical ecumenism and perennialism proposed by

---

18. R. C. Zaehner, *Mysticism Sacred and Profane* (London: Oxford University Press, 1957), 27.

19. Robert M. Gimello, "Mysticism in its Context," in Steven T. Katz (ed.), *Mysticism and Religious Traditions* (Oxford: Oxford University Press, 1983) 86.

20. Steven T. Katz, "Editor's Introduction," in Steven T. Katz (ed.), *Mysticism and Philosophical Analysis* (London: Sheldon Press, 1978), 1.

21. Huston Smith, in David Ray Griffin and Huston Smith, *Primordial Truth and Postmodern Theology* (Albany: SUNY Press, 1989), 61.

22. Charlene Spretnak, *States of Grace: The Recovery of Meaning in the Postmodern Age* (San Francisco: Harper, 1991), 9.

the above-mentioned scholars. They have tried to show that the varieties of mysticism cannot be reduced to a single common core of pure, undifferentiated experience, nor even to only two or three basic types of such experience. They have also questioned the dualist distinction between the experience itself and its interpretation. The content of mystical experience is contextual.

One of the leading lights of this discussion is Steven Katz, and in the following I will present some of his most important arguments.[23] Katz takes the epistemological assumption that there are no pure (i.e., unmediated) experiences or states of consciousness. "Neither mystical experience nor more ordinary forms of experience gives any indication, or any grounds for believing, that they are unmediated."[24] According to Katz, all experiences are mediated and in fact preformed or preconditioned by a complex, culturally acquired, sociopsychological mould consisting of concepts, beliefs, and expectations, which we human beings bring to the experience. The phenomenological content of all experience is shaped by a mediating framework. Mystical experiences have a specific content because mystics come to their experiences with certain religious concepts, beliefs, symbol systems, and expectations concerning what they will experience, which partially creates the content of their mystical experiences. Katz assumes that linguistic, social, historical, and conceptual contextuality affects the mystic before, during, and after the event to color or shape his or her experience. The context thus influences both the experience, the interpretation, and subsequent explanation.

Neither Christian nor Hindu mystics have experiences of an unidentified reality X which they describe in conventional and familiar concepts, labelling it Brahman or God. A Hindu has a Hindu experience and a Christian has a Christian experience because they have, at the least, a partially preformed Hindu experience of Brahman or Christian prefigured experience of God or Jesus.[25] The Hindu experience of Brahman and the Christian experience of

---

23. Besides Steven Katz, some of the more important contributors are Peter Moore ("Mystical Experience, Mystical Doctrine, Mystical Technique," in Katz [ed.], *Mysticism and Philosophical Analysis*), Robert M. Gimello ("Mysticism and Meditation," in *Mysticism and Philosophical Analysis*, and "Mysticism in its Context," in Steven T. Katz [ed], *Mysticism and Religious Traditions* [Oxford: Oxford University Press, 1983]). See also Hans H. Penner, "The Mystical Illusion," in *Mysticism and Religious Traditions*.

That religious experiences greatly depend on the context and interpretive concepts is also argued by Wayne Proudfoot in his *Religious Experience* (Berkeley: University of California Press, 1985). Proudfoot has influenced postliberal theologian George Lindbeck, who strongly criticizes an "experiential-expressive" model in favor of a "cultural-linguistic" alternative. Lindbeck denies a common core of religious experience, emphasizing rather that diverse interpretive schemes and languages evoke and mold different types of experiences. See George Lindbeck, *The Nature of Doctrine, Religion and Theology in a Postliberal Age* (London: SPCK, 1984), 40.

24. Steven T. Katz, "Language, Epistemology and Mysticism," in Katz (ed.), *Mysticism and Philosophical Analysis*, 26.

25. Steven T. Katz, "The Conservative Character of Mysticism," in Katz (ed.), *Mysticism and Religious Traditions*, 4.

God are not the same, phenomenologically speaking. In fact, as regards their phenomenological content, there are as many different kinds of mystical experiences as there are contexts.

Those who see mysticism as a key to the unity of all religions often regard the mystic as a rebel who challenges established religious authority and tradition. By examples from a wide variety of contexts, Katz tries to show that the mystics are more conservative than expected. They remain within their interpretative framework and, although at times in tension, they even reinforce the authority of the canonical texts through certain hermeneutical devices.[26] The certain agreed sources serve as important tools in theological and mystical education. Sacred texts, written in sacred languages and comprised of sacred alphabets as well as sacred words, do play important roles in the major mystical traditions of the world.[27]

Analyzing mystical texts, Katz shows that they reflect different ontologies. There are substantial differences between a Christian and a Buddhist or a Hindu view of ultimate reality which also shapes the form of the mystical quest and its goal, the definition of the problem and its solution. The preexperiential, inherited ontological structure enters into the experience itself.[28] Even a radical like Eckhart was in fact deeply trinitarian and Christocentric.

Another aspect of mysticism is the mystical "model" in every religious community or mystical movement within each community, those individuals who become norms for their tradition in a number of ways. These figures become ideals: "their individuality becomes categorical, their biographies didactic. The normative individual is the medium of a universal teaching; the instrument for the revelation of more general truths."[29] Paradigmatic figures of this kind can be human or divine, male or female depending on the context. Katz presents a number of roles and functions that the model can play and suggests finally that the models play an important role in providing our map of reality and of what is real and thus contribute heavily to the creation of experience.[30]

The common distinction between mystical experience and language, saying that the latter is inferior and an inadequate reflection of a specific religious tradition, is further questioned. The true unity of Being is said to transcend both linguistic expression and the very particularity that language entails.[31] But the main material we have from the major mystics is their writing and related linguistic creations which unavoidably include interpretive structures.[32] The refusal to accept that any predicates can be ascribed to the

26. Ibid., 30.

27. Ibid., 29.

28. Ibid., 40.

29. Ibid., 43.

30. Ibid., 51.

31. Steven T. Katz, "Mystical Speech and Mystical Meaning," in Steven T. Katz (ed.), *Mysticism and Language* (Oxford: Oxford University Press, 1992), 3.

32. Ibid., 4.

Absolute creates the consensus that language and the Absolute always remain "asymmetrical and incongruous."[33]

Katz points out that language has an essentially mystic task with the purpose of transforming consciousness. The Zen koans are linguistic means of correcting the errors of propositional and descriptive language that leads the mind to false ontic commitments about the substantiality of the self and the world of things. Through examples from Buddhism, Hinduism, Sufism, and Kabbalism Katz shows that language creates the operative process for the mystic ascent, language moves us from one level of consciousness to another, from ordinary awareness to mystical awareness. The Zen koan or the Hindu mantra Om are not propositional or descriptive, but their use involves propositional claims that are inherent in the respective tradition of which they are a part. The mantra Om is assumed to cause a desirable change which rests on the recognition that a causal law is operative in the metaphysical realm which is as certain and given as the law of gravity in the physical realm.

In all the major mystical traditions we see that language functions as a psychospiritual means of radical reorientation and purification: language is integral to mystical practice.[34] Language has power to achieve contemplative and cosmic ends. This is seen in the manipulation of alphabetical signs, the necessity of using the right names, formulations, the prayers prescribed by the tradition, the repetition of scriptures which are used in the ascent to new spiritual levels.[35]

The view of language as just a human convention, shared by many of the mystical ecumenists, is challenged by the fact that many of the world's most significant religious and mystical traditions begin with the belief that their language is sacred: the very language of God or Being. As such it has an ontic status decidedly different from merely immanent and conventional languages, making it capable of expressing transcendental realities in various ways. Among Kabbalists, Sufis, and Hindus the mystic possesses in language both the vehicle of divine/transcendental expression and one of the very sources of divine creativity.[36] Besides, in all religions there is some notion of an eternal and uncreated logos (void or *sunya* in the Buddhist case) of which the earthly scriptures may be taken as a manifestation.[37] This also challenges the notion that experience is primary.

Language also operates informatively in that it is used to describe the knowledge that is gained in the mystical moment. Starting with the Neoplatonic

---

33. Ibid., 6.

34. Ibid., 15. Christian mysticism has, for several reasons, a much less well-developed tradition of linguistically induced techniques, but there are some examples, such as the Jesus prayer and other motifs that are found in some parts of the Christian tradition as well, as Katz points out (15).

35. Ibid., 20.

36. Ibid., 16.

37. Harold Coward, *Sacred Word and Sacred Text: Scripture in World Religions* (Maryknoll, NY: Orbis Books, 1988), 166.

tradition, Katz finds, despite their own declarations regarding ineffability, that a collection of attributes of the Absolute and a definite logic of emanation are essential to the whole system. "The Neoplatonic mystic . . . appears to know more, far more, of the X of Xs than would at first seem possible given the systematic negations of Neoplatonic epistemology."[38] This is taken as paradigmatic for all mystical systems, despite the *neti neti* principle. They reveal, "however unintentionally, more of the 'truth' they have come to know in language than their overt negations of meaning and content would suggest."[39]

The arguments of Katz and like-minded scholars have created a lot of debate.[40] The critical material I have read so far has not convinced me that a contextual interpretation is fundamentally mistaken. Many seem to have accepted the basic approach, while seeking to sort out certain obscurities in the argumentation. Problems may also arise depending on whether you absolutize certain aspects of the theory. For my present purpose, without moving into technicalities, I find the contextual arguments very interesting as applied to the type of mystical claims one finds in New Age–oriented spirituality.

NEW AGE AND THE TRADITIONAL

With the above analysis in mind it is relevant to ask about the New Age relationship to traditions, texts, and other sources of external authority. An

---

38. Katz, "Mystical Speech and Mystical Meaning," 32.

39. Ibid., 25.

40. Some of the critical materials are the following: J William Forgie, "Hyper-Kantianism in Recent Discussions of Mystical Experience," *Religious Studies* 21 (1985): 205–18; Donald Evans, "Can Philosophers Limit What Mystics Can Do? A Critique of Steven Katz," *Religious Studies* 25 (1989): 53–60, Robert K. C. Forman, "The Construction of Mystical Experience," *Faith and Philosophy* 5 (July 1988): 254–67. Robert K. C. Forman has also edited the book *The Problem of Pure Consciousness: Mysticism and Philosophy* (New York: Oxford University Press, 1997, 1990) which is a response to Steven Katz. This book is reviewed in an excellent article by Michael Bagger, "Critical Notice: Ecumenicalism and Perennialism Revisited," *Religious Studies* 27 (1991): 399–412. D. Z. Phillips, "Mysticism and Epistemology: One Devil of a Problem," *Faith and Philosophy* 12 (April 1995): 167–88, seeks to clarify some aspects of the Katzian argumentation and also says that Katz, in treating forms of life as though they were interpretations, concludes that we must be agnostic about their truth. Phillips argues that confusions between forms of life and judgements within them lead Katz to conclusions which obscure the confessional character of truth in these contexts.

Some have argued that we cannot deny that states of pure consciousness may be possible to attain by means of different techniques, for example, in yoga or Zen. It takes place by means of a forgetting or bracketing of previous experiences and categories of understanding. The methods serve to eliminate prior conditioning. For a presentation of such an argumentation see Michael Peterson et al., *Reason and Religious Belief: An Introduction to the Philosophy of Religion* (Oxford: Oxford University Press, 1991), 25, and Foreman, "The Construction of Mystical Experience," 259. A counterargument would be: are not these techniques themselves a part of a linguistic-conceptual framework, and is not this reconditioning itself a kind of conditioning, albeit of a different sort?

important argument in Paul Heelas's analysis is that New Age, to a large extent, is a detraditionalized self-religion.[41] It rejects and transcends voices that speak with external and established authority from the past as well as voices belonging to the established order of contemporary society. The locus of authority is the individual or, more precisely, authority lies with the experience of the Self. Hence one can label many New Agers as "epistemological individualists" (Wallis).[42] One example is the New Age teacher Sir George Trevelyan. While drawing on a great bank of doctrine in one of his lectures, he still concluded with words like "this is what things look like to me," telling the audience to "only accept what rings true to your own Inner Self."[43] New Age is favoring the authority that comes from the Self itself. There is thus an Other, albeit lying within, which stands in a relationship of externality with regards to the utilitarian person (or ego) and which can thus serve as an authoritative foundationalism.[44]

To my mind, the New Age contains more explicit forms of Otherness vis-à-vis the Self. There are definitely epistemological tensions within this new spirituality, tensions between internal and external authority, between experiences and words and actual propositional positions. In these tensions I believe that new patterns of authority, theology, and tradition emerge. Having already shown that the New Age is deeply influenced by three formative forces and their respective attitudes toward mystical knowledge, I shall now go on to examine in more depth some important elements within this new spirituality.

THE THEOSOPHICAL TRADITION

The theosophical movement is without doubt one of the most influential factors behind the New Age and its precursors during the twentieth century.[45] Several hundred new occult organizations can be traced directly to Theosophy.[46] It was also the prime channel through which Hinduism and Buddhism were introduced into the West. The major figure behind the theosophical movement was Helena Petrovna Blavatsky. She taught that the key to true knowledge was not to be found in belief, dogma, or mere words but rather in personal intuitive experience. In these intuitive states she claimed to receive knowledge from a group of supernatural beings called the "Ascended Masters." Her remarkable insights set out to present "the archaic truths which are the basis of all religions," the ancient wisdom which does not exclusively belong to any of the traditions but is actually "the essence" of

---

41. Paul Heelas, "The New Age in a Cultural Context: The Premodern, the Modern and the Postmodern," *Religion* (April 1993): 109.

42. Heelas, *The New Age Movement*, 21.

43. Michael Perry, *Gods Within: A Critical Guide to the New Age* (London: SPCK, 1992), 147.

44. Heelas, "The New Age in a Cultural Context," 109.

45. Heelas, *The New Age Movement*, 44; Melton, "Whither the New Age?" 348.

46. Melton, "A History of the New Age Movement," 40.

them all, the various religious schemes now being made "to merge back into their original element."[47]

Blavatsky's mystical insights are far from ineffable; they are, rather, explicitly propositional. The major body of teaching is called "The Secret Doctrine" and establishes a set of fundamental "propositions" of ontic character:[48] an omnipresent, eternal, boundless and immutable PRINCIPLE . . . beyond the range and reach of thought . . . which antecedes all manifested, conditioned, being"; "the eternity of the universe in toto . . . periodically the 'playground' of numberless universes incessantly manifestating and disappearing" (the proposition affirms "the absolute universality" of this law of periodicity); "the fundamental identity of all souls with the universal oversoul . . . and the obligatory pilgrimage for every soul . . . through the cycle of incarnation (or 'necessity') in accordance with cyclic and karmic law."

Blavatsky presents herself as a champion of intuitive knowledge contrary to religion, especially the Christian one. Yet, her message contains both a set of dogmatic propositions about the cosmic order and assumptions about a common core of all religions, which, as it turns out, is Theosophy. Thereby she situates Theosophy in a unique and superior interpretative position, making it into a form of spiritual imperialism.

Blavatsky's insights did not come out of the blue. She had been deeply involved with Spiritism before she started the Theosophical Society and was a diligent student of the occult disciplines of the Western esoteric tradition. Several scholars have showed that very large portions of her major books were copied from other texts.[49] She studied Hinduism and Buddhism and incorporated these teachings, although she altered several of them, especially the concepts of karma and reincarnation, by adapting them to the central Western framework of her time, evolution.[50] It is chiefly because of Blavatsky that evolution has become a key myth in the alternative spirituality of the West, including the New Age.[51] Theosophy and its offshoots have all tried to integrate science, religion, and popular myth into an overall evolutionary mythology.

As a consequence of Blavatsky's revelatory and trancelike experiences with the "Ascended Masters," one can argue that the origins of a tradition emerged. As an increasing number of people became familiar with such experiences and the revelations associated with them, this material grew

---

47. Helena Petrovna Blavatsky, *Secret Doctrine: The Synthesis of Science, Religion and Philosophy*, facsimile ed., two volumes in one (Los Angeles: Theosophy Company), vol. 1: vii–viii.

48. Ibid., 1417.

49. Arlebrand, *Det Okända*, 146.

50. Robert S. Ellwood, "Theosophy," in Miller (ed.), *America's Alternative Religions*, 318, and Theodore Roszak, *Unfinished Animal: The Aquarian Frontier and the Evolution of Consciousness* (Faber: London, 1976), 118.

51. Irving Hexham and Karla Poewe, *Understanding Cults and New Religions* (Grand Rapids: Eerdmans, 1986), 42.

into a cumulative tradition.[52] As people enter into a trance and meet the "Masters," they will be brought into contact with this cumulative tradition and the values incorporated into it. Thus they experience what Blavatsky too experienced (and others after her). The mediumistic persons and their followers are therefore no empty vessels. Kranenborg also indicates that for some the content of such trance experiences remain congruous with Blavatsky's (and others') experiences, but in other cases new territories are charted. The tradition becomes a cumulative one since the doctrines revealed to Blavatsky (and others) is subject to elaborations by people who have undergone such experiences. Kranenborg traces the development within this tradition to such dynamic persons as C. W. Leadbeater, Krishnamurti, Rudolf Steiner, and Alice Bailey, and presents some of the elaborations.

In my own studies I have found that these elaborations do not compromise the overall ontological structure of the Blavatsky revelation. The need for a deeper experiential knowledge (gnosis) of the energetic and evolutionary cosmic process, including an identification of the individual soul with the ultimate impersonal principle, the law of karma and reincarnation, and the anticipation of a new world order has been ever present.[53] The similarities are striking. There are direct links from the cumulative theosophical tradition to the present New Age scene with its cosmology, ontology, and anthropology, including a Westernized belief in reincarnation and evolutionary optimism. New Age receives its theology from theosophy. And even if people do not move into altered states of consciousness of the Blavatsky type, they still have a discourse that is encoded in a number of written works that form a body of knowledge which serves as a framework in the mystical quest.

CHANNELING

The phenomenon of channeling is possibly the single most important and definite feature of the New Age.[54] Channeling is different from classical spiritism in that the medium is not communicating with deceased human beings but rather with higher entities in the spiritual world.[55] Most of the mediums of the twentieth century stand in a tradition going back to Blavatsky and her alleged contacts with the "Ascended Masters." People like

---

52. Render Kranenborg, "Revelation and Experience in the Theosophic Tradition," in Jerald D. Gort et al. (eds.), *On Sharing Religious Experience: Possibilities of Interfaith Mutuality* (Grand Rapids: Eerdmans, 1992), 151.

53. The more explicit belief in a New Age was most of all proclaimed by Alice Bailey (Arlebrand, *Det Okända*, 71), although both Blavatsky and Bailey anticipated the coming of a new "World Saviour" (Melton, "New Thought and The New Age," 20). Rudolf Steiner believed, for example, that Anthroposophy inaugurated a New Age.

54. Melton, "New Thought and the New Age," 21.

55. Arlebrand *Det Okända* 93, and Suzanne Riordan, "Channeling: A New Revelation?" in Lewis and Melton (eds.), *Perspectives on the New Age*, 105.

Alice Bailey (The Arcane School), Elisabeth Clare Prophet (Summit Lighthouse), Benjamin Creme, and many more have claimed to transfer teaching from spiritual entities. Bailey is particularly important since she was the first popularizer of the New Age concept in occult circles, although it did not become widely known until the 1960s.

David Spangler, who wrote the seminal book *The Birth of a New Age* (1971) and became a leading thinker in the early New Age movement, claimed to be a channel for an entity called "Limitless Love and Truth."[56] Channelers such as Jane Roberts, Helen Shucman, J. Z. Knight, Jack Pursel, and Kevin Ryerson have spurred the imagination of millions of New Age seekers.[57] And even if channeling is not favored in all segments of the New Age it definitely plays a very vital role on the scene, in Sweden at present a leading one.

The channeled material is critical of both modernity and religion for encouraging dependence on external sources of authority and is similar to Spiritualism whose proponents uncompromisingly "denounced the authority of churches over believers."[58] Alschuler argues that channeling represents a "transcendent education" that makes external authorities unnecessary and represents a democratization of prophecy.[59] The message is inherently mystical. We are encouraged to "go within," "follow our heart," "live in the now." Despite this we are being presented with a number of basic propositions. Our misplaced beliefs and teaching could thus be labelled an "antibelief belief."[60]

In spite of some discrepancies between the texts, we are provided with an overall explanation of the human predicament and a set of prescriptions designed to assist humanity in discovering its true destiny. The argument is based on certain assumptions about the nature of reality which these entities present from their presumably enhanced position.[61] They seek to con-

---

56. David Spangler, *Revelation: The Birth of a New Age* (Findhorn Foundation, 1976). The Findhorn Community in Scotland, where David Spangler worked for several years before going back to the U.S., has functioned as the example *par excellence* of a New Age community. It was founded by two people in the theosophical tradition.

57. In 1970, Jane Roberts of Elmira, New York, heralded a wave of increased spirit contact, going public with a book channeling material from a being called Seth (Jon Klimo, "The Psychology of Chanelling," *New Age Journal*, November/December, 1987, 35). This was followed by *A Course in Miracles* (1975), recording messages from Jesus via a psychologist, Helen Shucman. The 1980s saw a wave of channeled material, and actress Shirley MacLaine was the one who introduced the phenomenon to millions of people in the West through her books and the film *Out on a Limb*. Some of the other actors on the stage are J. Z. Knight, who has channeled messages from "Ramtha," Jack Pursel, who is the mouthpiece of "Lazaris," Kevin Ryerson, who claims to channel five different entities, and numerous others (Chas Clifton, "Changing Channels: An Irreverent Guide to Books about Channeling and Inner Awareness," *Gnosis: A Journal of the Western Inner Traditions* (1987): 13, and Elliot Miller, *A Crash Course on the New Age Movement* (Baker Book House, Grand Rapids, 1989), 155).

58. Riordan, "Channeling: A New Revelation?" 111.

59. Alfred S. Alschuler, "Recognizing Inner Teachers," *Gnosis: A Journal of the Western Inner Traditions* 5, (1987): 12.

60. Miller, *A Crash Course on the New Age Movement*, 169.

61. Riordan, "Channeling: A New Revelation?" 110.

vince us that we are not who we think we are and that much of our suffering can be traced to our mistaken identity. They claim to be here to awaken and remind us who we truly are, affirming the basic divinity of humanity and its ability to create whatever reality it desires.

Are these messages the timeless truths that they claim to be or are they a reflection of a specific cultural climate? Kinney poses a relevant question: "If channeled beings purport to be crosscultural and crosstemporal, why did so many mediums' 'controls' in the 19th century reflect that period's Christian milieu, while so many entities these days sound like they all are reading from the same handbook of 1980s new age aphorisms?"[62] Riordan believes that the similarities between several of the texts can be explained by the fact that most of these channelers prior to their respective experiences had endorsed the New Age worldview.[63] Miller says that in all, or nearly all, of the cases he has studied, some form of trance-inducing or occult activity had preceded the alleged contacts with the spirit guides.[64] There are also handbooks and manuals around that discuss the mental and physical changes associated with trancework, also including exercises on how to prepare one to receive one of the "higher entities" or "beings of light."[65]

The most influential of all the channeled texts is *A Course in Miracles*, "received" by Helen Shucman during a ten-year period as she listened to an inner voice introducing itself as Jesus. This heavy volume of nearly 1200 pages contains the *Text*, a *Workbook for Students*, and a *Manual for Teachers*. It has been called the "Bible of the New Age" and its teachings have been popularized by a number of writers, such as Gerald Jampolsky and Marianne Williamson. The latter has been called by *Vanity Fair* "God's woman in Hollywood" and *TIME* magazine has suggested that she is a "Mother Teresa for the 90s."

The work affirms mystical knowledge: "Knowledge comes from the altar within and is timeless because it is certain."[66] It emphasizes experience rather than theology. An often-used quotation from the Course is "a universal theology is impossible, but a universal experience is not only possible but necessary."[67] The message claims to deal with universal spiritual themes, seing itself as one version of the universal curriculum. There are others, but they all lead to God in the end. Although not claiming finality, it makes some rather definite claims which can be seen as a universal theory and even theology.

The Course affirms that "right perception is necessary before God can communicate directly to His altars."[68] The first part of the Workbook (fifty

---

62. Jay Kinney, "Unsolved Mysteries and Unanswered Questions," *Gnosis: A Journal of the Western Inner Traditions* 5 (1987): 7.

63. Riordan, "Channeling: A New Revelation?" 107.

64. Miller, *A Crash Course on the New Age Movement*, 164.

65. Clifton, "Changing Channels," 15.

66. Marianne Williamson, *A Course in Miracles: The Text, Workbook for Students and Manual for Teachers* (Tiburon, CA: Foundation for Inner Peace; London: Arkana, 1988). *The Text*, 41.

67. Ibid., *The Manual*, 77.

68. Ibid., *The Text*, 41.

lessons) thus centers on a radical redefinition of reality. The student is told to observe the ordinary sense world and repeat such phrases as "Nothing I see . . . means anything," "I do not understand anything I see," "These thoughts do not mean anything."[69] The second part of the Manual consequently focuses on the acquisition of true perception.

"The world you see is an illusion of a world. God did not create it, for what he creates must be eternal as himself."[70] The only thing God has created is the Son of God. But in a version of the fall myth, the Course declares that the Son of God in some mysterious way fell asleep and dreamed that he was separated from God and asserts himself as God. Because of his dream, when the Holy Spirit is sent to wake the Son this is interpreted as a judgement. In fear of judgement, the Son leaves the level of mind, the true meeting-place with God, and projects his dream of separation onto an illusory physical world where his dream ego is divided into innumerable egos which come to cling to a physical world of separation. Our world of false perception is thus "made as an attack on God."[71] The world, space and time, is born out of fear. The opposite of fear, according to the Course, is love, which is the only real. Williamson says that when we are not thinking with love, we are not thinking at all, since love is the only real. This world is actually a "mass hallucination" where fear seems more real than love, but fear is an illusion.[72]

The separation between God and humanity has in reality never happened; it is an illusion.[73] Atonement occurs when you realize that you never ever, in reality, have been separated from God. It is a cognitive change. "Forgiveness, salvation, Atonement, true perception, all are one. . . . True perception is the means by which the world is saved from sin, for sin does not exist."[74] Feelings of guilt are defined as "disordered thought" that needs to be corrected.[75] Forgiveness is likened to a "happy fiction; a way in which the unknowing can bridge the gap between their perception and the truth."[76]

Without moving into a more complete presentation of the teachings we have already seen enough to realize that the Course, despite its mystical orientation, delivers a distinct ontology, theology, anthropology, soteriology, and even epistemology. The message is conceptual and linguistic and yet on some occasions seeks to relativize words. A remarkable saying is: "God does not understand words, for they were made by separated minds to keep them in the illusion of separetedness."[77] As a contrast, the whole Workbook is full

---

69. Ibid., *The Manual*, 36.

70. Ibid., *The Manual*, 85.

71. Ibid., *The Workbook*, 413.

72. Marianne Williamson, *A Return to Love: Reflections on the Principles of A Course in Miracles* (San Francisco: HarperCollins, 1992), Reference made to the Swedish edition, *Åter till kärleken* (Orsa: Energica förlag, 1993), 40.

73. *A Course in Miracles: The Manual*, 5.

74. Ibid., *The Manual*, 85.

75. Ibid., *The Text*, 85.

76. Ibid., *The Manual*, 83.

77. Ibid., *The Manual*, 53.

of affirmations with a conceptual content like "I am God's Son. . . . The holy home of God Himself . . . His holy Sinless,"[78] "I am the light of The World."[79] One commentator of the Course, coming from a more gnostic context, points to the limitations of being locked into concepts we already know, such as the notion of an "I," etc.[80] Assuming they give a more direct contact with reality, he prefers sound without a conceptual meaning, like the mantras or names of God that the Kabbalists use.

The common folklore about Shucman is that, before the reception of the message, she was an atheist. In fact she was brought up "mystically inclined" and was also deeply influenced by metaphysical schools like the New Thought movement.[81] The various groups of this movement had a philosophy almost identical to the Course.

The book *A Course in Miracles* looks like a Bible, feels like a Bible, and functions like a Bible or devotional book with its prescribed and written lessons for each day of the year (365 in all), and contains the basic biblical vocabulary, thereby connecting to the Jewish and Christian tradition. And yet, through its radical reinterpretation of biblical concepts in line with the esoteric tradition it turns into a kind of gnostic gospel. Several seekers I have talked to have said that they never understood the Gospels before reading the Course. Its comprehensive interpretation of the human predicament has reached an almost canonical status in alternative spirituality. The text functions as an interpretative framework and external authority on the mystical journey. As it claims to supply a superior and true meaning of the message of Jesus, it also exercises interpretative power over Christians that hold on to the interpretative tradition of the church. The opinion that Christianity misunderstood the message from God is also present in several of the other channeled messages I have referred to, and they even deliver critical remarks on the Eastern religions,[82] opening up an interesting discussion on power and interpretation.

PSYCHOLOGICAL AND MYTHOLOGICAL METANARRATIVES

The mysticism of the New Age is further framed by quite distinct psychological and mythological interpretations of religion stemming from people with strong convictions. The influence of C. G. Jung (1875–1961) on the New Age scene is undoubted.[83] Marilyn Ferguson, who wrote the most com-

---

78. Ibid., *The Workbook*, 479.

79. Ibid., *The Workbook*, 102.

80. Richard Smoley, "Pitfalls of *A Course in Miracles*," *Gnosis: A Journal of the Western Inner Traditions* 5 (1987): 19.

81. Jon Klimo, *Channeling: Investigations on Receiving Information from Paranormal Sources* (Los Angeles: Jeremy P. Tarcher, 1987), 42. The New Thought Movement, starting in the nineteenth century, has not only influenced the *Course*, but is also an important source for the New Age (Melton, "New Thought and The New Age").

82. Riordan, "Channeling: A New Revelation?" 124.

83. Heelas, 1996, *The New Age Movement*, 46.

monly accepted statement of the New Age, points to a survey that identified Jung as the second most important source of this new spirituality, Teilhard de Chardin being number one.[84] Drury affirms that Jung's impact on New Age thinking "has been enormous, greater, perhaps than many people realize."[85] Arlebrand repeatedly refers to Jung's influence on different developments in the Western occult/esoteric tradition. Kinney writes that Jung developed a map of the psyche and a set of concepts that connects so well with the Western esoteric worldview that "even before his death the two had merged in many people's minds."[86] This may be due to the fact that his studies in Eastern religions, but most of all Gnosticism and alchemy, played an instrumental role in the development of his psychology.[87] Jung's interest in these subjects was probably stimulated by the Romantic movement, the nineteenth-century occult revival, and his maternal ancestry. The last-named was characterized by frequent involvement in the supernatural, and from his early years of personal experimentation, Jung retained an affinity for occult experiences throughout his life.[88]

Jung gives a basically psychological interpretation of religion. Beneath the ego, the conscious mind, he posits both an individual unconscious and a collective unconscious level. The deeper collective layer is not individual but universal, with contents and modes of behaviour that are more or less the same everywhere and in all humans.[89] It constitutes a common psychic substrate of a suprapersonal nature, present in all of us. The contents of the collective unconscious are known as archetypes. They are archaic, primordial types, universal images that have existed since the remotest times and manifest themselves in dreams and myths.

The ego develops in the three key stages of dependency, autonomy, and integration, which in turn correspond to different levels of religious experience and mythological images. Jung creates a connection between types of religious paths/traditions and psychological processes. Every position about truth, reality, the meaning of life, the nature and existence of gods—in short, every worldview—is itself "inevitably a position reflecting a certain psycho-

---

84. Marilyn Ferguson, *The Aquarian Conspiracy: Personal and Social Transformation in the 1980s* (Los Angeles: J.P. Tarcher, 1980), 420.

85. Nevill Drury, *The Elements of Human Potential* (Longmead, Shaftesbury: Element books, 1989), 25.

86. Jay Kinney, "Forever Jung," *Gnosis: A Journal of the Western Inner Traditions* 10 (1988/1989): 9.

87. This connection has by now been substantially documented by such writers as Stephan A. Hoeller, "Jung and The Occult," *Gnosis: A Journal of the Western Inner Traditions* 10 (1988/1989); Richard Noll, *The Jung Cult: Origins of a Charismatic Movement* (Princeton: Princeton University Press, 1994); June Singer, "A Necessary Heresy: Jung's Gnosticism and Contemporary Gnosis," *Gnosis: A Journal of the Western Inner Traditions* 4 (1987).

88. Hoeller, "Jung and the Occult," 22.

89. C. G. Jung, "Archetypes, Shadows and the Anima," in William Bloom (ed.), *The New Age: An Anthology of Essential Writings* (London: Rider, 1991), 114.

logical orientation."[90] Gods become symbols of the unconscious; religious language becomes a part of the language of the psyche. Religious thought does not tell us what the universe is, but reveals the way the psyche symbolizes itself; religious experiences translate into ways in which the ego undergoes certain transformations.[91] The human goal is self-actualization, which is a process in which you move toward a state of wholeness by integrating the conflicting contents and archetypal processes of the unconscious.[92] The Self is the central archetype, personified symbolically by a circle or a mandala, which are representations of wholeness. The foremost Western version of this archetypal Self is Christ.

Jung created a kind of psychological "metamythology" in which the diversities of religions are unified to one basic psychological reality behind all the religions. Religious symbols are being transformed into symbols of "the inner journey." Such a psychological perspective is perfectly in keeping with the esoteric tradition and its emphasis on self-development and a unified field beyond the ordinary world of appearance. The Jungian framework and its idea of self-actualization were taken up by humanistic psychology as it developed into the human potential movement, Transpersonal psychology, and the New Age. Leading chroniclers of this alternative spirituality affirm that psychology will have a major role to play in uniting the different spiritual traditions of the world: "Therapy will universalize the traditions."[93] A major thinker of Transpersonal psychology and the New Age can claim that different mythologies represent a type of sacred psychology through which each one of us can learn to contact the divine essence of our being.[94]

The Jungian internalization and universalization of religion in a psychological framework, coming to represent aspects of individual self-actualization, has had a lasting influence. And I believe that this Jungian metanarrative provides yet another important conceptual framework for the mysticism of the New Age. It is also one more interesting example of the exercise of interpretative power over the religions of the world, trying to squeeze them into one mould. The mythological approach of Jung has only briefly been dealt with so far. In the following discussion I will turn to another influential Jung-related individual.

Joseph Campbell was a major popularizer of a mythical and psychological interpretation of religion. He wrote a number of books, the best known probably being *The Power of Myth*, which was a companion volume to the 1988 six-hour public television series in the U.S. The book became a number-one bestseller that fuelled the imagination of not only New Agers but a wider audience. His earlier books inspired George Lucas to create the *Star*

90. William E. Paden, *Interpreting the Sacred: Ways of Viewing Religion* (Boston: Beacon Press, 1992), 50.
91. Ibid., 51.
92. Drury, *The Elements of Human Potential*, 24.
93. Roszak, *Unfinished Animal*, 18.
94. Drury, *The Elements of Human Potential*, 115, 123.

Wars film trilogy, after which they later became good friends.[95] Campbell came across as a wise old man and a remarkably gifted storyteller. He spoke into a Western culture that has lost its grand narrative and is now starving for new stories, even a grand one.

Campbell complimented the Oriental religions for a translation of mythological symbols into psychological references, "representing powers within the human spirit . . . which are to be developed and which can be evoked by contemplation and meditation on appropriate symbolic forms."[96] The Jungian influence on Campbell is indubitable, although there are some differences between them; Campbell also claimed to have the Indologist Heinrich Zimmer as his guru.[97] In his youth he attended a lecture by Zimmer that seemed to confirm the synthesis between North American Indian spirituality and the Catholicism he had practiced as a young boy.[98]

Like Luke Skywalker in the *Star Wars* movies, he trusted his intuition. When called a man of faith by the interviewer in "The Power of Myth,"[99] he immediately corrected him, saying that he does not have to have faith, as he has experience. Direct mystical experience is, according to Campbell, the highest form of knowledge. All the myths are telling us to turn within.[100] He quotes Jung who says that religion is a defense against the experience of God. As soon as the mystery is being reduced to concepts and notions, you short-circuit the transcendental experience.[101] Campbell was committed to a position he called "transtheological," which is about an undefinable, inconceivable mystery, thought of as a power that is the source and end and supporting ground of all life and being.[102] According to his epistemological position we cannot know anything about the transcendent. It is ineffable. God is beyond name and form, he says, calling on a quotation by Meister

---

95. Joseph Campbell and Bill Moyers, "The Power of Myth: An interview with Joseph Campbell" (with an editor's introduction), *New Age Journal*, July/August 1988, 58.

96. Campbell, quoted in Robert A. Segal, "Joseph Campbell on Jews and Judaism," *Religion* 22 (1992): 153.

97. See Segal, "Joseph Campbell on Jews and Judaism," 165, for examples and also the comment: "Where for Jung independent invention rather than diffusion inevitably accounts for the similarities among myths, for Campbell diffusion is at least as important a cause. Where for Jung myths serve to reconnect one to the unconscious, for Campbell they serve a host of additional, nonpsychological functions among them, linking one to the cosmos and society. Where for Jung the psychological ideal is a balance between consciousness and unconsciousness, for Campbell the ideal is a fusion of the two that amounts to sheer unconsciousness. Where for Jung myth is by no means the sole means to psychological nirvana, for Campbell it is." See also 161.

98. Joseph Campbell, *The Power of Myth* (New York: Doubleday, 1988). This reference and the following are made to the Swedish edition, *Myternas makt* (Stockholm: SvD förlag, 1990), 35.

99. Ibid., 318.

100. Ibid., 28.

101. Ibid., 321.

102. Ibid., 67.

Eckhart which says in effect that the ultimate is to leave one's notion of God for an experience of that which transcends all notions.[103]

Campbell attempted to create a global spirituality by often ignoring the historicogrammatical context of different stories or myths. We need to distinguish between the time-specific elements and the still relevant elements in their respective "truths," he says.[104] He notoriously pulls passages out of context, radically reinterprets concepts in his search for common patterns, which, he assures us, are there. All religions are true, if you view them as metaphors.[105] Reincarnation is thus made into a metaphor with the implicit meaning that we are more than we normally think we are.[106] The ascension of Christ means that he has gone inward, to an inward space, to the consciousness that is the source of all things, the kingdom of the heaven within.[107] Myths are metaphors for the inherent spiritual possibilities of humanity; all the myths are dealing with individual growth into maturity.[108] In a distinctly Jungian fashion he says that all the gods, all the heavens, all the worlds are within us.[109]

Campbell affirms a nondualistic ontology and theology:[110] ultimate reality is one. One of the tasks in life is to live with this insight, to be able to say, "I know the center, and I know that good and evil are simply temporal aberations and that in God's view there is no difference."[111] He creates a caricature of the Jewish and Christian concept of God by saying that we now know that there's no one upstairs: the old man has blown away and we have to find the Force within us.[112] We have to pass beyond our ordinary concept of Jesus, which becomes the ultimate barrier, and realize that we are all manifestations of the Buddha-mind or Christ-consciousness.[113] He thus delivers a specific christology as well as anthropology: God is within and we are our own creators.[114] Campbell says that a person who thinks he has found the ultimate truth is wrong.[115] The epistemological paradox is that, despite such claims and repeated affirmations of ineffability, he does seem to know a good deal.

Campbell in fact criticizes all religions, even if he has a particular aversion to the Western ones. In a discussion about his attitude toward Jews and Judaism, Segal says, "his central criticism of any religion is that it misconstrues its own myths. Campbell insists that the mythology of every religion

---

103. Ibid., 87.
104. Ibid., 229, quotation mark by Campbell.
105. Ibid., 98.
106. Ibid., 101.
107. Ibid., 99.
108. Ibid., 54, 68.
109. Ibid., 75.
110. Ibid., 87, 322.
111. Ibid., 115.
112. Ibid., 230.
113. Ibid., 321, 100.
114. Ibid., 251.
115. Ibid., 97.

preaches the nonliteral, nonhistorical, universalistic, matriarchal and mystical outlook that religions themselves typically miss."[116] He thereby elevates his own "transtheological" interpretation to a superior position with almost an imperial power of deciding real "truth."

A further comment on the mysticism of Campbell is that he uses words, language, and concepts, even though he denies the value of the very same phenomena. Even a metaphor is, of course, a conceptual qualification. He is also quite rational in his attempts to deny rational thought. If the transcendent is "unknowable and unknown," then how does Campbell know this? His work is further full of discussions about how to define mystical experiences and descriptions of mystical experiences although the "unknowable and unknown" entity is beyond all categories of thought. His "transtheological" metanarrative has had a considerable impact on the popular imagination and the New Age. The mysticism of Campbell seems to be as full of tensions as the previous claims presented in this paper.

MEDITATION AND HEALTH

The whole area of meditation in relation to health and healing cannot be adequately covered in a presentation like this. For the sake of simplicity, I single out Deepak Chopra, a bestselling author and one of the most influential persons within alternative and New Age–oriented medicine. He started out as a devotee of Maharishi Mahesh Yogi, the founder of Transcendental Meditation (TM), and his writing and speeches reached millions with the gospel according to Maharishi. After feeling marginalized by the medical establishment and public opinion because of this involvement, he left the movement in 1993 and started on his own.[117] By now he is a million-dollar success with more than half a dozen books, including fiction, and a position as educational director of The Chopra Center for Well Being in La Jolla, California. His latest project is The Wisdom Within, a personal program for "Total Well-Being" on CD-Rom. Chopra's official Website proclaims: "Your journey to infinite wisdom is now only a click away!"

Meditation is still his main cure for most things, although he also claims to revive an ancient Vedic way to health called Ayrvedic medicine that he took over from Maharishi. This particular medical care is a combination of old Indian insights and the whole TM program. Chopra's message is mostly dependent on the Neohindu teachings of Maharishi. By the end of the 1980s he remarkably regarded Maharishi's words as *sruti*,[118] i.e., having the same authority as the Hindu vedic scriptures! This astonishing claim is worth further exploration, but for now at least it reveals a clear connection with the Hindu tradition.

116. Segal, "Joseph Campbell on Jews and Judaism," 154.
117. Gregory Dennis, "What's Deepak's Secret?" *New Age Journal*, January/February 1994, 52.
118. Rune W Dahlén, *Myter och mantra: En bok om TM och Maharishi* (Örebro: Libris, 1992), 81.

Mystical knowledge is primary for Chopra. Through meditation we can reach a new form of awareness that "can change our belief systems," the goal of the meditation being "to transcend, to experience that pure awareness, that pure consciousness that is the source of the first fluctuation of thought, the first fluctuation of intelligence."[119]

In *Ageless Body, Timeless Mind* Chopra tells us that we have to abandon ten inaccurate assumptions in order to experience true health, including that[120] there is an objective world independent of the observer, and our bodies are an aspect of this objective world. Materialism is primary, consciousness is secondary. Our perception of the world is automatic and gives us an accurate picture of how things really are. Time exists as an absolute and we are captives of that absolute. No one escapes the ravages of time. Suffering is necessary; it is a part of reality. We are inevitable victims of sickness, aging, and death. These assumptions, he says, do not give a correct view of reality; they are only inventions of the human mind.[121]

The old "paradigm" needs to be replaced by a more "complete" and "developed" version of "truth" that signals the end of "the tyranny of senses".[122] The new paradigm includes the following assumptions:[123] there is no objective world independent of the observer; none of the objective facts that we normally presuppose about reality are of any major importance; consciousness is primary, matter is secondary; consciousness conceives, governs, constructs, and becomes matter, the totality of the physical world; the biochemistry of the body is a product of consciousness; concepts, thoughts, and emotions create the chemical reactions that uphold life in every cell; the human body is actually an expression, an epiphenomen of consciousness; we create our bodies as well as health and are not victims of aging, sickness, and death.[124] "Even growing old is a mass hallucination," Chopra says, "we live in a recreational universe and are made for happiness."[125]

Through the technique of TM you cleanse the mind from all negative mental content. You also transcend your sickness and reach a state that is not affected by disease, and that is the level of the Self.[126] The human Self, the microcosmos, is unchangeable and identical with the ultimate Self or Energy, the macrocosmos. This unchangeable inner Self is the real point of

119. Craig A. Lambert, "Quantum Healing: An Interview with Deepak Chopra," *New Age Journal*, July/August 1989, 49.

120. Deepak Chopra, *Ageless Body, Timeless Mind: The Quantum Alternative to Growing Old* (New York: Harmony Books, 1993). This reference and the following are made to the Swedish edition, *Tidlös till kropp och själ* (Stockholm: Nordstedts/Månpocket, 1996), 13.

121. Ibid., 15.

122. Ibid., 17.

123. Ibid., 16, 21.

124. Ibid., 48.

125. Dennis, "What's Deepak's Secret?" 94.

126. Deepak Chopra, *Perfect Health* (New York: Harmony Books, 1990). This reference and the following are made to the Swedish edition, *Perfekt hälsa* (Stockholm: Nordstedts, 1991), 124, 126.

reference for any experience. All other points of reference are bound by change, decay, and loss.[127] The mantras used to reach this absolute state are not chosen for their cognitive meaning but for their particular sound.[128] This sound is in the same frequency as the primordial sound, the energy vibrations of bliss that uphold all creation.[129]

The specific way to mystical mastery and insight prescribed by Chopra is an echo of the teachings of Maharishi. This in turn is deeply embedded in the Hindu advaita tradition, in spite of fervent attempts to secularize the whole method. The mantras are in fact not mere sounds but names of Hindu gods; the initiation ceremony is a Hindu devotional ritual.[130] The practical part of Chopra's *Perfect Health* includes some of the basic techniques of yoga as well as a practice of saluting the Hindu sun god, Surya,[131] one of the most basic devotional rites in Hinduism. Chopra also vindicates his particular approach to healing by repeated references to quantum physics, saying that his basic presuppositions are perfectly in keeping with the writings of such people as Einstein, Bohr, and Heisenberg.[132] This line of argument is common in the New Age. In fact, the quantum language functions as a cultural and religious broker, exchanging the metaphysical capital of the past for a coin that suits the present.[133] Also in Chopra we find a distinct set of assumptions about reality that functions as an interpretative framework for the mystical journey. He is actually telling us what to believe and not to believe. He is, moreover, deeply rooted in the Hindu tradition.

CONCLUSIONS AND FURTHER REFLECTIONS

It is now time to sum up some of the epistemological tensions we have seen so far within New Age mysticism, and also to use this summary as an occasion for some further reflection within the field. First, all the examples studied above reveal that certain forms of commitment, education, training, and experimentation had an early influence, most likely shaping their respective forms of mystical knowledge. Second, the persons or phenomena referred to also reflect a pattern of thought we find in Eastern religions, Western occult tradition, and New Age: the fundamental dilemma of the human predicament is a lack of knowledge; the problem is of a cognitive kind. While the necessary new knowledge is said to be of the experiential sort, it is still knowledge and, as we have seen, includes a whole array of rather radical conceptual claims. Because of the shared premise of the need for cognitive reorientation, it is next to impossible to maintain the primacy of the experiential in these versions of mysticism.

---

127. Chopra, *Tidlös till kropp och själ*, 47.
128. Chopra, *Perfekt hälsa*, 125.
129. Ibid., 130.
130. Dahlén, *Myter och Mantra*, 13, 18.
131. Chopra, *Perfekt hälsa*, 260.
132. Chopra, *Tidlös till kropp och själ*, 16.
133. Albanese, "The Magical Staff," 77.

Third, the necessary reconditioning of the human also, on many occasions, involves an extensive use of language. The foremost example in our presentation is the set of affirmations being used in *A Course in Miracles*. The widespread use of affirmations in the New Age as a whole shows that language with a conceptual content is thought to have transformational power. But even the more nonconceptual affirmations or mantras that are being used of course operate, as Katz points out, from a specific ontological context or framework.

Fourth, the mystical inclination of the New Age is inspired by our present cultural climate of expressivism, but even more by the perennialism that has been taken over from Neovedantism, Theosophy, and its developments in a psychospiritual direction within Transpersonal psychology. From these sources the New Age also inherits a fundamental ontotheological and conceptual structure that is being replicated by various teachers and groups. The theological elaborations and modifications one can observe do not substantially change the basic structure; neither do variations in practices and vocabulary, some, like *A Course in Miracles*, having a more Christian language. The similarities are definitely more striking than the differences. The psychological and mythological interpretations of people like C. G. Jung and Joseph Campbell strengthen the monistic model, making it more personally and culturally relevant in a psychological society.

Fifth, all the points above imply that different forms of external authority are at work. What about texts? In several cases, one can find that messages that have been channeled from spiritual entities come to exercise a considerable authority on groups and individuals, the prime example being *A Course in Miracles*, which for many has an almost canonical status. Channelers, persons with renowned spiritual insight, gurus, astrologers, and the like are also examples of significant forms of authority external to the Self that can shape experience. The influence of the role model as a formative factor in the mystical quest, taken up by Katz, would be an interesting field of further research on the New Age. Almost every presentation that I have heard from leading New Agers has been in the form of a personal story, thereby creating patterns for the mystical journey of the listeners.

Sixth, can we speak of a tradition within the New Age? The individualist and eclectic use and abuse of techniques and thoughts from a variety of religions and traditions would seem to lead to a negative answer. But the New Age brings a whole set of paraphernalia from the Western esoteric tradition and Theosophy, presupposing the existence of the arcane, the esoteric, hidden wisdom, and an inner secret tradition. This assumption, together with the distinction between esoteric (inner, deep) and exoteric (outer, superficial) truth, form an epistemological metanarrative that most New Agers adhere to. They are important elements in the interpretative tradition. They have also influenced the psychological and mythological interpretations that have become so popular.

The presence of a fundamental ontological framework, the existence of which I have demonstrated above, further indicates that we here have some sort of tradition at work. Differences and similarities are revealed, depending on whether you move on the margins of thought and practice or whether you move toward the core. Despite the fact that different teachers and individuals may draw on various authorities as they speak, together they are creating a new, albeit diverse at many points, tradition of spirituality in the West. As many people seek a new spiritual direction for their lives, they are being presented with a pattern that provides not only food for thought but also a framework for mystical experience.

A leading expert in the field of new religions, Gordon Melton, has prophesied that we will soon see an institutionalization of New Age. People cannot endure the endless eclecticism and experimentation that is going on and feel a need for more stable orders. One writer in *Gnosis*, probably the most scholarly magazine on the subject, argues quite strongly for the inescapable need to forge a new religious orthodoxy.[134] Focusing on one particular aspect of this emerging metaphysical understanding he singles out the "you create your own reality" hypothesis, saying that we individually and collectively have the power to create and cocreate both our subjective, psychological realities and our objective, physical realities!

The postmodern West is in the middle of a reconstruction of traditions, a kind of reconstitution of itself. Aspects of this process may be interpreted as being a part of the postmodern plea for the Other. Many seek to reclaim the past and actually try to reconstruct different traditions. This paradoxically leads to new traditions and assumptions of central motives and common cores. The shamanism that is being taught and practiced today within neopagan and New Age circles is actually an innovation, operating with the concept of a core shamanism that stands above and differs from the diverse patterns that we find in various cultural settings.[135] This neoshamanism also functions like a new religion on its own. One of the most prevalent forms of neopaganism is found in the attempt, by different groups and thinkers, to recreate ancient European pre-Christian religions.[136] This includes assumptions about a primal Goddess religion, which includes a rehabilitation of the feminine, and different groups that reclaim Odinism, Asatru, and Norse Paganism.

While some suggest that neopaganism is a part of the New Age (Drury), others suggest that it is a separate phenomenon (Kelly). Neopaganism prides itself on being more pluralistic than the New Age, denouncing perennialism in favour of polytheism and radical difference.[137] In a major study Adler writes that neopaganism "is perfectly willing to throw out dogmas" and yet she also presents a set of "basic beliefs" that most people in her book

---

134. Jordan S. Gruber, "You Create Your Own Orthodoxy," *Gnosis: A Journal of the Western Inner Traditions*, Summer 1990.

135. Hammer, *På spaning efter helheten*, 122.

136. Margot Adler, *Drawing Down the Moon: Witches, Druids, Goddess Worshippers, and other Pagans in America Today* (Harmondsworth: Penguin/Arkana,1997), 233.

137. Aidan A. Kelly, "An Update on Neopagan Witchcraft in America," in *Perspectives on the New Age*, 138, 147.

share:[138] "the world is holy; nature is holy; the body is holy; sexuality is holy; the mind is holy; the imagination is holy; you are holy; thou art Goddess, thou art God; divinity is immanent in all Nature; it is as much within you as without." Neopaganism contains a similar sort of paradox as the New Age. Celebrating experience, it yet carries convictions of a creedal nature.

Seventh, the previously mentioned epistemological metanarrative of esoteric and exoteric truth also raises the issue of power. Mystical experience is held to provide access to an underlying core of common truth behind all religions. This esoteric, higher Truth is superior to the exoteric truths of the various religions. An implicit consequence of this is that ordinary believers in the religions of the world have not so far fully understood their own religion. Without even being aware of it, many Western New Agers place themselves in elevated positions evaluating the beliefs of billions of people throughout the world as inferior.[139] The claim to deliver unifying frameworks of a monistic kind, irrespective of the particular, we see also in channeling, Jung, Campbell, and Chopra. The New Age quest for unity denies real plurality and in the process comes to exercise a sort of spiritual neo-imperialism.

Another related example is the imposition of a so-called core shamanism, referred to above, over the varied forms of shamanism in the world. The New Age and related groups, in a postmodern way, also utilize whatever they find interesting in native religions. But the voice of the Other is now beginning to be articulated in various ways. One example is the protest by North American Indians at The World Parliament of Religions in Chicago 1993.[140] Their message to the New Age was: "First you stole our land, now you steal our religion, our sacred rituals and ceremonies and sell them as lucrative commodities on the religious market." The easygoing New Age spirituality could, from this angle, be interpreted as a form of neocolonialism. In its seemingly postmodern plurality, as noted above, it also paradoxically assumes a higher universal Truth. This of course falls back on the belief that, because ultimate reality is One, diversity and difference are a mental disease of which we all need to be cured. All the talk of harmony and unity can conceal a problem of power that lurks as a shadow within the New Age.

Eighth, taking the discussion a bit further, the tension between orthodoxy and orthopraxis is worth a brief comment. While the Western religions have tended to affirm orthodoxy, Eastern ones and neopaganism tend to be more orthopractical. By practising yoga, meditation, or shamanistic techniques you gradually enter into a certain understanding of the cosmic order. It is a

---

138. Adler, *Drawing Down the Moon*, 135, ix.

139. The Western esoteric tradition is the main source of inspiration. A lot of material on esoteric versions of, e.g., Christianity and Buddhism is prevalent in New Age bookstores. *A Course in Miracles* comes across as an esoteric version of Christianity.

140. Notto R. Thelle, "Et postmoderne religionsparlament Chicago 1993," *Norsk Tidskrift for Misjon* 1 (1994), 51. See also "Spiritual Seekers Borrow Indian Ways," *New York Times*, December 27, 1993.

learning by doing, and as the methods themselves are a part of an ontological structure, one can argue that a specific framework of interpretation progressively comes to be embraced, including also conceptual knowledge.

It is my impression, gathered from interviews with New Agers, that the entrance into the New Age most often is brought about by some technique or therapy that promises release from forms of unease or critical situations. As time goes by, a need for a deeper understanding of the practice is felt, books are read, seminars and lectures attended. The individual is then drawn into an educational process of conceptual knowing that also, most likely, shapes the experiential.

Ninth, how do we cope with the fact that large numbers of people in the West seem to live outside of religious traditions? Also, Ninian Smart has commented, how do we handle the evidence for experiences which seem to hit people out of the blue, even though they do not belong to a given tradition?[141] Smart asks that we should not confine religious experience to given traditions. He also makes an analogy between religions and ideological systems, such as Maoism, saying that they may have similar functions. Ideological systems may thus also serve as a framework for experience.

How do we interpret a postmodern Western culture in which ideological systems of the grand type no longer exercise a formative influence? Is it possible to pin down some cultural trends or patterns of discourse that have any lasting power? Any attempt to answer the above questions would necessarily become quite lengthy. At the great risk of overgeneralising, I would suggest that two of the most influential linguistic systems of the West are science, especially the natural sciences, and psychology. In trying to trace the cultural contextuality of the New Age, I have found that its combination of quasiscientific and therapeutic-expressivist approaches are factors that make it extremely culturally relevant.[142]

According to the sociology of religion, a conversion is more likely to take place if a person experiences a dissatisfaction with his or her personal situation and/or circumstances in society. The growing number of discontents in the West can at present find new patterns of identity in the framework of a booming New Age spirituality. As expressed by an increasing number of media celebrities, films, handbooks, and novels, the potential for identity in a situation of personal and/or communal crisis will grow. The phenomenal success of the New Age novel *The Celestine Prophecy* by James Redfield is an illuminating example.[143] The story is poor literature, but it presents powerful ideas. With a quasi-scientific and therapeutic linguistic system it presents a powerful metanarrative explaining the history of humanity, including modernization and the present turbulent time, telling us that we are just on

---

141. Ninian Smart, "Understanding Religious Experience," in Katz (ed.), *Mysticism and Philosophical Analysis*, 11.

142. Johansson, "New Age," 212.

143. James Redfield, *The Celestine Prophecy: An Adventure* (New York: Warner Books, 1994). In the following, I also refer to James Redfield/Carol Adrienne, *The Celestine Prophecy: An Experiential Guide* (New York: Warner Books, 1995).

the verge of a major breakthrough into a new phase in history, a New Age. The accompanying handbook, the *Experiential Guide*, removes the illusion that this is just another piece of fiction. The author is actually presenting a theological tract, albeit in a narrative form.

In describing his conversion to Christianity, C.S. Lewis often refered to *Phantastes*, a novel by George MacDonald. The novel had, he said, long before his conversion "baptized his imagination." I suspect that the books by Redfield, Shirley MacLaine, Deepak Chopra and associates, as well as other pieces of imaginative art, at present "energize" the imagination of a large number of discontents in the West.

Drawing this long discussion to a close, I believe we can say that the Self spirituality of the New Age by no means operates with a purely internal Other. The mystical knowledge of the New Age is also determined by forms of external Otherness as prior commitments and education, overt claims to cognitive change, conceptual structures that operate from an ontotheological framework, linguistic aids, the presence of some sacred texts and/or teachers, and even something that could be called a tradition or interpretative framework. And in the presentation I have also found patterns which show that different forms of neo-imperial power are exercised over the Other. Orthopraxis, as well as different forms of culturally relevant narratives, also contribute to determine the nature of New Age mysticism.

NEW AGE KNOWLEDGE AND MISSIOLOGY

We now return to our friend the film director we met at the beginning, who explicitly claimed to know by pure intuition that some particular verses in the Bible were later additions. This man has, in fact, for several years studied *A Course in Miracles*, a text that, as we saw, consciously sets out to reprogram our perception of reality. The subtext to his intuitive knowledge is thus another text, quite different from the Bible. The reading of the Bible is being made with a pair of glasses received from the Course. While chastizing the church and Christians for being dogmatic and not relying on intuitive insight, he is himself equally dogmatic. And in the process he personifies a paradox that is present in the Western context which today represents one of the greatest challenges to the mission of the church.

There is a remarkable spiritual hunger in the West which calls the church to a perceptive response. The once countercultural spirituality of the New Age is now even becoming a part of the mainstream; it is, in other words, establishing itself as a major interpretative religious framework in Western culture.[144] The church is, at the same time, being disestablished as we approach the

---

144. Some argue that the New Age is gradually growing into a religion, both in the substantial and functional sense. With its recognition of a sacred sphere, apart from everyday life, its growing appeal to sacred texts, sacred sites and sacred objects, it bears the marks of the more established religions, according to Hammer, *På spaning efter helheten.*

end of "Christendom." And with it the dominion or sovereignty of the Christian religion over the West is dying.[145] The spiritual hunger, the shift of power and the changing epistemological predicament we are discussing in this book present missiology with new challenges and opportunities.

A missiology of Western culture must seriously reflect on the conditions for and content of an agenda for dialogue with seekers who orient themselves from within a New Age framework. The dialogical nature of the encounter is necessitated not least by the historical record of "Christendom." The abuse of power is constantly held up as an argument against Christian belief by the New Age. The countercultural character of the Christian movement thus needs to be reclaimed, not only for sociological and theological reasons, but also for missiological ones. In this endeavor, I believe that recent epistemological reflections on power, tradition, and community play an important role. With the increased awareness of the contextual nature of knowledge, the church is thrown back to its own tradition in order to seek an understanding of truth that is noncoercive. In facing the challenge from the New Age, I believe that the synthesis of insights and practices between the Radical Reformation tradition and Alasdair MacIntyre is of particular value. It addresses the problem of power seriously, describes the church as a countercultural community, and, thus, becomes missiologically relevant in this encounter.

Epistemology also informs missiology in that the new awareness of the contextual nature of experience and knowledge can create new conditions for the desired dialogue; this may be the main missiological outcome of my presentation. As the church in the West today is being challenged by the claims of intuitive knowledge and mysticism presented by advocates of alternative spirituality, dialogue can take on new dimensions in which the New Agers are being challenged to make explicit their commitments, conceptual frameworks, textual dependencies, tradition(s), in short, their external sources of authority. A simple dualism between experience and interpretation, between inner and outer, as I have argued, can no longer be maintained.

This deepening of dialogue gives us new possibilities for intertraditional conversations, taking us beyond simplistic positions in which the church represents dogma and the New Age immediacy. While many NewAgers do not have any epistemological awareness and freely pick and mix whatever seems suitable, I believe that a discussion of dependencies, the meaning of words, and the content of belief can make a real dialogue possible. Analogies then emerge between New Age religion and the Christian tradition, allowing for real communication.

While the content of the conversation can be as varied as there are situations, I would like to mention some possible points for an agenda in relation to our topic. Although pluralist New Agers claim that the One Gospel has swallowed up the many, repressing difference and the Other, they do not

---

145. Douglas John Hall, *The End of Christendom and the Future of Christianity* (Valley Forge, PA: Trinity Press International, 1997), ix, 33.

discuss the implicit problems of their own position. Both the New Age assumption of a common core of higher Truth and its monistic denial of ulti-mate diversity and difference turn out to be an oppression of the Other.

The ultimate truth that All is One denies the full reality of a world of difference. New Age terms for the unity of humanity turn out to be rather imperial: the many are swallowed by the One. And even if the Christian gospel has been made a tool of imperialism, it contains challenging cor-rectives. Lesslie Newbigin reminds us that at the heart of the gospel is a "denial of all imperialisms, for at its center there is the cross where all imperialisms are humbled and we are invited to find the center of human unity in the One who was made nothing so that all might be one. The very heart of the biblical vision for the unity of humankind is that its center is not an imperial power but the slain Lamb."[146] Ultimate truth is not a denial of the Other, but a suffering for the Other in the real world of dif-ference and distress.

This self-giving in love reflects a Christian understanding of the nature of ultimate reality. The conception of God as a being-in-communion in which the three persons of the Trinity, Father, Son, and Spirit, are mutually and freely constituting one another in love has a particular missiological rele-vance. In the conversation with a spirituality which seeks a remedy for post-modern pluralism and fragmentation by turning to the One and dissolving the Other, we bring our belief in a triune God who is both unity and a dynamic plurality. A discussion of the epistemological predicament leads us to an ontology which preserves the particular, replacing an ontology of power with an ontology of love. The doctrine of the Trinity may in fact be a resource so far unexplored as we try to deal with the problems and possi-bilities of contemporary pluralism.[147] It is not only the ontological founda-tion for the unique particularity of every human being, it may also present us with "the transcendental condition for interreligious dialogue, the ontolog-ical condition that permits us to take the other in all seriousness, without fear, and without violence."

A trinitarian ontology also responds to the epistemological predicament in general, and the New Age in particular, since it affirms the relational and per-sonal character of all knowledge. While the New Age at one level talks a lot about relationships and personal knowledge of the experiential-expressivist kind, New Age knowledge is, at heart, neither relational nor personal. Ultimate truth is an intuitive insight about one's own identification with the nonrelational, impersonal reality of the universe. A trinitarian epistemology

---

146. Lesslie Newbigin, *The Gospel in a Pluralist Society* (Grand Rapids: Eerdmans, 1989), 159.

147. This is the working hypothesis of the book *The Trinity in a Pluralistic Age: Theological Essays on Culture and Religion,* Kevin J. Vanhoozer, (ed.) (Grand Rapids: Eerdmans, 1997). The quotation in the above paragraph is from Vanhoozer's essay in that volume, "Does the Trinity Belong in a Theology of Religions? On Angling in the Rubicon and the 'Identity' of God," 71.

affirms the relatedness of the material, the personal, the social, and the cultural realms in an overarching framework that simultaneously allows each to be itself.[148]

Knowledge arises not by abstraction but by our indwelling in and our engagement with and relatedness to the world. It is a knowledge by acquaintance which grows out of a concrete relation in which the created order reflects the intensely relational and personal character of the triune God. A trinitarian response to the epistemological predicament reconceives the relations of God, self, and world, and thus becomes missiologically relevant in the dialogue with the New Age. The relational and personal language can be a bridge to the conversation, as the Christian community seeks to affirm that a relational and personal understanding of knowledge at a deeper level corresponds to a relational and personal view of ultimate reality.

This view of knowledge also connects with the intense quest for identity which we find in the New Age. A trinitarian contribution to this conversation is informed by the belief that we as persons are more than individuals, that we as persons are who we are through our relations to others, relations that do not erase but establish particularity. A Christian understanding of ultimate truth is a knowledge about our identity as relational beings and, ultimately, our identity in relation to a God who is being-in-communion.

Most of my suggestions above could be interpreted as an attempt to draw the New Age onto logocentric grounds as they involve a dialogue on the meaning of words, concepts, and fundamental assumptions. If such a conversation is going to be fruitful, however, it must first be supported by a faith community that confirms that the gospel is true also in practice. Such a missiological insight has gained deeper dimensions through our epistemological survey, in which the close connections between truth, community, and practice have been pointed out. In the encounter with a New Age spirituality which constantly plays down the significance of words it becomes even more relevant. While retaining the cognitive content of Christian faith and an optimism regarding dialogue, we must also remember that embodied truth is often more convincing than spoken truth. Truth as practice, as a way of life, becomes important as we meet a spirituality which emphasises individual pragmatic "livability," most often beyond community and demands for consistency. Second, an authentic conversation must entail a sharing of the experiential. The New Age claim to have firsthand knowledge, to know truth by personal experience, is challenging to a church which has accommodated itself to modernity and its loss of transcendence. A Christian community which enters into dialogue with the New Age needs to reflect a living encounter with God, a knowledge of the truth by personal experience, in order to be relevant in the contemporary context.

My concluding missiological suggestions combine countercultural and

---

148. My presentation of trinitarian thinking is an echo of Colin E. Gunton, "Knowledge and Culture: Towards an Epistemology of the concrete," in Hugh Montefiore (ed.), *The Gospel and Contemporary Culture* (London: Mowbray, 1992). The application to the New Age is made by myself.

trinitarian themes, words, and practice. How the church can face the end of modernity, the end of "Christendom," and the resurgence of new spiritual tradition(s), which I have briefly described, is of course a topic for a more extensive discussion. In another, more lengthy presentation, I have suggested some points that may be important in this encounter.[149] These challenges involve a refocusing of both theology and practice.

---

149. See Johansson, "New Age," 228–41.

CHAPTER TEN

The Ends of the Earth and the End of Time

Bringing Together Missiology and Epistemology

BERT HOEDEMAKER

SEPARATE WAYS

Missiology and epistemology are unlikely bedfellows; their backgrounds and histories suggest they would not even be on speaking terms. To be sure, both are at home in modern Western culture: missiology as the reflection on the foundation and strategies of the modern missionary movement, epistemology as the reflection on the foundation and possibilities of true knowledge. To the extent that the "foundation" in each case remained unquestioned, the two disciplines shared the self-confidence of the culture. On the other hand, precisely that self-confidence kept them travelling on their separate ways. It took a predicament *on both sides* to make them aware of each other.

Before the advent of the predicament, neither missiology nor epistemology had experienced the plurality of traditions and belief systems as a great problem. Missiology had always assumed that it was possible to conceive of a network of communication which is universal in principle, which "reaches to the ends of the earth" and encompasses the whole of humankind, and that it was possible to believe that something like *salvation* would fit these dimensions. Epistemological foundationalism had always assumed that a foundation of unquestionable beliefs would eventually be stronger than the divisive forces of plurality. Now, however, against the background of a widely felt loss of universal frameworks, the impact of pluralism has made a major difference.

For missiology, this difference expresses itself above all in a new awareness of the impenetrability of the *cultural* world of humankind. For epistemology, the difference means the impossibility of defending and justifying the beliefs of one particular tradition as true or applicable for all human beings. The two predicaments are not identical but similar. They recognize each other from a distance, as it were. Their actual point of encounter needs to be spelled out in more detail.

MISSIOLOGY AND THE PROBLEM OF CULTURE

Missiologists customarily describe their discipline as a study of "the expansion and growth of the mission of the Church in all its dimensions,"[1] or even as "the study of the worldwide church's divine mandate to be ready to serve this God who is aiming his saving acts toward this world."[2] In these definitions, "mission," which is often defined as "God's own cause,"[3] is not necessarily identical with "apologetics" in the sense of defending the truth of one particular faith *vis-à-vis* others, although this is included; the main point is the successful crossing of frontiers, the ability of "the faith" to take root in a variety of contexts. Epistemological questions are not dominant in this approach. The awareness that "the faith" actually represents *only one belief system among many*, and that this in itself constitutes a major problem, is a much more recent phenomenon. It arises out of a general "postmodern" mood and is strengthened by the epistemological predicament. But it is not as such a missiological problem. The predicament that is peculiar to missiology is much more the result of a new, more sophisticated look at the phenomenon of *culture*.

When missiology first became interested in the systematic use of the concept of culture, in the first half of the twentieth century, it came under the influence of functionalist theories which regarded "culture" as a relatively independent system of mutually cohering elements. Luzbetak,[4] Schreiter,[5] and Taber[6] argue that the functionalist concept of culture became a dominant tool in missions and missiological research,[7] and that this approach fits in well with the affinity of the missionary movement, as well as of missiology, to relatively closed, "primitive" tribal cultures. The experience gained with these cultures became the starting point for the more systematic treatment of the problem of culture in relation to mission.

This methodological one-sidedness, however, predictably created a certain blindness to phenomena such as cultural change, intercultural communication, and secularization, which have increasingly claimed attention during the last two or three decades. The one-sidedness likewise created the

---

1. L.J. Luzbetak, *The Church and Cultures: New Perspectives in Missiological Anthropology* (Maryknoll, NY: Orbis Books, 1988), 14.

2. J. Verkuyl, *Contemporary Missiology; An Introduction* (Grand Rapids, MI: Eerdmans, 1978), 5.

3. So H.W. Gensichen in K. Müller, *Missionstheologie* (Berlin 1985), 17.

4. Luzbetak, *The Church and Cultures.*

5. R.J. Schreiter, *Constructing Local Theologies* (Maryknoll, NY: Orbis Books, 1985); also, "Anthropology and Faith: Challenges to Missiology," *Missiology* 19 (1991): 283–94.

6. C.R. Taber, *The World Is Too Much with Us: "Culture" in Modern Protestant Missions* (Macon, GA: Mercer University Press, 1991).

7. "Missionary anthropology" thus became, for good or ill, an adaptation of functionalism: cf. Taber, *The World Is Too Much with Us*, 94.

possibility of using the polarity *gospel/culture* in a precritical way, ignoring the hermeneutical problem of the prior intertwining of faith formulations with religions and cultures, and underestimating the difficulties implied in the effort to define "gospel" as an independent entity over against "cultures," especially when cultures are viewed as processes of signification. Indeed, this precritical use of the gospel/culture polarity appears ineradicable, even where the complexity of the relation between the two poles is acknowledged.

Luzbetak, who insists on using cultural anthropology exclusively in the service of the "church-in-mission,"[8] tends to dismiss semiotic theories of culture on the grounds that they are too abstract, too far away from the daily "nitty-gritty" of missions.[9] And even Schreiter's work, which has the merit of introducing missiology to more sophisticated theories of culture, shows traces of an uncritically used polarity. To be sure, Schreiter does break up the massive concept of "church tradition" by viewing tradition as a "series of local theologies";[10] on the other hand, however, "tradition" remains a basically given reality, as is evident from his comparison of "tradition" with the "language system" as it appears in Chomsky's linguistic theory.[11]

The point of the newer approaches to culture, however, is not that they challenge missiology to produce more sophisticated reflection on the basis of the same gospel/culture pattern. The point is, rather, that these approaches show that the reality of culture as a process of signification and of intercultural communication as a struggle for common meaning is highly problematic in itself; that it is itself, to put it in theological terms, in need of redemption, of salvation.

The "epistemological predicament" is not only constituted by abstract problems of knowledge, rationality, and truth. These problems in turn reveal the predicament of people who have lost common points of reference, common frameworks of meaning, and whose configurations of "making sense of the world" are constantly at odds with each other. It is at this point that the traditional gospel/culture polarity breaks down definitively. In its concentration on the need to utilize cultural studies for the proclamation of the "message," traditional missiology has always stopped short of the question of how the proclamation of the message might itself be a salvific element within and for intercultural human communication as such. In its concentration on the need to connect the *one* gospel to the *many* cultures, it has been inclined to lose sight of the need to (re)identify the message in relation to the problematic nature of cultural plurality. Cultural plurality was seen and used as an instrument in the service of "inculturation," rather than seen as the problem itself.

---

8. "We are concerned about cultures so that the Church may be as perfect a channel of grace as possible" (*The Church and Cultures*, 397).

9. Ibid., 155.

10. Schreiter, *Constructing Local Theologies*, 32.

11. Ibid., 113ff.

THE POSSIBILITY OF ENCOUNTER

Precisely at this point—the problematic nature of cultural plurality—a fruitful encounter between missiology and epistemology comes into view. The contemporary epistemological challenge to missiology is to take seriously those views of culture in which the epistemological predicament expresses itself, and to develop its self-understanding accordingly—for instance, by raising the question as to how the traditional missiological occupation with "cultures" might be interpreted and reconstructed from the point of view of contemporary discussions.

In French poststructuralism, for example, cultural studies tend to become complicated hermeneutical philosophies which implicitly and retroactively question the ways in which missiology has dealt with the plurality of cultures. It is here that missiology is challenged to shed its epistemological naiveté, together with its typically "modern" confidence in the superiority of Western Christianity. It might then redefine itself in a direction such as the following: "Missiology focuses on the investigation of conditions and possibilities for the communication of the Christian gospel in the context of cultural and religious plurality and secularization, and on the effort to provide theological justification for such communication." A definition like this might serve as a bridge between what missiology has always been and what it is called to become.

Conversely, the traditional missiological insistence that it is possible to conceive of a network of communication which reaches to the ends of the earth and encompasses the whole of humankind, and that it is possible to believe that something like *salvation* fits these dimensions, might provide a framework in which some epistemological quandaries can be (re)defined and refocused: a metaperspective in which the whole field of culture, religion, and secularization is somehow *theologically* understood. There may still be ways to formulate this perspective apart from (lost) "modern" presuppositions.

ASYMMETRY AND CONFLICT

It is not an exaggeration to say that the epistemological problems which come to the fore in the predicament continue implicit in missiology: they are hidden in the ways in which missiology struggles with the question of universal truth in its encounter with cultural plurality. The struggle has led to various strategies of dealing with the gospel/culture polarity, such as the "kernel-and-husk" approach, which emphasizes translation,[12] and the "inculturation" approach, which envisions a dialectic between the unity of the church and the permanent transformation of cultures in the direction of the unity of humankind.[13] The concept of *contextuality*, which has become

---

12. E.g., D.J. Hesselgrave and E. Rommen, *Contextualization: Meaning, Methods and Models* (Grand Rapids: Eerdmans, 1989).

13. A. Roest Crollius and Th. Nkéramihigo, "What is so new about inculturation," in *Inculturation* (working papers on living faiths and cultures), vol. V (Rome, 1984).

popular in recent decades, can be used for both approaches; but, viewed against the background of its own specific history, it thematizes the gospel/culture problem in a more radical way.

"Contextuality" is related to the position adopted by many non-Western theologians over against traditional approaches which interpret the non-Western world on the basis of preconceived images of the "other" culture, or which consider non-Western history to be a derivative of the Western "mainstream." What these theologians defend is neither the value of non-Western cultures as such, nor particular theologies that have emerged in those cultures, but, more fundamentally, the right to seek a direct link between the core convictions of the Christian faith—the *Missio Dei*, God's plan of salvation for the world, creation and incarnation—and one's own historical and existential experience, independently of the acquired *foreign* schemes of interpretation. Non-Western theologians wish to free themselves from the defining, judging, and also somewhat disparaging attitudes that come from a theological tradition established over centuries.

In these discussions, the concept of *context* takes on polemical traits. It does not refer simply to social and cultural conditioning, but rather to a conjunction of religious, social, and cultural histories which becomes the breeding ground for a conscious faithful choice of position by Christians, in which traditional "self-evident" ways of thinking are criticized in a fundamental way.[14]

In the challenge to deal with this more radical version of the problem of cultural plurality, summarized in the term *contextuality*, missiology can be enlightened by those approaches to culture that emphasize the power play, the "fight for symbolic domination" by which all cultures and subcultures are characterized. In turn, it can enlighten those approaches by showing that the *asymmetry in intercultural communication*, which is exposed in the discussion of contextuality, is a global manifestation of "culture" in that sense. In other words, *in the discussion of contextuality the problem of culture as such is thematized on a global level.*

THE EVAPORATION OF THE CONCEPT OF CULTURE

The missiological experience of contextuality, and of culture and intercultural communication *as an arena of conflict*, ties in with the definition of culture as a process of signification which is characterized by change and negotiation. Culture is "a dynamic process of radiation, adoption and confrontation, reception, modification, rejection, reconstruction and invention."[15] The same might be said of intercultural communication, as there

---

14. E.g., G.H. Anderson and T.F. Stransky (eds.), *Mission Trends no. 3: Third World Theologies* (New York and Grand Rapids 1976); also S.B. Bevans, *Models of Contextual Theology* (Maryknoll, NY: Orbis Books, 1992); V. Küster, *Theologie im Kontext: zugleich ein Versuch über die Minjung-Theologie* (Nettetal, 1995); L.A. Hoedemaker, *Theologiseren in Context* (Kampen, 1997).

15. A definition used for a political discussion on "culture" in the European Community.

seems to be "no master narrative that can reconcile the tragic and comic plots of global cultural history."[16] In these definitions, the concept of culture is only applicable to larger units (Scottish, Southern, African culture, and so on), if it is agreed that "culture" in those cases refers to a provisional relative fixation of certain configurations of meaning, and particularly certain configurations of *power*.

At this point the epistemological problems which had remained implicit and hidden in missiology have a chance to come out into the open. Recent approaches to culture find an echo in those versions of the epistemological predicament that exhibit a strong affinity to the study of *language*. There is a suspicion here of "logos" and "subject"—a preference for speaking of structures and systems which are inherently unstable and which depend for their validity on their relation to other "texts"—and an inclination to reduce epistemology to anthropology.

Generally speaking, a tendency to connect the search for truth with competition among communities is widespread among postmodern philosophers. Even McIntyre, who maintains the possibility of (fractal) justification, focuses in his definition of "a living tradition" on the *social embodiment* of the argument.[17] But its strongest version is the view that the social network in which 'definitions of the real' are created is by definition a *dispute de pouvoir* (Bourdieu)[18] and that any given system of truth oppressively denies "the other."

The convergence between epistemology and the study of culture is significant for missiology. In the convergence, large concepts such as "culture" or "system of meaning" tend to evaporate. They are, as it were, broken up, reduced to basic human elements of search, struggle, conflict, and creativity. Both on the personal level, in the fight for symbolic domination, and on the global level, in the asymmetry, the dominance, the oppressions, and the contextual interruptions, the convergence thematizes not only the provisional nature of any claim to truth, but the precariousness of human existence and human communication beyond that. There are eschatological implications in this precariousness, insofar as it is right to associate "truth" with complete, uninhibited sharing.

ESCHATOLOGICAL OPENNESS

The reference to eschatology is deliberate. In the argument pursued here, "culture" is presented as *eschatologically open*, which means that a definition of culture in terms of "process" and "battle" does not make sense unless it

---

16 James Clifford, *The Predicament of Culture* (Cambridge, MA and London: Harvard University Press, 1988), 15. According to Clifford, the cultural process is motivated by the need to "make a real difference" (p. 275).

17. A. McIntyre, *After Virtue* (Notre Dame: University of Notre Dame Press, 1984), 207.

18. P. Bourdieu, *Ce que parler veut dire* (Fayard, 1982), 148: definitions of the real manifest "le pouvoir quasi divin sur la vision du monde." Also: "(la réalité) . . . est le lieu d'une lutte permanente pour *définir* la 'réalité,'" (p. 142).

implicitly refers to some ultimate order in which all fragmented human com-munication finds its coherence and purpose. In some contemporary approaches to culture this implicit reference can be traced without much dif-ficulty. Clifford Geertz's famous description of the Balinese cockfight is a good example.[19] According to Geertz, the cockfight is a reminder of the mar-gins of uncertainty and tragedy which are still present in an otherwise rela-tively fixed social order. Even if everybody shares the code which makes the cockfight function as a rite of social cohesion, it is still a code that contains in itself the possibility of change and reversal. Insofar as it is meant to exor-cise this "other possibility," the fight is also an instance of collective religion, of collective coping with anxiety, finitude, and guilt. In this perspective, one might even speak of a *double* eschatological openness: the social system is only a provisional result of an ongoing fight for symbolic domination *and* the system itself is a way to cope with the precariousness of life. Both inter-pretations refer to forms of salvation that "lie ahead."

Missiology can develop its own way of speaking about "eschatological openness" in the thematization of the problem of culture on a global level. Against the background of the remarks made above about asymmetry and conflict, a distinction can be made between two frontiers at which this prob-lem manifests itself. There is, first of all, the frontier that is constituted by the predominance of Western ways of thinking, which has provoked and still provokes theological revolt. At this frontier, Western theologians are forced to bring home to themselves the uncritical way in which Western cul-ture and Western theology have projected Western presuppositions on to "the others" and in the process legitimized much global injustice (a major theme of liberation theology). The second frontier is constituted by the inevitability of "Western" rationality predominating in the economic and political systems which structure global society. This is the frontier between global secularization and global (cultural and religious) plurality. It presents a challenge for both Western and non-Western theology, as it implies the marginalization of many cultural and religious traditions, even within "Western culture" itself.

Taken together, the two frontiers enable us to see that the problem of plu-rality presents itself in missiology in the form of a quest for a more complete and more authentic communication among a greater number of human beings and traditions. Precisely here lies its eschatological openness. It is an openness which reminds one of the traditional missionary vision of "the ends of the earth": all nations and all cultures unite in "truth."

But this eschatological openness is an openness of battle, of the self-asser-tion of forms of religion, faith, and theology—and thus also forms of *cul-ture*—that are denied or run over in the asymmetry of cultures. There cannot be a unity or eschaton on the conditions *only* of the "modern" con-cept of the unity of humankind, which is a product of Western rationality (although even this "secularizing" rationality has its valid eschatological

---

19. C. Geertz, *The Interpretation of Cultures* (New York: Basic Books, 1973), 412–53.

points. The destructiveness of dominant systems, particularly of *this* dominant system, needs to be countered by other systems of signification in which human beings reach for the truth, from the bottom up, in a permanent struggle of humankind against any asymmetry.

There will be much "religion" in this struggle, and not only "Christian" religion. It will continually be marginalized by the power of secularizing rationality and yet not give up its claim of presenting a more complete perspective for the unity of humankind. This is the eschatological openness of contextual self-assertion. The suspicion of dominant systems which characterizes it reminds one of the suspicion of contemporary French philosophers with regard to metanarratives and all manifestations of "logocentrism." This suspicion, too, can be interpreted as a basic eschatological openness, the major point of which is that the discourse concerning "the other" should not be closed prematurely. In a sense, "the other" is the eschatological category here. *Différence* is a hopeful term.[20]

ESCHATOLOGY AND MISSIOLOGY

The difficulty with the use of the term "eschatology" in relation to epistemological issues is that the term easily takes on a very general meaning. It is then understood to refer to the open-endedness of human life and to the dependence of the process of truth-seeking on "future" justification. In other words, it easily becomes trivial. For missiology it is, however, crucial to insist on the theological substance of the term. The traditional meaning of eschatology is teaching about the "last things": resurrection, eternal life, judgment, redemption. In much modern Western thinking, this tradition has become intertwined with a philosophy of history that speaks of human freedom and the development of justice and peace through the "rational" conquest of nature.[21]

Partly in reaction to this, dialectical theologians have sought to define "the eschaton" as the absolute limit of human existence, as the point where the sovereign God touches human history in judgment and challenge. This rigorous move rescues aspects of biblical eschatology but hardly seems to leave room for last *things* or events; rather, eschatology has come to refer to eternal questions and open answers.

More recently, there have been efforts to bring eschatology back as a fundamental category and a determining framework for theological thinking, for instance in the work of Moltmann and Pannenberg. In these efforts modern Western thinking and dialectical theology are in some sense reconciled: faith and life are understood in the perspective of the promise of a *coming* revelation. In any case, the theological consensus is that the notion of the

---

20. This point is elaborated as a common concern of Derrida and Lévinas by D. Cornell, *The Philosophy of the Limit* (New York and London, 1992).

21. C. Walther, *Eschatologie als Theorie der Freiheit: Einführung in neuzeitliche Gestalten eschatologischen Denkens* (Berlin and New York, 1991).

coming of God to redeem the creation is essential; it will not do to understand eschatology as merely referring to the final destiny or *telos* of human searching. This does not deny, however, that it still makes sense to conceive of a correlation between divine activity and the human predicament. In this sense, the precariousness of human life can be understood as correlating with the coming of God, much as the networks of human guilt become available for interpretation in the perspective of the gift of forgiveness.

There has always been a strong affinity between missiology and eschatology, for "mission" has been largely understood as the establishment of a link between the world and the "coming kingdom." In the nineteenth century, especially in the United States, this affinity led to various forms of millennialism, in which revivalism and a sense of national predestination often joined forces.[22] In the twentieth century, especially in Europe, the affinity was strengthened by a revival of biblical-eschatological thinking under the influence of Karl Barth and the New Testament scholar Oscar Cullmann.[23] The point here was a positioning of mission "between the times": mission was not to be seen as an extension of the church but rather as an announcement of the coming kingdom. In this view, mission is based directly on God's action: it is a sign of God's gathering, reconciling, and redeeming activity. Everything is future-directed: "the walls of history are held apart by mission" (Cullmann).

Curiously, this revival of eschatology did not lead to further reflection on *how* the coming of the kingdom relates to the dynamics of world history. On hindsight, it looks like an intratheological debate about the shift of emphasis from *church* to *kingdom*.[24] The most promising impetus toward further reflection was perhaps given by Hans Hoekendijk with his attention on salvation as a "worldly" category. But he never elaborated his insights systematically.[25] In other words, while eschatology obviously belongs to the regular equipment of missiology, it needs further development—particularly in the context of contemporary approaches to intercultural communication. Although the concept of "culture" also belongs to the regular equipment of missiology, its instrumentalization has tended to hide its "eschatological substance" from view.

---

22. G. Marsden, *Fundamentalism and American Culture: The Shaping of 20th Century Evangelicalism* (New York, 1980); W.R. Hutchison, *Errand to the World: American Protestant Missionary Thought and Foreign Missions* (Chicago and London: University of Chicago Press, 1987).

23. O. Cullmann, *Christus und die Zeit* (Zürich, 1946); W. Freytag (ed.), *Mission zwischen Gestern und Morgen* (Stuttgart, 1952); L. Wiedenmann, S.J., *Mission und Eschatologie: Eine Analyse der neueren deutschen evangelischen Missionstheologie* (Paderborn, 1965).

24. D. Bosch, *Transforming Mission: Paradigm Shifts in Theology of Mission* (Maryknoll, NY: Orbis Books, 1991), interprets the debate in the traditional framework of the balance between the "already" and the "not yet." In that way he can argue that "extreme eschatologization" leads to the neglect of world; cf. 505–10.

25. See Bert Hoedemaker, "The Legacy of J.C. Hoekendijk," *International Bulletin of Missionary Research* 19 (1995): 166–70.

In the argument presented here, the eschatological figure of thought is indispensable. It is needed for the effort both to present a framework, or metaperspective, for the process of intercultural communication and to give a theological perspective for engaging with the dynamics of plurality and unity in which humankind, including Christianity itself, is involved.

PANNENBERG ON ESCHATON AND TRUTH

It might be profitable at this point to glance a little more closely at the "eschatological holism" of Pannenberg. Pannenberg seeks to (re)structure the whole system of Christian doctrine in an eschatological perspective, on the basis of the key insight that the vindication of God's self-revelation in Jesus Christ presupposes and requires the entire unfolding of history.

For our argument, two elements in this systematic theology need particular attention. The first is that all events that are called "revelatory" need to be seen in the perspective of provisionality, of *prolepsis*: i.e., they still await their final verification. Christian faith operates on the basis of the assumption that these events, particularly the Christ-event, will be proven right when everything is brought to light "at the end."[26] The second element is that there is a certain correspondence between the movement of God-in-Christ towards his creatures and the directedness (*das Angelegtsein*) of the creatures towards completeness (*Ganzheit*).[27] Knowledge of God, Pannenberg insists, is indispensably connected to insight into the human longing for salvation (or the human "knowledge of possible salvation").

There is a correlation here between eschatology and anthropology that might be fruitful for our argument. The difficulty is, however, that most of this thinking is focused on "revelation" and "proof." In other words, this eschatology is meant to produce a *systematic theology*, which creates a coherent framework for the substance of Christian faith. In *missiology*, this focus would inevitably lead to apologetics, and from there probably to a certain blindness to the questions that have been central to our argument so far. Of the two elements that we selected in the previous paragraph the second is clearly subordinate to the first in Pannenberg's thinking. In a missiology that is eschatologically structured, however, this would have to be the other way around. The fulfillment of the human longing for completeness or salvation would not as such be further *proof* of the truth of God's self-revelation, as it is for Pannenberg, but it would include truth as one of its aspects. Also, the plurality of humankind and the ongoing battle for truth would themselves be aspects of the *Angelegtsein* of human beings to God; this is not the case in Pannenberg's approach.

Missiology needs a certain distance from the vindication of the truth of the Christian faith. Its task is not to give an apologetic argument for Christianity

---

26. See esp. W. Pannenberg et al., *Offenbarung als Geschichte* (Göttingen, 1961); and *Grundzüge der Christologie* (Göttingen, 1964).

27. Especially in the section on eschatology, in *Systematische Theologie*, vol. 3 (Göttingen, 1993), 583–96.

as a worldview, although it presupposes the belief that the Christian message is preeminently suited to guide human beings on the way to salvation. It is called, rather, to reflect *theologically* on the place of Christian faith in the larger context of humankind. What, then, is this place from a missiological point of view?

ESCHATOLOGY AND ETHICS

The first point to be made is that the introduction of eschatology into missiology as proposed in the argument thus far means that the effort to round off the discourse of the Christian faith as a universe of its own is suspended in and interrupted by communication with others. To be sure, the starting point is Christian faith. More precisely it is the reference to the (eschatological) *coming of God* as it is emphasized in the Christian faith. However, this eschatological starting point works backwards, as it were, on the Christian self-understanding.

Eschatology always means suspension of truth. From the point of view of Christian faith this is not suspension in the general sense of relativizing all truth, but in the specific sense of binding it to the condition of *eschatological performance*, i.e., of taking "the other" seriously. To put it another way, from a missiological-eschatological point of view the Christian tradition is not a universe in itself which "absorbs the world," in the sense of its being recognized as the discourse in which the world "makes sense" (Lindbeck), but it is the product of a continuous dialectic between self-structuring and reference to the unity of humankind. Christian statements of faith are expressions of this dialectic: context and dialogue participate in the shaping of their substance.

This middle road between insularity and relativity is the essence of mission and not only produces hopeful engagement in serious dialogue, but also challenges other traditions to do the same. It is, for want of a better term, called *eschatological performance*. Understood in this way, "mission" moves between the experience of incommunication, misunderstanding, incompatibility of traditions on the one hand and the eschaton of complete human communication on the other.

But there is more that can be said. This eschatological reinterpretation of mission implicitly focuses on a dynamic which is present in the gospel and which may be characterized as *gathering and multiplying*. This binary term should be understood to refer to several important elements in Christian believing and thinking: the bringing together of the people of God and the reaching out to the ends of the earth, Jesus' call to focus on the coming kingdom and his attitude of taking each individual with utmost seriousness, and the eschatological action of God, in which all things are brought together in the perspective of unity, truth, and justice, and in which plurality is an enrichment rather than a threat.

"Gathering" suggests the sustained effort to establish complete humanization, in opposition to all religious and political power that stands in its way. "Multiplying" suggests the unlimited acceptance of human beings as they are. The dynamic to which the binary term refers turns against the violence that seeks either uniformity or fragmentation. It presupposes the hope that a sustainable combination of unity and diversity, of justice and plurality, in spite of all the human failures in this respect, might yet be possible.

With this elaboration we arrive at the most basic aspect of the problem of plurality, communication, and truth: the *ethical* aspect. In the sketch of the epistemological predicament, reference has been made to the ethical intentions of some "logoexcentric" positions, such as those of Derrida and Lévinas. For them, "the other" is the limit of all knowledge and the permanent presence in the face of which there can be no final or definitive representation of reality. Similarly, "eschatological performance" means both taking "the other" seriously in his, her, or its particularity and permanently resisting the temptation to be ahead of God's final revelation.

There is one final point. The ethical focus on "the other" calls to mind the notion of *reconciliation*. This is an eschatological notion *par excellence*, which has always been essential for the self-understanding of the Christian faith. It is a basic Christian conviction that no analysis of the human condition is adequate unless it is placed in the perspective of the need for reconciliation that exists between individuals, but also between peoples, nations, classes, races, and sexes. There are unsolved problems from the past, such as unavenged victims and accepted injustices, just as there is continuing estrangement and enmity as a seemingly inevitable by-product of the organization of human life. All this indicates a fundamental *openness* of history. In other words, open *ethical* questions in need of an *eschatological* perspective remain. "Unity of humankind" is not a simple moral directive to which human beings can respond by (re)organizing their lives. It is an expression which summarizes the depths of the human problem and it is, therefore, necessarily linked to "reconciliation."

The metanarrative of the Christian faith may not be the only place in which eschatology and ethics in this sense are brought together in a coherent and convincing way, but it cannot be ignored. It is the business of missiology to apply it to the problem of pluralism, to encourage mission as "eschatological performance" and, by this means, to take the epistemological predicament seriously.

CHAPTER ELEVEN

Toward an Epistemologically Responsible Missiology

BERT HOEDEMAKER

THE POINT OF ENCOUNTER

What happens to missiology when foundationalism becomes suspect? What if missiology would begin to reconsider its basic epistemological assumptions and move a little closer to the other pole: relativism? Would it still be recognizable as *missiology* in the sense of reflection on the indisputable mandate for *mission*?[1]

Various forms of relativism have always threatened the self-evidence of the missionary movement. There have always been voices questioning both the possibility and the legitimacy of transcontextual communication of religion and faith, and criticizing the assumption that the Christian message is universally applicable. For missiology, however, this has always been an external threat rather than an internal debate. There was hardly any internal epistemological uncertainty. In that respect, the present predicament creates a new situation.

Today, the uncertainty is characteristic of modern Western culture as a whole. Epistemologically, missiologists too are challenged to work out a position on the spectrum between classical foundationalism and radical relativism and to consider the implications of that position for the meaning of mission. If one opts for some version of holism, coherentism, or traditionalism, what does that mean for notions such as proclamation or prophecy? At first sight, these notions are replaced by dialogue, mutual learning, and

---

1. This chapter represents a careful interpretation of the discussion of the working group on epistemology at its last meeting and an attempt to make a programmatic statement on the outcome of the group's work over four years. The group is happy to endorse this expression of its work in general terms; at the same time, individual members might have reservations about some of the particulars.

respect for the other "system," in the acknowledgment that none of us has a unique relation to ultimate truth. But is that all there is to say? The instinctive counter-question raised by the missiologist would be: Is there no point at which dialogue ends and yields to the monologue of preaching, to the uniqueness of the Word? And is there no way to discriminate between belief systems, between traditions that may be equally coherent but not necessarily equally true?

We have a clear point of encounter here between epistemology and missiology. There is a complication, however. Missiology has always had more affinity to cultural studies than to philosophy. The implications of this obvious fact are not without significance for the present discussion. Traditionally, the missiologist does not deal with "belief systems" or "traditions" but with cultures. And while cultures may sometimes present themselves as coherent stable systems of custom, belief, and ritual, behind this apparent coherence one observes human searches for meaning and identity which are often opaque and constantly in flux and in combat.

Mission as intercultural communication has always concentrated on that second level. That is the reason why its methods have been manifold and its results often unpredictable. Mission is not in the first place a discussion between beliefs or traditions, but an effort to present the gospel as a live option in the midst of the complexities of daily life. The encounter with the baffling issues of culture and pluralism, therefore, will drive the missiologist not *primarily* toward questions of justification and truth, although these are ultimately inescapable, but toward a closer analysis of intercultural communication.

In passing, it should be noted that the experience with cultural pluralism and recent developments in cultural studies make clear that simple and clear-cut ways of speaking about culture are *passé*. There is a certain messiness about culture in today's world: borderlines become fuzzy, syncretisms abound, there is hardly any place left where one can observe a culture in a pure, original, uncontaminated form. "Culture" has come to mean not a stable system but an ongoing process in which change and interaction and permanent struggles for domination are the major characteristics. That is bound to have its effects on missiology; it will drive it even further away from clear epistemological discussion of traditions and belief systems. In this respect, missiology has its own predicament about pluralism.

In traditional reflections on the missionary movement, pluralism was both an obstacle to be overcome in the common perspective of the kingdom of God and a reflection of the abundant creative action of God. Pluralism meant three things: diversity as an aspect of a good and promising creation, fragmentation as a continuing sign of alienation of human beings from each other and from God, and a redeemed manifoldness, or reconciled diversity, as part of the content of eschatological expectation.

Now that pluralism has become a *predicament* that threatens the self-confidence of the movement, what remains of this theological approach? It is easy to say that without at least some kind of transcending common perspective any missionary movement would be pointless. But such a common perspective is now less easily regarded as something within reach. It has become an eschatological notion even more than it already was. The gap between missionary movement and final divine action seems to have grown wider.

In a sense, missionary theology has always been strong on eschatology. It has often operated on the assumption (sometimes based on a specific interpretation of Matt. 24:14) that the final completion of all things in the biblical sense would be linked to the successful crossing of all frontiers between cultures and religions. In other words, the eschatological "answer" to pluralism was understood to have two aspects that were closely related: there would be universal understanding, one framework of communication for the whole of humankind, related to the spreading of the gospel; *and* there would be ultimate truth, in the final self-revelation of God. As the predicament of pluralism is probed more deeply, this eschatological answer may still hold, but it will be severely challenged.

Contemporary missiology, then, faces the challenge of a new look at intercultural communication and a reconsideration of its traditional approach to pluralism and eschatology. This in itself constitutes an impressive agenda; and it exists even prior to and apart from the presence of any epistemological predicament. The epistemological predicament reinforces the missiological agenda by its own specific impact. Understood in this way, the encounter between epistemology and missiology is inescapable, necessary, and significant.

Missiologists cannot dodge the epistemological predicament by simply saying that it describes one of the ills of Western culture which must be cured by the proclamation of the gospel. Rather, the predicament forces them to rethink the relation between given belief and unity of understanding. Is there a straight unbroken line between the two, as a classical foundationalist position would hold? Or is there no relation, as the relativist would say? If we reject these extreme options, what remains? How would an eschatological perspective affect positions that we might choose between the extremes: holism, coherentism, traditionalism? Conversely, how would an emphasis on otherness, dialogue, and mutual learning affect traditional understandings of mission? In the encounter of predicaments, is there a way in which subjectivity, particularity, and skepticism can become constructive ingredients in missiology? Can pluralism be regarded as a promise, as a way to salvation, rather than merely as a threat and an obstacle?

To describe the point of encounter between missiology and epistemology in this way implies an emphasis on the continuing necessity of rational justification of faith positions on the one hand, and an emphasis on the continuing significance of the missionary perspective on the other. These choices are not self-evident. They exclude, for instance, an approach to religion and faith that privileges feeling and intuition and therefore, according to some of its proponents, rises above the need for rational justification. They also exclude an approach which capitalizes on secularization and refers all questions of religion and faith to the realm of private eclectic consumption; in this case pluralism is reduced to a supermarket, a world of possibilities without obligation. Both these approaches basically deny the significance and the urgency of the predicament. They underestimate the necessity of rational debate and of struggle for common vision in a world that depends on communication.

EMPHASIS ON ESCHATOLOGY

To say that missiology is invited to test its tradition of eschatological thinking in the discussion about the epistemological predicament is valid and important; but it should not cause us to overlook that this contribution meets with certain "eschatological" tendencies already present in the epistemological debate itself. The mapping of the predicament that is attempted in the preceding chapters almost inevitably provokes ways of speaking that might (derivatively) be termed eschatological: there is a reference to tradition-transcending notions and perspectives, and even to the possibility of an ultimate unity of understanding in which at least the counterproductive aspects of pluralism will be overcome. The two "eschatologies" should be drawn together very carefully.

The eschatology that is an inalienable part of the Christian faith speaks of the coming of God, of a final unambiguous divine self-revelation, of a judgment, of a final separation of good and evil, and of the redemption of the faithful. On the level of the individual it speaks of resurrection and eternal life; on the cosmic level it speaks of a new heaven and a new earth. All this is inseparably connected to the second coming of Christ: it has its foundation, in other words, in the givenness of Christ, in his life, death, and resurrection. By contrast, the eschatology that is implied in epistemology is much more formal. Here, eschatology is understood in terms of final completeness of knowledge, indisputable vision of truth, and unity of understanding. This eschatology is, in a sense, the transcendental condition for the "success" of any partial knowledge and communication. It is a tacit presupposition of daily life which counts upon the possibility that even simple thoughts and actions have some relation to a truth that will ultimately be accessible to all human beings.

It might be objected that it is premature to call this presupposition "eschatology," that the two eschatologies have little to do with each other, and that it is artificial to establish a relation between them. In historical perspective, however, this objection does not hold. In the emergence of modern culture, Christian eschatological models of thought were historicized and appropriated to account for the progress of humanity in terms of knowledge and liberty. In much Christian theology, moreover, traditional eschatology allied itself with a philosophy of history that spoke of the development of justice and peace through the rational conquest of nature. This alliance can and perhaps should be criticized, but it cannot be made to disappear. Even in the self-reflection of the modern missionary movement, in which crossing of cultural and religious frontiers was linked to the coming of the kingdom, traces of this alliance can be observed.

How do the two "eschatologies" relate to each other against the background of the epistemological predicament? The statement that the relation between given tradition and ultimate truth is a complicated pilgrimage, a learning process in which other belief systems play important roles, will create a certain distance, an open space between the givenness of Christ and the final "coming of God." The space between them becomes a space of learning, of dialogue, of conversions. This idea appeals strongly to the notion of *internal* eschatological criticism which is already present in the New Testament and which becomes visible in Jesus' self-relativizing references to the coming Kingdom of God as well as in the distinctions between provisional, partial believing and final, complete seeing. Here lies an important connection.

Christian faith and proclamation may, and will, choose its foundation in the givenness of Christ; but a missiological reflection which takes the epistemological predicament seriously will highlight the eschatological dimensions of this foundation and urge the Christian faith to take these seriously. The result will be a missionary theology that works backwards, as it were, from eschatology to pneumatology to christology. Such a theology will not ignore the foundation but it will not use it in a "foundationalist" way. That means that the givenness of Christ is a belief that does not stand by itself but derives its significance from the other beliefs to which it has come to be (and continues to be) connected in the construction of the Christian tradition.

Missionary theology will illuminate the givenness of Christ from the point of view of an eschaton that engages all positions, including Christian belief systems, in a permanent process of mutual learning and *in that way* links them to ultimate universal truth. For the Christian there is no eschatological faith without Christ; but precisely this eschatological faith—highlighted, emphasized, and strengthened by the epistemological predicament—precludes final answers to the question of his significance.

On the basis of this general starting point, different positions are still possible with regard to the nature of the eschatological self-relativization of the Christian faith and the extent to which the first fruits of ultimate truth are already given to the Christian community. Similarly, the starting point does not predetermine a position on universalism: the emphasis on eschatology proposed in the preceding argument does not necessarily imply it. On these issues the discussion will have to continue. In any case, the effort to reorder elements of faith in the perspective of "*emphasized eschatology*" seems epistemologically responsible and missiologically fruitful.

THE SPIRIT OF THE COMING GOD

The epistemological predicament questions the self-evidence of the relation between given belief and unity of understanding. Missionary theology will have to reconsider this relation in its own way, using as much of its own tradition as possible. The proposed eschatological reordering of elements opens the way to do precisely this: not only does it do justice to the epistemological predicament, it also enables missiology to capitalize on its own heritage of eschatological thinking.

How does one envisage the relation between given belief and unity of understanding in the perspective of emphasized eschatology? Logically and traditionally, this question leads into the area of pneumatology. The Holy Spirit serves as the link between divine life and human life, between an unambiguous eschaton and an ambiguous present, between a redeemed and an unredeemed plurality, between the kingdom of God and a community that seeks to maintain its identity through the complexities of intercultural communication. The lifeline that the Holy Spirit is for the community is not a guarantee of truth in the simple, straightforward epistemological sense of the term; for it is not immune to the profound confusions of cultural and religious pluralism. Neither is the lifeline permanently discernible; it manifests itself now and then, and it does not protect the community from the necessity of reinterpreting its tradition in the light of new learning experiences.

Indeed, reinterpretation of tradition is one of the dimensions of belief in the Holy Spirit that is highlighted by the contemporary predicament. In the New Testament, the book of Acts is, in this respect, the pneumatological document *par excellence*. Integration of the mission to the Gentiles into the patterns of the then existing community was a revolutionary move which could only come about under the pressure of the Holy Spirit—more precisely, under the influence of the spark of recognition which was established between new events and given interpretive frameworks (as in the Cornelius story). What happens here and on similar occasions is more than an expansion of given faith by the accumulation of new experience; nothing less is at stake than a restructuring of the faith itself. The community, by its own exercise of discernment ("the Holy Spirit and us"), becomes the locus of transition and restructuring; only as such is the community also the link between past and future.

Pneumatologically speaking, "mission" is not a simple action of carrying a given message to the ends of the earth; it is, rather, the engagement in an eschaton-directed process of reinterpretation of that message. "Eschaton-directedness" here means several things. It means, first of all, attention to the dynamics of culture and intercultural communication, to the places where human searches for meaning are imprisoned in closed worldviews or run into blind alleys. Second, it means the presentation and justification of the "given message" in the context of that attention, in dialogue with other meaning-giving systems and traditions, in a common learning process focused on reconciliation and unity of understanding. Third, it means the introduction of a spirit of reconciliation into the epistemic dialogue itself; for in the eschatological encounter of different belief systems much more is at stake than the making of propositional points only.

These last remarks already draw our attention to the significance of ethics in the reconsideration of missionary theology. The fruits of the Spirit are not described in cognitive terms as elements of belief systems, but in moral terms as ingredients of life, as virtues and attitudes. The Holy Spirit, as the link between an unambiguous eschaton and an ambiguous present, "will prove the world wrong," not about the truth of given systems or traditions, but "about sin and righteousness and judgment" (John 16:8). In other words, this link between divine and human life is a link of judgment, a test of the readiness and the ability of human beings, but also of systems and traditions, including the Christian tradition, to take the eschaton of reconciled diversity seriously even in the present situation of pluralism. In that perspective, presenting Christ to the world implies not only, and perhaps not even primarily, the defense of one belief system among many; it implies above all the praxis of the Spirit, the praxis of reconciliation, the praxis of the link between unredeemed and redeemed plurality.

Obviously, a triadic if not trinitarian structure remains crucial when missionary theology is reconceived in an eschatological perspective. The Spirit of the coming God links up with Christ, and in this movement keeps the community moving in history, learning, crossing frontiers, transcending its own constructed traditions, enjoying glimpses of truth. There is a mutual confirmation here between God, Christ, and the Spirit. The threeness, the nonidentity, of God, Christ, and the Spirit is reflected in the historical space of the community, its precarious existence, the activity of reinterpretation in which it is engaged, the learning and the surprises to which it is exposed. At the same time, it is the oneness of the three on which the life, the future, and the continuing missionary identity of the community depend.

CHRIST IN THE CONTEXT OF THE SPIRIT

Against the background of the epistemological predicament as analyzed in the present book, pneumatology might appear as a relativizing factor that encourages a movement away from foundationalism in the direction of radical relativism. To a certain extent that is, of course, the case: emphasized eschatology tends to draw out those dimensions of pneumatology that highlight the adventure character of the Christian community in a pluralist world. It would be wrong, however, to conclude that this approach necessarily and automatically leads to a relativizing of the meaning of Christ, or to see Christ merely as eschatological reference. Here, too, several different positions are possible, including those that would emphasise Christ as the given embodiment of universal truth. In all these positions the givenness of Christ remains crucial. But it will not be a givenness outside of and prior to the work of the Spirit; it will be a givenness that is manifest again and again in the context of the pilgrimage of the community through a world of limited belief systems and incomplete knowing.

It follows from this "pneumatological contextualization" of Christ that his givenness is never purely formal. The historical fact of Jesus' existence is, theologically speaking, not the only significant factor. It is also significant that Christ has entered into the history of a *community*, which is an ongoing history of remembering, interpreting, expecting, and witnessing. In other words, Christ has become part of a web of belief: he is being remembered and interpreted in connection with other elements of belief as one who redirects human lives toward God and toward the coming kingdom in a unique way.

Only by way of this qualitative givenness, only through the presence of the Spirit in the community, is Christ now given to history in general: as question, challenge, and judgment, as part of the learning process of humanity. Needless to say, the faith that Christ will be vindicated in the end is the *raison d'être* of the Christian community. But this faith is vulnerable like clay jars; it needs to be subjected to reordering, restructuring, learning, and dialogue if it wants to remain itself. The line between the given Christ and his ultimate vindication is not a straight and self-evident line; only in eschatological hindsight will it be fully visible.

For a christology that is designed from a missiological point of view which takes the epistemological predicament seriously, all this probably implies that metaphysical schemes about "natures" and "states" of Christ are not by themselves enough, as these often betray foundationalist presuppositions. A better way might be to focus on the traditional christological metaphors of *incarnation* and *kenosis* and to develop those in the pneumatological context sketched above.

Incarnation means that the Word of God becomes flesh and blood in a very particular configuration of human life. What has eschatological validity becomes present in a specific piece of history, and its true character is recognized and embraced by faith. A theology that reflects on this faith may choose to isolate this specific piece of history—"it happened then and there"—and then choose to understand the Holy Spirit as the link between this crucial event and all generations following. But this is not necessarily the only way. The flesh and blood of Christ, his specific life and witness, can also be understood to mean that the Word of God needs multiple particular configurations in order to remain Word of God and in order to be heard at the end of time. This does not make Christ the symbolic summary of all human searches for meaning. That would take him out of history and trivialize the problem of pluralism. Rather, it makes Christ the bearer of the promise that, at least, some particular contextual choices of position in a plural world—with all the dialogue and the struggle that these choices entail—are part and parcel of the pilgrimage to ultimate truth.

Kenosis means that healing and reconciliation take place through radical entrance into the confusion and violence of the world. The term suggests a movement from high to low status, from wealth to poverty, from being lord to being slave. It has become an image for Christ as the one who leaves divine fullness behind in order to enter into the world of suffering and who is then raised up, exalted, by God (Phil. 2:6–9). Here again, the metaphor can be used to refer to the once-for-allness of the appearance of Christ, to the unique quality of this appearance, meant to be set apart and imitated by his followers. It could, however, also be used to articulate the insight that the appearance of Christ reveals the cost of reconciliation and the violent nature of the world that needs to be reconciled.

When we speak of an eschaton of "reconciled diversity," this does not refer to the achievement of consensus or compromise in the world of diverging opinions and beliefs. That would also trivialize the problem of pluralism and reduce dialogue to an academic game. Pluralism has an "underside" of lives and histories immersed in estrangement and hostility. Reconciliation in human diversity does not only mean that persons or even belief systems find some common ground of agreement or mutual recognition, but also that the age-old estrangements and hostilities—between races, cultures, religions—are themselves addressed.

This effort to approach christology from the point of view of emphasized eschatology might be summarized as an effort to hold together the determinate meaning and the open significance of Jesus Christ. There is a givenness in the incarnation, which remains the starting point of the Christian community; but this givenness has the nature of an eschatological reality. It can only remain "given" when it is reappropriated and reinterpreted. This reappropriation and reinterpretation are open and problematic; they are part of the life of faith in a world of seemingly incommensurable traditions, limited belief systems, and incomplete knowing.

MISSIONAL ECCLESIOLOGY

What is the church, missiologically speaking? Simply to say that the empirical church is or should become a "missionary church"—in the sense that it should be dynamically related to its context—will not do; one needs to be more specific about the effects of emphasized eschatology on more commonly accepted approaches to ecclesiology. In eschatological perspective, the church is the end-time community, called to life by the Spirit, moving between the historical and contextual givenness of Jesus Christ on the one hand and final revelation on the other. It is a community, travelling from context to context, emerging in different cultural spaces, putting up signs of the coming kingdom and providing safe environments for people who try to make sense of their world with the aid of the gospel. It lives on the basis of the pneumatological contextualization of Christ.

Traditionally, there are four ways in which church and eschaton are related. One is implied in the notion of pilgrimage: the church is constantly held in motion and challenged to reinterpret and reappropriate its past by a divine call that always remains "ahead." A second way is characterized by the integration of eschatology into ecclesiology in the form of a reference to mystery and promise. This approach regards the church as the prologue to the eschaton, and it emphasizes a sacramental presence of cosmic redemption, particularly in the celebration of the Eucharist. A third way is the distinction between the visible and the invisible church: until the end of time the true followers of Jesus Christ are mixed with others, and only a final divine judgment can separate the two. The fourth way is the self-transcending reference of the church to humankind: the ultimate vision here is a redeemed, reconciled humanity rather than a triumphant church. In connection with the perspective developed in the preceding pages, these eschatological qualifications of ecclesiology can become highly significant for missiology. They provide the church with good reasons, both for self-relativization and for stubbornness in hope.

A brief look at existing ecclesiological typologies might help to visualize a little more closely what is meant by the eschatological qualification of ecclesiology. Dominant among the typologies is the one based on a comparison of systems of church order. The opposite ends of the spectrum here are episcopalianism and congregationalism, and, analogously, maximal and minimal attention to the question of historical succession of ministerial authority. Then there is, of course, the approach based on spirituality, with a range from "sacramental" to "charismatic": from an attachment to ritual forms to preference for the free play of the Spirit. (This typology does not necessarily run parallel to the one first mentioned.) Third, there is the sociological (Troeltschean) church-sect scheme, which can conceivably be combined with the (Niebuhrian) Christ-culture typology. Here the focus is on the ways in which the social embedding of churches is incorporated and reflected in their institutional organisation and social teaching. All typologies refer to aspects of ecclesiology that need to be taken into account if one wants to connect ecclesiology to missiology.

A more eschatologically informed approach will qualify the ministry typology, not necessarily by pressing for a "free church" or by moving into the direction of congregationalism, but by addressing the general issue of the relation between ministry and laity and the meaning of ministerial authority when this is connected to incarnation and kenosis in the sense described above. As far as spirituality is concerned, the approach will probably encourage an understanding of sacrament that supplements *anamnesis* (remembering Christ) with *epiklesis* (invoking the Spirit). Finally, an eschatological approach will reconceptualize the church-culture scheme by raising the question what it means to be "in culture," that is, to be part of ongoing human searches for meaning and identity, as the community that anticipates reconciled diversity.

Only on the basis of this general qualification of ecclesiological typologies can we venture the thesis that the eschatological perspective creates a typology of its own, with two extreme positions on either end of the spectrum. At one end we find the church defined by its beginnings, by the apostolic tradition, by an original message that must be safeguarded and expanded to the ends of the earth and till the end of time. This is a church for which pneumatological contextualization means mainly linear growth, both quantitatively and qualitatively. At the other end we find the church defined not by its givenness, but rather by its emergence, as ecclesiogenesis, as *ad hoc* discovery, as the product of a faithful struggle with a context, as the decision of believers who construct a tradition and communicate with others who are involved in similar struggles, both synchronically and diachronically. This is a church built on hope, on anticipation of reconciled diversity rather than on memory alone in the sense of an unhistorically rigid attachment to revealed truth. An eschatological missiology must locate itself appropriately along this spectrum.

The typology sketched here allows for a wide range of positions between the two extremes. These positions are held together by the specific ways in which the eschatological perspective qualifies ecclesiology as a whole. In that way even the positions that are inclined to emphasize the importance of "givenness of tradition" would not necessarily become identical with analogous positions in the other typologies, but they would still see the givenness as part of a "pneumatological contextualization." They, too, would affirm that the only way we can speak of a final identity of the church is in eschatological hindsight, at the end of a complex journey through a culturally plural history.

There is yet another way of reflecting on the relation of eschatology and ecclesiology. Much traditional ecclesiology is structured according to the four *notae ecclesiae*, the marks of the church mentioned in the Nicene Creed: unity, holiness, catholicity, apostolicity. What happens when these marks are considered in the light of emphasized eschatology? Unity and catholicity would not be seen as attributes of the church per se, but as ways in which the church foreshadows the reconciled diversity that is characteristic of transformed humanity eschatologically.

Reconciled diversity refers to the situation in which there is no longer a contradiction or even a tension between gathering together around one center and spreading out in an endless variety of life-forms and causes. The church is "one and catholic" insofar as it manages to bring together these two basic movements in as balanced a way as possible. Likewise, holiness reflects and foreshadows the ultimate rejection of evil which is implied in the redeemed unity of humankind; it works itself out in the difficult ecclesiological questions of tolerance and discipline, exclusion and embrace. Apostolicity, finally, refers to the faithfulness of the church to its beginnings—beginnings that can be understood as a specifically given foundation in Christ which needs to be preserved, or as an original sentness which needs to be reappropriated from context to context.

A missional ecclesiology is not a doctrine of the church in which everything is subordinated to a mandate for missionary activity which supposedly precedes, supersedes, and encompasses all community building. Neither does it refer to a theology that places everything that the church is and does under the umbrella concept of *missio Dei*. It is an effort to reconsider the theological self-definition of the church in the perspective of an emphasized eschatology and in that way to help concrete communities of Christians to relate their identity to their experience of the predicament of pluralism.

POSSIBLE THEMES FOR CONTINUING DISCUSSION

Obviously, the discussion rendered in the previous pages is only a beginning; it is a first step in the encounter between an analysis of the contemporary epistemological predicament and a rethinking of the strengths and weaknesses of missionary theology. The discussion does not claim to present even a first sketch of a systematic theology that might result if the encounter is continued, expanded and deepened. It intends to indicate a direction in which a missiology for Western culture might move if it wants to pay serious attention to the philosophical crises of that culture. The following themes are presented with the intention of clarifying that direction a little further. The views brought forward in the course of that clarification should be considered as possible conceptual developments rather than as necessary implications of the working group's discussion.

GOSPEL AND CULTURE

What precisely do we mean by *culture* and *intercultural communication*? How do we speak theologically about "human searches for meaning which are themselves often opaque and constantly in flux and in combat"? What does it mean to relate the gospel to those searches? How does the epistemological predicament inform and qualify the current use of the gospel/culture polarity? The first thing to be said here is that the usefulness of the polarity as such is called into question. The emphasis on pneumatological contextualization and on the necessity of learning and reinterpretation, defended as a necessary implication of the missiological response to pluralism, undermines the possibility of defining "gospel" as an independent entity over against "cultures" and calls for a different hermeneutic.

An epistemologically responsible missiology can no longer use a frame of thought in which it is held to be self-evident that we bring "the gospel" from outside to "culture," as all understandings of "gospel" are part of the phenomenon that is being addressed. Rather, the question to be focused on in missiology is threefold: (1) How does the growing awareness of the predicament of pluralism and truth in fact influence new interpretations of the Christian tradition, and how can a responsible analysis of this predicament guide this process of interpretation? (2) How do new interpretations of the Christian tradition in fact qualify the perception of the human pilgrimage to truth and the vision of "the end," and how can a responsible theology support this? (3) How can the (possible) role of a Christian faith-involvement in human searches for meaning be defined? In this threefold question the term "culture" evaporates as an unambiguous point of reference. The term may remain indispensable for the description and analysis of the ways in which searches for meaning and pilgrimages to truth interact and in the process create different traditions and belief systems, but the missiological focus is on the searches and the processes themselves, as well as on the universal (eschatological) perspective in which these can be seen.

From this point of view, current approaches that list general characteristics of modern culture over against general characteristics of the gospel, with the intention of calling the church to conversion from too much "inculturation" to faithfulness to the gospel, appear inadequate. There is insufficient probing of the predicament here, and a lack of analysis, both of what is behind the façade of modern Western culture and of the extent to which the church is part of its problems.

Unity of Humankind

In the description of the eschatological point of reference in the preceding discussion, there were in fact two converging perspectives. One was the coming of God, God's unambiguous self-revelation, judgment, and promise, the appearance of final truth. The other was the perspective of universal understanding, of a humankind beyond pluralism, at least beyond a pluralism that keeps generating misunderstanding and violence. The term "reconciled diversity"—borrowed from ecumenical discourse—emerged to describe both perspectives together. It was suggested that the missionary movement was already familiar with the convergence of the perspectives, and that it remains an important task for missiology to find a responsible theological basis for it.

It is tempting to use the term "unity of humankind" here, because it expresses an overarching vision within which also the imagery of Christian eschatology can be made understandable. The term will need considerable qualification, however, for three reasons. First, it has become associated with the "project of modernity" and as such has come under suspicion; the term can be used to disguise attempts to "unify" the world on the basis of a particular ideology. The unification of humanity in one economic market- and growth-oriented system, for example, is not necessarily consonant with Christian eschatology. Second, from a Christian theological point of view the term 'unity of humankind' is often associated with the assumption that humankind can redeem itself, that the attainment of unity and reconciliation is an immanent historical process. Third, there is a proper question about 'unity' being an acceptable term for Christian eschatology, on the grounds that it does not account adequately for the biblical notions of judgment and separation.

These doubts about the adequacy of the term "unity of humankind" have to be taken very seriously. The conditions under which the term might yet be useful for an epistemologically responsible missiology need to be spelled out with great care. At least two of those conditions can be mentioned briefly.

In the first place, it should be clear that final and decisive unity is unthinkable apart from a reality-transcending perspective that always implies some measure of judgment. There is an analogy here with what is sometimes experienced and described as the fragmentation of the human self. The experience of fragmentation is accompanied by a unifying intent, a longing for oneness; but this oneness is only conceivable from a point of view that transcends time, history, and life. The crucial point in the term "unity of humankind," then, is not the realization of this unity at some point in history, but the consistent orientation toward this unity as the "end." In the second place, "unity of humankind" should be understood not only to unite humanity in its present state, but to include its complex histories of alienation, misunderstanding, hostility, and violence. Pluralism of traditions and belief systems contains these complex histories in itself.

Unity, reconciliation, the redemption of pluralism in this broad sense can, therefore, only be conceived as an eschatological event that encompasses the whole world and all history. Incidental dialogical encounters, the emergence of common ground, or the overcoming of hostility in particular situations does not come anywhere near this total unity. Faith in the unity of humankind is only realistic, so the Christian would argue, if it takes the form of surrender to the perspective of divine forgiveness.

BELIEVING, LEARNING, AND PROCLAIMING

Mission has often been described straightforwardly as the crossing of the frontier between belief and unbelief. Is that description still tenable in a discourse about belief systems that are involved in a learning process? Has it now become impossible to envisage the "victory" of a particular belief system as it continues to convince others and in the process grows in multicultural depth and expression?

The question here is to what extent the epistemological predicament produces a relativism that, in spite of all nuance, ultimately destroys the very starting point of missiological reflection. The answer is that whatever relativism may be produced externally by the predicament is echoed and corroborated by the internal eschatological criticism that is peculiar to the Christian faith. The self-relativizing references to the coming kingdom and to complete knowing (and being known) illustrate this internal relativism. Traditionally, a few exceptions notwithstanding, theology does not link this "modesty of faith" to pluralism. Now that this link presents itself as a good possibility for an epistemologically responsible missiology, however, it is inevitable that the relation of believing, learning, and proclaiming will be reconsidered.

A Christian belief system that is engaged in a learning process together with other belief systems will attach great importance to the recognition of similar self-relativizing mechanisms in others. It will look for analogies and similarities, not primarily in propositional content but in what may be termed *eschaton-directedness*. This will result in a dialogical style in which the consciousness of existing alienation and misunderstanding is deepened and which focuses on reconciliation and forgiveness. From here, one's own beliefs may be revisited with a view to reinterpreting and deepening them with the aid of the other's eyes. This implies that doctrinal distinctions between belief systems become less significant in their function of determining the measure in which one is right and the other is wrong. They remain significant in their function of calling each other's attention to the specific ways in which faith in the final eschatological reconciliation is articulated and a corresponding dialogical style is encouraged.

In this kind of pilgrimage of mutual learning there is room for proclamation, for the sharing of basic insights. But this proclamation will no longer proceed on the assumption that in essence there is nothing to learn or to receive. Such an assumption ignores the difficulties but also the possibilities and the promises of pluralism. A belief system that takes pluralism seriously and embarks on the adventure of mission will not make itself impenetrable and unassailable, but it will include itself in the preliminary nature of belief implied by the eschatological perspective.

THE FOCUS AND STRUCTURE OF MISSIOLOGY

Traditionally, both mission and missiology are focused on transfer and reception, proclamation and conversion. The problems to be considered with regard to mission are usually arranged around this point of concentration. Missionary communication, understood in this way, is seen as decisive for the growth of Christianity, for the continuity between existing tradition and new form, and between established faith and wider inculturation. The generally accepted business of missiology is, accordingly, the description of the history of missionary efforts so conceived, the search for relevant scriptural foundations, and the elaboration of practical strategies for mission. More recent items on the missiological agenda, such as the function of eschatology and ethics or the feedback to the self-understanding of the missionary church, are additions to this focus rather than incentives to change it.

Is the traditional missiological paradigm of transfer and reception, proclamation and conversion, still adequate? Or should we perhaps begin to reformulate the missiological questions in a framework of intercontextuality and eschaton-directedness? Against the background of the discussion rendered in the previous pages this becomes a real possibility. It is conceivable that the missiological focus will shift to the issues of appropriation of tradition, intercultural communication, and contextualization, and that missionary communication as traditionally understood will merely be regarded as the upbeat to that main theme. In other words, when pluralism and eschatology become the central points of reference, missiology will be more inclined to concentrate on a synchronic perspective (communication between different traditions and systems) than on a diachronic perspective (continuity between existing tradition and new form).

This is not to suggest that missiology should no longer concern itself with what has always been its *raison d'être*: the basic belief that there is a movement of the Word into the world which needs to be supported and made visible by living communities that actually cross frontiers with a vision of the "coming kingdom" and the "ends of the earth." Missiology cannot ignore or deny this basic belief, but is called to reflect on its status in the context of pluralism and eschaton-directedness. This reflection will seek to relate the basic belief to the shift of focus suggested above.

All this implies that we will have to distinguish two different levels of reflection within missiology. One will concentrate on the basic Christian belief and on the coherence of the systems to which it belongs. The other will concentrate on the ways in which the basic belief comes into contact with other systems, frameworks, and contexts, and on the ways in which it can appropriate the challenges of pluralism. It would be a misconception to see the second (meta)level merely as prolegomena to the first. Rather, a permanent back-and-forth movement between the two levels remains essential. It is this back-and-forth movement which can ultimately free missiology from remnants of foundationalism.

If this restructuring of the discipline of missiology makes sense, it should be embedded in efforts to deal theologically with the definition of *culture* and the phenomenon of *intercultural communication*. One of the most important effects of the shift of focus suggested above is that it loosens the grip of the gospel/culture polarity and helps missiology to concentrate on *human culture* as the totality of spaces in which meaning is formed and understandings of the gospel are articulated, and in which *all* existing Christian traditions are available for testing and reconstruction.

Conceived in this way, an epistemologically responsible missiology might yet be able to come out of the closet of exotic appendices to the theological curriculum and move up to the status of "fundamental theology."

CONCLUDING REMARKS

The relation between an analysis of the epistemological predicament and a reconception of missiology can be understood in more than one way. One way is to see the predicament as a problematic development in modern Western culture to which missiology is forced to respond if it wants to remain credible. Another way, however, would be to see it as an opportune challenge to missiology to revisit its own tradition of eschatological thought and spirituality and put it to use in new and creative ways. It might even be possible to use epistemological responses to the predicament as a stimulus for missiology to move beyond some of its own stalemates. One of the major stalemates that has emerged in different forms is the opposition between a spirituality of missionary conquest and a skeptical relativism. At this point, the careful epistemological searching for positions between the extremes of classical foundationalism and radical relativism could be a great help.

It is important to keep this in mind when the question of the limited significance of the epistemological predicament and of epistemology as such comes up. It is, after all, a Western cultural hangup, and non-Western missiology may not be inclined to occupy itself with it. And even within Western culture, the predicament may signal the end of epistemology. It may be an implication of postmodernism that epistemology is ousted from its influential position. All this, however, cannot obscure the fact that pluralism is a universal problem with which the Christian faith will have to come to terms. The experience of tension between the reality of cultures and religions on the one hand and traditional Christian claims on the other is not limited to one culture only. Seen in this perspective, the discussion about an epistemologically responsible missiology has great ecumenical relevance.

Epilogue

J. ANDREW KIRK

The purpose of appending a final statement is limited and modest. The group wishes to put on record its own opinion of which major areas, related to the epistemological challenge and Christian mission, require ongoing exploration. Others may find additional or alternative themes which, in their opinion, are more important.

Having worked with these issues over a number of years with a degree of intensity and with the benefit of a highly stimulating process of interaction, the group has come to the conclusion that the unfinished work[1] can be distributed under four main headings: *the justification of beliefs, the question of truth, the relation of knowing and doing (belief and action), and intercultural communication.* We will look briefly at each one.

THE JUSTIFICATION OF BELIEFS

Although for some the question of justification is no longer a major issue, the majority still see it as a fundamental problem, particularly in the area of ethical decision making. If the search for a foundation which is immune from error, doubt, and refutation, and which does not suffer from an infinite regression, is no longer fruitful, how are beliefs to be defended where clear conflicts of interpretation and incommensurable stances are being adopted? If it is no longer possible to appeal to universally recognised criteria to justify beliefs, can justification take place only within a particular self-contained and self-authenticating tradition of understanding?

The epistemic move from knowledge pictured as a building arising from unshakable foundations to an interconnecting web isolated from other webs raises the essential question of the possibility of any intertraditional dialogue. For example, where there is a serious clash of ideologies whose influence in the public arena has a marked effect on the lives of vulnerable

---

1. To affirm that there are still some knotty issues which deserve further exploration does not deny that the group has made some real progress in bringing together epistemological analysis and missiological concerns.

people, is it sufficient to point to their internal consistency? After all, the ideology of racism or nationalistic xenophobia could be shown to be coherently intelligible within the framework of its own presuppositions and yet, in the eyes of most people, wrong and reprehensible. On what basis, however, can such ideologies be judged to be unwarranted?

In practice, does it not happen that judgements are made which tacitly assume some independent reference point from outside the tradition which can be used critically to show that the beliefs are not justified? Otherwise, it is perfectly possible for beliefs to be thoroughly rational and justified within their own tradition of discourse and yet not true. Alternatively, pushing the boat further from its moorings in some kind of primary anchorage, do not beliefs become little more than an appendage of aesthetics—a matter of taste, according to the sector of society with which one has chosen (momentarily) to identify oneself?

More particularly, does it not seem strange that some kind of foundationalist view of justification is so suspect among many Christian thinkers, seeing that the thrust of the biblical message is metanarrative on the grandest scale? And can Christianity survive as a presumed coherent and overarching explanation of reality without being able to appeal to its own warrant as a given which cannot be further justified, but which can be meaningfully challenged from other beliefs?

These are some of the questions which have been intensely debated within the group. They arise within the disciplines of both philosophy and theology in different ways. One way forward might be to explore how each can both learn from the other and contribute its own critical insights into resolving some of these problems.

THE QUESTION OF TRUTH

We have noted the wide variety of ways of understanding the truth question. Although there is no consensus within the group about which of these ways might constitute a primary understanding, we all recognize the intimate logical connection between truth and error and the impossibility of being able to recognise wrong and evil without a firm basis for discovering truth. But is it possible to speak meaningfully about accessibility to truth, in the sense that one can be confident about grasping the truth here and now, even if in an incomplete form? Or is the discovery of truth always something waiting to happen, like a journey into unknown territory whose outcome is always hidden from view?

A number of other crucial questions have been raised. There is, for example, the issue of being able to distinguish between programmatic definitions of truth and the criteria for recognising truth. Probably the group would agree that some of what are taken to be alternative versions of truth are, in reality, ways of establishing the credibility of truth claims (e.g., pragmatic theories).

Then there is a strong common assumption abroad in contemporary Western society that truth claims have as their chief end a manipulative and coercive power over others: in other words, that they are made in the interests of maintaining relations of domination by some individuals or groups over others. If this suspicion could be substantiated, then truth would be opposed to freedom and power would always be a negative force in human life. On the other hand, it could be cogently argued that there is no way of avoiding the exercise of power; and the view that it is always corrupt and corrupting is both unduly cynical and empirically uncorroborated. Could the tables be turned, perhaps, by arguing that being able to judge whether or not power is being used to oppress or exploit requires a notion of truth?

There is the question, which may seem obvious and yet which raises deep philosophical difficulties, of the commonsense view of truth. This is the view that we know truly most, if not all, of those things which as ordinary human beings we think we know and which, if we did not know them, would make ordinary living impossible. This view seems to possess a certain practical validity in that even those who question such a view of truly knowing are compelled to act as if they really hold to the truth of certain realities when going about the ordinary affairs of life. Such a view does not, however, answer the question of *how* we know these truths or, indeed, how we would evolve safe criteria for being able to distinguish between the true, the imaginary, and the illusory.

Finally, within a Christian framework we discussed the truism that truth has an eschatological reference, in the sense that, if there is an end to the present time-space sequence that we experience, it will become clear retrospectively at that point what is true in the nature of belief and action and what false. A universally conclusive pronouncement on truth and error requires a universal vantage point from which it may be delivered. History will be its own infallible interpreter, once it has run its full course.

For the time being, however, the eschatological perspective may not be much help. It assumes what still has to be argued and substantiated, namely, that history is teleologically driven. Where is the evidence that history is moving inexorably toward a climax rather than repeating itself continually in an "eternal return"? If eschatology is, by definition, based on a future reality, of what interest is it to present living? At least within classical Christian understandings of the dynamic of history what will be (true) at the end has already been anticipated partially (but truly) at one supreme moment of history, but also to a lesser extent at other moments. The eschatological reference, if taken by itself, seems merely to postpone the question of truth claims or, perhaps, to beg the question.

THE RELATION OF KNOWING AND DOING, BELIEF AND ACTION

The exact nature of the relation between epistemology and ethics was a question constantly on the agenda of our discussions. This can be seen in most, if not all, of the constructive essays. There was a keen consciousness that serious doubt about the accessibility of truth and the justification of beliefs could lead inexorably to a relativism in the area of moral values and practice.

None of the group thought that this movement was inevitable, that the only way of halting the slide down the slippery slope of relativism was by maintaining a classic foundationalist position. Nevertheless, the issue of moral certainty and clarity is of such supreme importance in a number of contemporary matters to do with such subjects as human sexuality, the defense of life, and the evils of torture, slavery, and racial and gender discrimination that an undifferentiated equality of opinion and action is not defensible. Relativism can easily lead to a casual tolerance which really masks an uncritical indifference to suffering and evil.

The group also wondered whether methodologically and practically ethics as a discipline is prior to epistemology. This might be true for two different reasons. First, right living, whilst intimately related to right believing, is the more powerful medium of communication. Put another way, the way we actually live—our life-style, our particular modes of behaviour, and our practical commitments—is indicative of our beliefs, i.e., it shows what we hold to be the most important aspects of life. Second, the consistency between belief and action is an important criterion of truth claims, even though it may not be a definition of truth. Within the context of a conflict of interpretations about the meaning of life and concrete ethical choices, the ability to maintain a consistency between practice and its theoretical defense may be a decisive way of testing systems of belief.

INTERCULTURAL COMMUNICATION

Unfortunately, culture has become an ideological weapon in a pluralist world, not least in the controversial arena of human rights, either to confirm the superiority of one historical process (theories about "the end of history") or to confirm the relativity of all cultural forms and norms. Neither of these two positions seems prima facie to be tenable: the first because it acts as judge and jury of its own achievements and ultimately reduces history to banality; the second because it would eliminate all appeal to inalienable goods and rights in human society and thus remove a cogent force in defense of justice and freedom for powerless people. This being so, the use of culture as an argument (or weapon) in defense of certain positions and practices has to be revalorised in contemporary political, ethical, and missiological debate.

Current discussion of the value and place of culture tends to emphasize difference. Why should difference be valid as *the* starting point? Why not accentuate a common humanity across racial and ethnic boundaries—a commonality which is not the theoretical conclusion of some esoteric anthropological idea, but one rooted in real life experience? If a multiplicity of voices, images, forms, values, and worldviews is a feature of the contemporary world (not just in the West), what happens to the continuity of identity through time? Or is such an ambition a manifestation of a slave mentality that baulks at the exercise of a radical liberty prepared to move continually back and forth between different identities, or from one identity to another? Is the whole matter of roots just a question of fashion and image, as we allow ourselves to pick and choose from the immense variety of possibilities offered by the professional purveyors of styles, trends, and tastes and by the "spin-doctors," the contemporary high priests of designer politics, tailor-made social attitudes and contrived linguistic correctness?

Within the framework of Christian commitment what, if any, is the missiological place for apologetics (i.e., for the defense and propagation of the faith against rival views of life)? What is the relation in communication between proclamation, dialogue, and testimony? In what circumstances might one be more appropriate than another, and why? Finally, given the uncertainties about foundations and truth, how is prophecy (that mode of biblical communication rediscovered so vehemently by sectors of the church in recent years) validated as a persuasive announcement of judgement and salvation?

All of these questions under these four rubrics, and many more that could be imagined, are directly touched by the epistemological predicament of contemporary society which we have attempted to lay bare in this study. To ignore them is to render oneself missiologically naive and impotent. We have reiterated a number of times that the challenge of the times also gives to Christian faith an unusual opportunity, modestly and in penitence to review the cogency of its communication within and to a culture racked by epistemological uncertainty, economic confusion, and ecological indecision. Would that many more, with due humility and trepidation, were willing to join the fray!

Select Bibliography

Alston, W. *Perceiving God: The Epistemology of Religious Experience.* Ithaca: Cornell University Press, 1991.
———. *A Realist Conception of Truth.* Ithaca: Cornell University Press, 1996.
Bernstein, R. *Beyond Objectivism and Relativism.* Philadelphia: University of Pennsylvania Press, 1983.
Bertens, H. *The Idea of the Postmodern: A History.* London: Routledge, 1995.
Bevans, S. B. *Models of Contextual Theology.* Maryknoll, NY: Orbis Books, 1992.
Bloor, D. *Knowledge and Social Imagery.* London: Routledge, 1976.
Bosch, D. *Believing in the Future: Towards a Missiology of Western Culture.* Valley Forge, PA: Trinity Press International, 1995.
———. *Transforming Mission: Paradigm Shifts in Theology of Mission.* Maryknoll, NY: Orbis Books, 1991.
Clayton, P. *Explanation from Physics to Theology: An Essay in Rationality and Religion.* New Haven: Yale University Press, 1989.
Clifford, J. *The Predicament of Culture.* Cambridge, MA: Harvard University Press, 1988.
Coady, A. J. *Testimony: A Philosophical Study.* Oxford: Clarendon, 1992.
Dancy, J. *Introduction to Contemporary Epistemology.* Oxford: Blackwell, 1985.
Dancy, J., and E. Sosa. *A Companion to Epistemology.* Oxford: Blackwell, 1993.
Davis, S. T., ed. *Philosophy and Theological Discourse.* New York: St. Martin's Press, 1997.
D'Costa, G. *Theology and Religious Pluralism.* Oxford: Blackwell, 1986.
Derrida, J. *Of Grammatology.* Baltimore: Johns Hopkins University Press, 1974.
———. *Writing and Difference.* Chicago: University of Chicago Press, 1978.
Devitt, M. *Realism and Truth.* Oxford: Blackwell, 1991.
Dummett, M. *Truth and Other Enigmas.* Cambridge, MA: Harvard University Press, 1978.
Farrell, F. B. *Subjectivity, Realism and Postmodernism.* Cambridge: Cambridge University Press, 1994.
Feyerabend, P. K. *Farewell to Reason.* London: Verso, 1989.
Fodor, J. *Christian Hermeneutics: Paul Ricoeur and the Refiguring of Theology.* Oxford: Clarendon, 1995.
Frame, J. *Apologetics to the Glory of God: An Introduction.* Phillipsburg, NJ: Presbyterian & Reformed Publishing Co., 1994.
Geertz, C. *The Interpretation of Cultures.* New York: Basic Books, 1973.
Gergen, K. *The Saturated Self: Dilemmas of Identity in Contemporary Life.* New York: Basic Books, 1991.
Gouwens, D. J. *Kierkegaard as Religious Thinker.* Cambridge: Cambridge University Press, 1996.

Guerriere, D., ed. *Phenomenology of the Truth Proper to Religion*. Albany, NY: SUNY Press, 1990.

Gutmann, A., ed. *Multiculturalism: Examining the Politics of Recognition*. Princeton: Princeton University Press, 1994.

Gutting, G., ed. *Paradigms and Revolutions*. Notre Dame: University of Notre Dame Press, 1980.

Haack, S. *Evidence and Inquiry: Towards Reconstruction in Epistemology*. Oxford: Oxford University Press, 1993.

Hacker, P. M. S. *Wittgenstein's Place in Twentieth-Century Analytical Philosophy*. Oxford: Blackwell, 1996.

Harvey, V. *The Historian and the Believer: The Morality of Historical Knowledge and Christian Belief*. Philadelphia: Westminster Press, 1966.

Hauerwas, S. *After Christendom*. Nashville: Abingdon Press, 1991.

Hawkes, D. *Ideology*. New York: Routledge, 1996.

Helm, P. *Belief Policies*. Cambridge: Cambridge University Press, 1994.

Hesse, M. *Revolutions and Reconstructions in the Philosophy of Science*. Bloomington: University of Indiana Press, 1980.

Hesselgrave, D. J., and E. Rommen. *Contextualization: Meaning, Methods and Models*. Grand Rapids: Eerdmans, 1989.

Hick, J. *An Interpretation of Religion*. New Haven: Yale University Press, 1989.

Hiebert, P. G. *Anthropological Insights for Missionaries*. Grand Rapids: Baker, 1985.

———. *Missiological Implications of Epistemological Shifts: Affirming Truth in a Modern/Postmodern World*. Harrisburg, PA: Trinity Press International, 1999.

Hoedemaker, B. *Secularization and Mission: A Theological Essay*. Valley Forge, PA: Trinity Press International, 1998.

Hutchison, W. R. *Errand to the World: American Protestant Missionary Thought and Foreign Missions*. Chicago: University of Chicago Press, 1987.

James, W. *The Meaning of Truth: A Sequel to Pragmatism*. Cambridge, MA: Harvard University Press, 1975.

Kearney, R. *Modern Movements in European Philosophy*. Manchester: Manchester University Press, 1994.

Kierkegaard, S. "On the Difference Between a Genius and an Apostle." In *The Present Age and Two Minor Ethico-Religious Treatises*, edited by Alter Lowrie and Alexander Druanda. Oxford: Oxford University Press, 1940.

Kirk, J. A. *Loosing the Chains: Religion as Opium and Liberation*. London: Hodder and Stoughton, 1992.

———. *The Mission of Theology and Theology as Mission*. Valley Forge, PA: Trinity Press International, 1997.

Kirkham, R. L. *Theories of Truth: A Critical Introduction*. Cambridge, MA: MIT Press, 1992.

Kuhn, T. *The Structure of Scientific Revolutions*. 2d ed. Chicago: University of Chicago Press, 1970.

Kvanvig, J. *The Intellectual Virtues and the Life of the Mind*. Lanham, MD: Rowman & Littlefield, 1992.

Lakatos, I. "Falsification and the Methodology of Scientific Research Programmes." In *The Methodology of Scientific Research Programmes*, edited by John Worrall and Gregory Currie, 8–101. Cambridge: Cambridge University Press, 1978.

Lehrer, K. *Knowledge*. Oxford: Oxford University Press, 1974.

Lévinas, E. *Totality and Infinity*. Pittsburgh: Duquesne University Press, 1969.

Lindbeck, G. *The Nature of Doctrine: Religion and Theology in a Post-Liberal Age*. Philadelphia: Westminster Press, 1984.

Lury, C. *Consumer Culture*. Cambridge: Polity Press, 1996.

Luzbetak, L. J. *The Church and Cultures: New Perspectives in Missiological Anthropology*. Maryknoll, NY: Orbis Books, 1988.

Lyon, D. *Postmodernity*. Buckingham, England: Open University Press, 1994.

MacIntyre, A. *After Virtue*. 2d ed. Notre Dame: University of Notre Dame Press, 1984.

———. *Three Rival Versions of Moral Enquiry: Encyclopaedia, Genealogy, and Tradition*. Notre Dame: University of Notre Dame Press, 1990.

———. *Whose Justice? Which Rationality?* Notre Dame: University of Notre Dame Press, 1988.

Margolis, J. *The Truth about Relativism*. Oxford: Blackwell, 1991.

Matson, W. *A New History of Philosophy*. 2 vols. San Diego: Harcourt Brace Jovanovich, 1987.

McCarthy, T. *The Critical Theory of Jürgen Habermas*. Cambridge, MA: MIT Press, 1978.

McNaughton, D. *Moral Vision: An Introduction to Ethics*. Oxford: Blackwell, 1988.

Mitchell, B. *The Justification of Religious Belief*. London: Macmillan, 1974.

Moltmann, J. *The Way of Jesus Christ: Christology in Messianic Dimensions*. Minneapolis: Fortress, 1993.

Montmarquet, J. A. *Epistemic Virtue and Doxastic Responsibility*. Lanham, MD: Rowman & Littlefield, 1993.

Murphy, N. *Anglo-American Postmodernity: Philosophical Perspectives on Science, Religion, and Ethics*. Boulder, CO: Westview Press, 1997.

———. *Beyond Liberalism and Fundamentalism: How Modern and Postmodern Philosophy Set the Theological Agenda*. Valley Forge, PA: Trinity Press International, 1996.

———. *Theology in the Age of Scientific Reasoning*. Ithaca: Cornell University Press, 1990.

Murphy, N., and G. F. R. Ellis. *On the Moral Nature of the Universe: Theology, Cosmology, and Ethics*. Minneapolis: Fortress, 1996.

Nathanson, S. *The Ideal of Rationality: A Defense within Reason*. Chicago: Open Court Press, 1994.

Newbigin, L. *The Gospel in a Pluralist Society*. Grand Rapids: Eerdmans, 1989.

Niebuhr, R. *Christ and Culture*. New York: Harper and Brothers, 1951.

Norris, C. *Deconstruction: Theory and Practice*. London: Methuen, 1982.

Phillips, D. Z. *Faith after Foundationalism*. London and New York: Routledge, 1988.

Plantinga, A. *Warrant and Proper Function*. New York: Oxford University Press, 1993.

———. *Warrant: The Current Debate*. New York: Oxford University Press, 1993.

Polanyi, M. *Personal Knowledge: Towards a Post-Critical Philosophy*. London: Routledge and Kegan Paul, 1958.

Puntel, L. B. *Wahrheitstheorien in der neueren Philosophie. Eine Kritisch-Systematische Darstellung*. Darmstadt: Wissenschaftliche Buchgesellschaft, 1978.

Putnam, H. *The Many Faces of Realism*. Lasalle: Open Court Press, 1987.

———. *Reason, Truth and History*. New York: Cambridge University Press, 1981.

Quine, W. V. O. *From a Logical Point of View: Logico-Philosophical Essays*. Cambridge, MA: Harvard University Press, 1953.

Rescher, N. *The Coherence Theory of Truth*. Oxford: Clarendon, 1973.

Romain, D. *Thinking Things Through: Critical Thinking for Decisions You Can Live with*. Mountain View, CA: Mayfield Publishing Co., 1997.

Rorty, R. *Philosophy and the Mirror of Nature*. Princeton: Princeton University Press, 1979.

———. *Consequences of Pragmatism*. Minneapolis: University of Minnesota Press, 1982.

———, ed. *The Linguistic Turn: Recent Essays in Philosophical Method*. Chicago: University of Chicago Press, 1967.

Runzo, J. *World Views and Perceiving God*. New York: St. Martin's Press, 1991.

Schreiter, R. J. *Constructing Local Theologies*. Maryknoll, NY: Orbis Books, 1985.

Searle, J. *The Construction of Social Reality*. New York: New York University Press, 1995.

Segundo, J. L. *Faith and Ideologies*. Maryknoll, NY: Orbis Books, 1984.

Sessions, W. L. *The Concept of Faith: A Philosophical Investigation*. Ithaca: Cornell University Press, 1994.

Shenk, W. *Write the Vision: The Church Renewed*. Valley Forge, PA: Trinity Press International, 1995.

Silverman, H., ed. *Questioning Foundations: Truth/Subjectivity/Culture*. New York: Routledge, 1993.

Steiner, G. *Real Presences*. Chicago: University of Chicago Press, 1989.

Stenmark, M. *Rationality in Science, Religion and Everyday Life: A Critical Evaluation of Four Models of Rationality*. Notre Dame: University of Notre Dame Press, 1995.

Stout, J. *The Flight from Authority: Religion, Morality and the Quest for Autonomy*. Notre Dame: University of Notre Dame Press, 1981.

Taber, C. R. *The World Is Too Much with Us: "Culture" in Modern Protestant Missions*. Macon, GA: Mercer University Press, 1991.

Thiemann, R. *Revelation and Theology: The Gospel as Narrated Promise*. Notre Dame: University of Notre Dame Press, 1984.

Thiselton, A. C. *Interpreting God and the Postmodern Self*. Grand Rapids: Eerdmans, 1995.

Thompson, J. B. *Studies in the Theory of Ideology*. Cambridge: Polity Press, 1984.

Toulmin, S. *Cosmopolis: The Hidden Agenda of Modernity*. New York: Macmillan, 1990.

Touraine, A. *Critique of Modernity*. Oxford: Oxford University Press, 1995.

Tracy, D. *The Analogical Imagination: Christian Theology and the Culture of Pluralism*. London: SCM Press, 1981.

Trigg, R. *Reality at Risk: A Defense of Realism in Philosophy of Science*. Totowa, NJ: Noble Books, 1980.

van Huyssteen, J. W. *Essays in Postfoundationalist Theology*. Grand Rapids: Eerdmans, 1997.

van Til, C. *A Christian Theory of Knowledge*. Phillipsburg, NJ: Presbyterian & Reformed Publishing Co., 1969.

Vanhoozer, K. J. *Is There a Meaning in This Text? The Bible, The Reader, and the Morality of Literary Knowledge*. Grand Rapids: Zondervan, 1998.

Verkuyl, J. *Contemporary Missiology: An Introduction*. Grand Rapids: Eerdmans, 1978.

Volf, M. *Exclusion and Embrace: A Theological Exploration of Identity, Otherness and Reconciliation*. Nashville: Abingdon Press, 1996.

Walker, R. C. S. *The Coherence Theory of Truth: Realism, Anti-Realism, Idealism*. New York: Routledge, 1989.

White, A. R. *Truth*. London: Macmillan, 1971.

Williams, M. *Groundless Belief: An Essay on the Possibility of Epistemology.* New Haven: Yale University Press, 1977.

Williams, S. N. *Revelation and Reconciliation: A Window on Modernity.* Cambridge: Cambridge University Press, 1995.

Wink, W. *Engaging the Powers.* Minneapolis: Fortress, 1992.

Wittgenstein, L. *Philosophical Investigations.* New York: Macmillan, 1953.

Yoder, J. H. *The Priestly Kingdom: Social Ethics as Gospel.* Notre Dame: University of Notre Dame Press, 1984.

Zagzebski, L. *Virtues of the Mind: An Inquiry into the Nature of Virtue and the Ethical Foundations of Knowledge.* Cambridge: Cambridge University Press, 1996.

Contributors

Philip Clayton is Professor of Philosophy and Chair at California State University (Sonoma). His books include *God and Contemporary Science* and a two-volume work in German on modern philosophical theology.

Bert Hoedemaker is Professor of Ecumenics and Missions at the University of Groningen, the Netherlands. He studied at Utrecht and Yale, held a teaching position in Jakarta, Indonesia, and was a member of the Faith and Order Commission of the World Council of Churches for fifteen years. His books include *Secularization and Mission*.

Lars Johansson is a Lecturer in Philosophy at Örebro Theological Seminary, Sweden, and Director of Forum for Faith and Society. He is currently doing research on the question: Whatever happened to the New Age?

J. Andrew Kirk has been Dean of Mission at the Selly Oak Colleges, Birmingham, England, for the last nine years. He is now the Director of the Center for Missiology and World Christianity in the University of Birmingham's Department of Theology. He worked for twelve years in Argentina. His current research is in the areas of epistemology and mission and Latin American missiology. His books include *What Is Mission? Theological Explorations*.

Nancey Murphy is Professor of Christian Philosophy at Fuller Theological Seminary, Pasadena, California. She holds doctorates in both philosophy and theology. Her research interests focus on the role of modern and postmodern philosophy in shaping Christian theology and on the relations between theology and science. Her books include *Theology in the Age of Scientific Reasoning*.

Andy F. Sanders is Associate Professor of the Philosophy of Religion at the University of Groningen (The Netherlands) and a member of the Center of Theological Inquiry (Princeton). He specializes in religious epistemology and wrote *Michael Polanyi's Post-Critical Epistemology*.

Kevin J. Vanhoozer was for eight years Senior Lecturer in Theology and Religious Studies at New College, University of Edinburgh. He now holds the post of Research Professor of Theology at the Divinity School of Trinity International University, Deerfield, Illinois. He is the author of *Is There a Meaning in This Text? The Bible, the Reader, and the Morality of Literary Knowledge*.

Index